THE JOY OF EFFORT

A Biography
of R. Tait McKenzie

THE JOY OF EFFORT

A Biography of
R. Tait McKenzie

Jean McGill

distributed by

Clay

PUBLISHING COMPANY
LIMITED
BEWDLEY, ONTARIO

"The House of Helpful Books"

ISBN 0-9690087-4-0

Printed and Bound in Canada by
The Alger Press Limited
Oshawa, Ontario

To the late Edwin C. Guillet

CONTENTS

Foreword

Robert Tait McKenzie—Rab, Rob, or R T M—as he is referred to in the text, was born in a rural manse near Almonte, Ontario, in 1867 and died seventy-one years later in Philadelphia. Almost half of his life was spent in the new Dominion of Canada: the other half in the United States. He entered the medical faculty of McGill University, Montreal, in 1885 and remained there about twenty years as a student, demonstrator in anatomy, director of physical training, instructor in gymnastics and during much of this time he also conducted private practice in orthopedic surgery. For fifteen months during this period he was resident physician to the Governor General of Canada, Lord Aberdeen, while his duties at the university were performed by an assistant. In 1904 he was offered and accepted an appointment at the University of Pennsylvania as director of the new gymnasium and professor in the faculty of medicine and he remained there for the rest of his life, except for a brief period of service with the British Army during World War I.

From boyhood he was active in athletics and this formed a bond with a neighbour, Jim Naismith, who preceded him, first to McGill and later to the United States where he became a leader in the physical education movement and invented the game of basketball. McKenzie followed in the same path, winning athletic honours at McGill and establishing a progressive program in physical education. Through his medical studies he became interested in the treatment of deformity through exercise and contributed to the new science of Anthropometry, which relates the physical potential of the human body to its proportions. As these activities progressed he became increasingly concerned with preventive medicine and the promotion of good health among the general population.

Meanwhile he also developed skills as a painter and sculptor. While at McGill, he gave a series of lectures on "Artistic Anatomy" at the Montreal Art Association and several of his paintings were hung in the annual exhibitions. He also made several masks, using prominent athletes as his models, to illustrate differences in facial expression when under stress. In 1900 these were used to illustrate a paper entitled: *The Facial Expression of Violent Effort, Breathlessness and Fatigue*, which was read before several learned or scientific societies. The masks brought favourable comment both in the United Kingdom and the United States and he was sufficiently encouraged to show his first figure in the round, the Sprinter, in New York and, afterwards, at the Royal Academy in London and the Paris Salon. This demonstrated a new dimension of his talent. He had embarked on another career which was to lead to the very pinnacle. His masterpieces include: The

Youthful Franklin, The Call, General Wolfe, The Boy Scout, The Joy of Effort, The Triumph of Wings, and many others.

Jean McGill's book is no conventional biography. In his later years, R T M spoke of writing his reminiscences but the project never materialized, although he was approached by several publishers with this in view. However, he kept a diary for many years and corresponded with a wide circle of friends. From these sources Miss McGill has drawn many excerpts which enrich her narrative.

Moreover, Miss McGill is well-qualified for the task she has undertaken. Also a native of Lanark County, she is familiar with the countryside in which McKenzie spent his boyhood and to which he returned as a summer resident at the end of his life. In 1930 he visited Almonte to discuss with friends the erection of a suitable memorial to his former schoolmaster, P.C. McGregor. While there he discovered an abandoned mill which he purchased and named "The Mill of Kintail." To this retreat he came each summer and shared its relaxed atmosphere with his devoted wife who was an accomplished pianist. Together they practiced their arts, she in her music room, he in his studio where he continued to create masterpieces such as the commemorative plaque for the Olympic Games. The Mill now serves as a Museum, displaying the models of many of his works and after his death a Cloister-on-the-Hill, an attractive outdoor chapel, was erected nearby as a tribute from his friends and admirers in Philadelphia. With these scenes, Miss McGill is perfectly familiar and this has given her confidence and sympathy in dealing with her subject.

My own appreciation of R T M goes back to the nineteen-twenties, when he had become a sort of legend at McGill. The Canadian Intercollegiate Athletic Union had purchased a reproduction of the "Sprinter" as its championship trophy and in those years it was frequently in our trophy cabinet at the Student Union. It was one of his earliest masterpieces produced while he was still at McGill and several McGill sprinters had posed as models. One was Dr. Fred J. Tees, who was honorary-president of the football club and did much to carry on the McKenzie tradition of amateurism among our athletes. In this he was joined by Dr. Arthur "Dad" Lamb, who was Director of Physical Education and a close friend of McKenzie. For those of us on the teams, there was a deep admiration and respect for McKenzie's versatility and talents as well as his opinions about physical fitness.

When the American-Scottish memorial was erected in Edinburgh in 1927 a wave of pride swept through the university and this was repeated when other memorials and the Olympic Shield were completed. By then McKenzie had become an international figure but his roots in Canada were deep and he had a special place at McGill. This became evident to me in the nineteen-fifties when, as Director of the Institute of Education, I was made responsible for the McGill School of Physical Education, which had been founded in 1912 and developed within the McKenzie tradition by "Dad" Lamb. To my surprise, I found that the custom had been established for the students of each graduating class to visit the "Mill' before receiving their degree. This pilgrimage of about 150 miles is still continued. McKenzie's principles of sport and of education have become part of the School's tradition, respected alike by staff and students.

I did not myself visit Kintail until 1970, when I was a resident of Ottawa. My wife and I drove out into Lanark County one summer's afternoon and shared the beauties of this unusual retreat with Major and Mrs. Leys who resided there as curators. Reporting our discovery in correspondence with the late Cyril James, McGill's principal from 1939 to 1963, I drew an excited reply that he had visited the site on several occasions to share his memories with an old friend whom he had known intimately at the University of Pennsylvania. As a matter of fact, he said, "I was able to persuade a generous benefactor to purchase the last statue McKenzie carved." He was referring to "The Falcon", a six-foot study of the memorial to aviation called "The Triumph of Wings" and it stands on the terrace of the McLennan Library on the McGill Campus.

Like it, I hope this book may strengthen the ties between McGill and one of her most distinguished sons, bringing new power to his influence in our own and future generations.

Bobolinks,
Choisy, Québec   David Munroe*
August 1, 1975
*deceased 1976

Introduction

Robert Tait McKenzie was primarily an educationist. He believed that education should involve an equal and simultaneous development of physical, mental and spiritual aspects of man, and that one aspect could not be developed at the expense of another without seriously imbalancing the whole person.

This was the basis of his lifetime involvement in physical education for he perceived that when the mind was housed in a well-functioning, vigorous and well-exercised body, the mental and psychic natures could more ably express the excellence hidden in man. And McKenzie believed profoundly in this Divine seed within man—this potential for perfection.

Like Leonardo de Vinci whose writing he sometimes quoted he felt profoundly "I am fearfully and wonderfully made."

McKenzie began life without any show of genius or academic ability yet by persistence in his ideals, he achieved excellence in sculpture, renown in physical education, esteem in physical medicine, and both respect and love in personal life.

At 62, he was described by Christopher Hussey, an early biographer, thus:

> He is very like one of his sculptured athletes: spare of words and movement, alertly sensitive but unemotional, with an acute intelligence, impatient of artistic top-hammer, but keen and resourceful. He has the Highlander's rooted mistrust, be he Spartan or Scot, of softness whether of mind or body. Bred in a hard school . . . he conceives man confronted with the necessity of overcoming nature by thought and self-control. He gives the impression of facing life like a lightweight boxer, balanced, watchful to seize any momentary opportunity and any means of getting through his adversary's weak defences. The unique position he holds today of both world-wide authority on physical efficiency and a sculptor of international reputation, has been achieved by a will like flexible steel, amazing keenness and a charm of mind.

McKenzie loved life and its challenges. Socially he had a great capacity for fellowship and enjoyed the company of his fellow man. He took great pleasure in his sculpture for here he could graphically illustrate the ideals he held in mind. But his greatest ambition lay in the field of physical education where he hoped to leave a clear-cut path for others to follow.

He deplored the "creeping professionalism" invading amateur sport in his day. The last thirty years have extended that professionalism in North America and made the multitudes observers of sport. Yet McKenzie would have been encouraged by the awakening during the 1970's to our dismal physical state and revival of gymnasiums and physical fitness programs for all and sundry.

It would have made his heart glad to observe of an early morning the joggers of various ages on our city residential streets.

Jean McGill

Acknowledgments

A special tribute to the late Edwin C. Guillet who advised on the handling of the material and read the completed manuscript, and to Grace Nicholls who also read the manuscript and gave helpful advice.

Thanks to two former associates and students of Dr. McKenzie— Joe Brown and Dr. Boris Blai—for their generosity in granting interviews and sharing their recollections of Dr. McKenzie with me.

My appreciation for information and courtesies extended by: Miss Edith Emerson, Curator of the Violet Oakley Foundation; Dr. Dick Sutcliffe, Treasurer of the St. Andrew's Society of Philadelphia; Mr. Charles Savage of North East Harbor, Maine; Mr. Wayne Johnson of the Medallic Art Company; Brookgreen Gardens, North Carolina; Mrs. Christopher Hussey, Mr. T. Kovacs, Mr. Lawrence Hayward, Mrs. David Gillies, Mr. Alfred Petrie, Mr. Joseph Lippincott, Jr., Mrs. Bess Barron, Mr. Thomas O'Neil, Miss Julie Heiton, Mrs. Dawn Knutsen, Mr. C.R. Blackstock, Mrs. Carol Erb, Dr. Rebecca Weinstein, Mrs. Louise Hulzig, Mr. D.G. Keddie, and the late Mr. Hal Kirkland.

Acknowledgment of the assistance of the following in supplying files on R. Tait McKenzie: The National Library of Scotland, Edinburgh; Wellcome Medical Library, London, England; Inverness Public Library, Inverness, Scotland; Edinburgh Public Library; Westminster Library, London, England; Osler Library, McGill University, Montreal; Montreal Museum of Art; Archives of McGill University, Montreal; Toronto Reference Library; Hart House, University of Toronto, Toronto; University of Toronto Athletic Association; Almonte Public Library; Free Public Library of Philadelphia; Historical Society of Philadelphia; John P. Robarts Library, University of Toronto.

The Author also wishes to thank the following organizations who supplied information through correspondence and/or illustrative material: The American Association for Health, Physical Education and Recreation; The Canadian Association for Health, Physical Education and Recreation; Teacher's College, Columbia University; Amherst College; Yale University; Harvard University; The Metropolitan Museum, New York City; The National Gallery of Canada; The Mississippi Conservation Authority; The National Portrait Gallery of Edinburgh; The Town of Cambridge; The National Education Association, Washington; The College of Physicians of Philadelphia; the Royal Victoria Hospital, Montreal; Janesville Public Library, Janesville, Wisconsin; The City of Darien, Ga.; *The Scots Magazine*; The London *Times*; The San Jose *Mercury News*; *Country Life Magazine*; Church of Scotland Assembly Office; National Capital Commission, Ottawa; Canada Post Office.

Special thanks to Mr. James F. Dallett and his congenial and helpful staff at the Archives of the University of Pennsylvania, and to Mr. Richard Sherman, Secretary of the University of Pennsylvania for their generosity in giving permission to freely use material from the R. Tait McKenzie Papers. Also thanks to the Lloyd P. Jones Gallery at the Gimbell Gymnasium, University of Pennsylvania, for supplying photos from their collection of Dr. McKenzie's sculpture.

Appreciation to the late Dr. David Munroe former Dean of Arts at McGill University for writing the Foreword.

A special acknowledgment goes to the Canada Council for making possible research in England and Scotland, and completion of the writing of this biographical study, and to the Ontario Arts Council for assistance during later revisions.

Jean S. McGill

List of Plates

CHAPTER I

The Formative Years

Robert Tait McKenzie was born in 1867—the year the provinces joined in confederation to become The Dominion of Canada.

His father, Rev. William McKenzie, was minister of the Free Presbyterian Church in Ramsay township, Lanark county, about 30 miles from Ottawa, the capital of the new dominion.

Rev. William McKenzie had been sent out to Canada by the Presbytery of Edinburgh in 1857, a recent graduate of New College, Edinburgh, and a thirty-two year old bachelor. He spent his first winter assisting Dr. Simon Fraser at the Côte Street church in Montreal, occasionally lecturing at the New Presbyterian College. The next summer he explored Ontario, preaching his way from place to place as was the custom of itinerant ministers.

Originally a Highlander from Cromarty, William's father, the Rev. Patrick McKenzie, had gone to preach in the Lowland Anti-Burgher parish at Kelso, near Edinburgh, and here William had grown up.

Like his father he adhered to the Free Church of Scotland and in Ramsay township found a landscape and community of Scots with whom he felt at home. They needed a pastor for their new rural church. They liked his quiet personality and fine, zealous sermons and offered him charge of the new church. He accepted and a year later returned to Edinburgh to marry Catherine Shiells.

Forty years before, Ramsay had been settled by Scottish weavers and tradesmen from Lanarkshire. Irish settlers had arrived a few years later driven out of Ireland by the potato famine and incredible poverty, and brought to Canada under an emigration plan of the Honourable Peter Robinson. Most of the pioneers were unfamiliar with farming but settled down to learn the hard way how to clear, work and till the land. It was to such a community that William McKenzie brought his bride from sophisticated Edinburgh.

Two children were born to the McKenzies before the arrival of Robert Tait in May 1867. A year later the family moved to Almonte.

Rev. William McKenzie had ministered to the congregation of St. John's Presbyterian church of Almonte for three years prior to this and the burden of the two parishes had sorely taxed his strength for he had been a tireless worker in his community as well as their "preacher" on Sundays. When it became evident that his health was being undermined, the two congregations agreed to unite and close the Ramsay township church.

University of Pennsylvania Archives

TAIT McKENZIE'S FIRST HOME. Church and manse on 8th line of Ramsay Township. Water-colour sketch by McKenzie about 1888.

Almonte was then as it is now, one of the prettiest towns in the Ottawa Valley with winding tree-lined streets and the Mississippi River meandering through it. The town had grown around a picturesque cascading waterfall which provided power to run several mills. The largest, the Rosamond Woollen Mill, produced fine woollen tweeds to ship to Britain and other lesser fabrics for the domestic market.

The McKenzies lived at the south-west end of the town in a white brick manse opposite the Presbyterian church. Rural and village life blended happily in their lives.

> When I was three or four years old, my mother had a serious illness and was taken home to Scotland for treatment, by my father and we were farmed out to members of his congregation. Robert Young's farm became a second home. Its fine stone house shaded by a veranda on three sides, the fragrant lilacs in its garden, its hedges and beehives, were places of delight. The patient collie on its treadmill worked the churn. Its spacious barn housed the products of the well-tilled fields and the stable-pump and horse-trough supplied the horses and cattle.*

The McKenzies were often the guests of "Grandfather Young" as they called him for he was grandfather to three orphan children who lived with him—Peter, Annie, and James Naismith.**

---

*Unless otherwise indicated, all quotations in this chapter are taken from the autobiographical notes of R. Tait McKenzie. University of Pennsylvania Archives.
**James Naismith was inventor of basketball.

Visits to the farm were looked forward to with joyful anticipation, the daily school round in Almonte was not. "Robbie" as the little McKenzie was called, did not get on well with his first schoolmaster, Mr. McCarter. McCarter had been a blacksmith before he took up teaching and he wielded the strap in school much as he might have wielded a hammer in the blacksmith shop. He was nicknamed "Juno" by the students because of his ferocity.

Sixty years later when McKenzie spoke in the Almonte high school to a group of students, he recalled his early days there with mild pleasure until he came to recollections of McCarter. As he told of the schoolmaster beating both boys and girls, his voice quavered with anger. As for himself:

> Looking back with the eye of memory I see a rather delicate child, sensitive at being called pale-faced, a roamer of the woods and fields with a mind filled with the romance that Sir Walter Scott and Fenimore Cooper alone could instil, going unwillingly to school, distracted by thoughts of the *Deerslayer*, making clothyard shafts from the straight cedar rails looted from the fences of unwilling farmers, feathered with care to be sped by bows of rock elm against squirrels, chipmunk or groundhog, the wild pigeon then still with us, the partridge sitting low on its branch, and failing all these, even the domestic hen . . .

Years later Robbie's brother William recorded the public school experiences under McCarter with these poignant lines:

THE MEESERABLE TOOL

Wi' the vera spunk o' leevin' this laddie was aglow,
    He loved the summer sunshine, an' the blawin' caller air;
Wee creatures o' the forest gied him mony things tae know,
    Sae for him tae be in prison wasna fair.

The schoolroom had a stuffy smell wi' dust o' yesterdays,
    The place was thrang, the 'oors were long an' weary went the time
The maister aye a giant seemed, ower-michty tae gie praise,
    The business had nae reason and nae rhyme.

When 'rithmatick was forward, the lad heard many words,
    And saw unmeaning figures chalked upon the blackened wa',
His mind was in the shady woods, an' list'ning tae the birds
    He micht hae said he wasna there ata'.

The maister was a handy man, blacksmithin' was his trade,
    Wha bellows, fire an' anvil left for teachin' weans at school,
Each time the lad was stupid-like he'd hear the same tirade,
    Eh, Rabbie, ye're a meeserable tool!

. . . .

The leaves maun fa', then comes the snaw, ere Spring's wi' us again;
    Auld fashions pass an' life renewed's aye wantin' better tools
The liliputians o' the school grow up tae weel-faured men.
    An' Nature picks for use ane o' the fools.

Ane whom she picks for usefu'ness is docile in her hand,
    An' eager wi' a diligence that coonts nae toil or pain;
An' mean men shalna judge him, for afore kings he shall stand
    Wi' his ain gift enriched, an' not wi' gain.

That ane was Nature's freend indeed, *the meeserable tool*
    What stum'led at the crossin' o' the *Assinorum Pons;*
But he was rich wi' diligence an sib tae Wisdom's rule,
    An' formed his thochts wi' age-endurin' bronze.

The sculptor's hands had skilfu'ness the blacksmith couldna ken,
    Wha hammered on his anvil since that meeserable lad;
Thae hands that fashioned beauty's form, pictured ideal men
    Tae mak' the hearts o' tens o' thousan's glad.

Fortunately when Robbie was eight years old, a new school was built on Martin Street to accommodate both public and high school classes. William and Agnes were then high school students and Robbie accompanied them to the new school where his teacher was a Miss Neilson. He thus escaped the dreaded McCarter who remained at the old school.

> On our way to school, we had a plunge in the pool shaded by an old elm from whose hanging branches the orioles swung their cunning nest and a shallow stretch of the river known as 'Rockbottom' served as a safe school for the more timid.

> When winter came we skated over the frozen stretches of river, creeks and ponds, screwing the wooden skates to the heels of our boots and binding them with straps that made our feet ache with cold, or clamping on the "Acme" skates that were supposed to stay on without straps and represented the last word in mechanical perfection.

In the new school, Robbie found a more sympathetic teacher in Miss Neilson, who took an interest in his talent for drawing. When the local newspaper advised that a visiting drawing master was coming to Almonte, Miss Neilson suggested that Robbie benefit by professional instruction. His parents agreed and the boy was introduced to watercolour sketching. Thus at an early age he acquired the sketching habit which remained with him all his life and formed a basic training for later work in sculpture.

Tragedy hit the McKenzie family in 1876. Overworked and ill for some time, Rev. William McKenzie died at the age of 52. With two children in high school, Robbie in public school, and a new baby expected, Mrs. McKenzie had scarcely time to grieve as she tried to cope with the financial situation in which she found herself. Her husband had been much loved by the entire community and the townspeople came to her rescue, helping in many ways in addition to raising money for a new house, for now the manse must be vacated for the incoming pastor.

John Bertram, married to her sister, Helen Shiells, was a prosperous lumber merchant in Peterborough. He too came to the little family's rescue, but Mrs. McKenzie was a true Scot, and proud. Henceforth the children had to run errands and do odd jobs after school to augment the family income. It was the end of the leisurely life for the little McKenzies.

Whether the arrival of his baby brother, Bertram, or the arrival of the circus was more exciting to Robbie the summer of 1876, is unknown. The year was, in any event, one of the milestones of his life for he faced death and birth at close hand during the year and was also introduced to an idea that was later to germinate in young adult life.

Shortly before the birth of his brother, in June the "New Golden Menagerie Circus" came to town. Robbie saw for the first time, acrobats in action. No stocky, muscle-bulging strong men were these, but lean, trim, sinewy figures of men who depended upon perfect timing and balance to perform amazing feats on the high wire. Watching them fly through the air with the greatest of ease, the boy saw how a man of small stature and slight build could reach great heights in physical achievement. Ashamed of his undersize and delicate physique, some hope stirred in Robbie's breast as he watched the trapezists.

Though he watched the phenomena with interest, he did not associate the performance with athletics. The word "athlete", he recalled later in life, would at that time have meant Donald Dinnie's exploits at the Caledonian games, or Ray Moe MacLennan, Glengarry County's pride who could leap over three horses, the center one being sixteen hands high, and throw a 10-pound blacksmith's hammer further than a man could fling a finger stone of his own choosing.

There was also the professional pedestrian like Harry Bethune who planted himself in a small town, talked up an interest in sprinting at the barber shop and livery stable, showed his remarkable speed to a chosen few, got up a matched race backed by the local sports eager to make money on a sure thing and either crossed or double-crossed them as the financial situation required.

At school we ran, jumped and played tag and prisoner's base. Once two of us ran continuously from the school to our home at the other end of the village, but that was just to see if we could do it.

We formed a lacrosse club and practiced on the common which formed the grazing ground of the village cows, a perilous playing field as may be readily believed, and in winter we found that by mounting a high fence and jumping off with our heads well tucked in, we could land in a sitting position without any apparent injury, the discovery of the principle of the front somersault. But it was not till I came home from my first year at college that I could show my former companions in the old circus ring itself that one can run, leap in the air, turn over and land on one's feet without falling.

With spring came the great lumbering drives down the rushing waters of the Mississippi to the Ottawa River. There was a timber slide in Almonte providing great excitement for young and old.

The drive of sawlogs down the swollen stream was a dramatic event. The agile river men would leap from log to log, levering them off the rocks with their peevies and shoving their noses with their pike poles into the slides that passed the Falls and rapids down which they slid with increasing speed, to plunge and rise again, to shake the water from their heads, to float gently into the calm waters of the lower bay. And when all was done there was the final running of the slide . . . the crews of the long, high-pointed red York boats, to the beating of pans and kettles, shouts and laughter.

As he grew older, Robbie joined other daring youngsters in leaping the logs, testing their skill in balance and agility.

We stepped lightly from stick to stick as they sank under our weight, till we could come to rest on a big one. Sometimes we would come suddenly to a space of clear water too late to stop and then we had to throw ourselves belly down across one and warily regain our place on top. Good exercise it was and practical for it had an element of risk without which the sporting spirit is lacking.

The sinister power of the rushing water was brought to us by the drownings that were recounted to us as warning as we learned the risks men run in their contest with Nature.

Visits to Robert Young's farm were more frequent as the McKenzie children grew older and were able to help with farm chores. Here Robbie learned much of use to him later in life.

I learned to ride a horse bareback, hanging on surreptitiously to such tufts of the mane that were within reach, especially when the trot of the thirsty horse to the water-trough made the problem of balance acute, and so I learned to harness a horse, milk a cow, and even a little later to hold a plough.

On the farm the spirit of competition found its outlet in the daily task of the harvest field and in them Jim Naismith, the eldest, was the hero. Jim could stand astride an unbound sheaf of wheat with a band in his hand. I wonder how many men now living know how to draw from a sheaf the handfuls of stalks to make a band, twist the heads so they will not slip, bring the stalks around the sheaf dextrously, tuck in the bases so that the sheaf can be forked into the wagon without pulling apart? Jim could as I said stand astride his unbound sheaf, the band in his hand, take another sheaf already bound, throw it high in the air, and before it came to earth, could show the other securely bound and set on end.

Such feats as this took the place of athletic sports and our heroes were the men who could make their team of horses pull a load where another had failed, who took pride in lifting the heavy end of the log, who could tame a wild colt, run a straight furrow with his plow, handle a canoe, shoot straight, or make a tree fall where he wanted it to lie.

The Young farm lay along the Mississippi River.

The Spring nights on the farm were often spent in spearing fish in the shallow water that flooded the low banks of the river. The lurid gleam of the jack filled with splattering pink knots, the paddler seated in the stern of the punt, the spearman with his poised trident, the sudden lunge, and the gleaming scales of the fish as it was thrown on the floor of the boat, brought us romance, and tragedy was not absent when on one unforgettable pitchblack night we beached the punt quietly on the low bank of the meadow, a lighted lantern concealed in an empty firkin, carefully covered, Jim with his gun across his knees and I holding the nose of the punt against the bank, waiting in silent anticipation for what was to happen. Presently we heard the rush of frightened feet coming toward us and the flock of sheep came stampeding by. I raised the lantern high and there was a sudden startled pause as I saw reflected in the phosphorescent light startled eyes. The gun cracked and a neighbour's dog, long under suspicion for sheep killing, dropped in his tracks.

Once Robbie coming home in a springless cart over a rocky road, placed his gun butt down, holding the barrel in his hand. A sudden heavy jolt of the cart touched it off. The sharp bark of the gun sounded in his ear and he recovered his hat torn and smoking with part of the rim shot away. It was a good lesson for the young marksman.

By the time I was fourteen, I had my own birch bark canoe, lined with cedar and strengthened by thwarts of hickory, calked with resin, its ends rising to a high point—a beautiful craft. And I learned to drive it with a single paddle against the wind. With a companion, we navigated the river to its mouth 35 miles away, running the rapids, portaging the mill dams and falls, and camped at Marshall's Bay on the great Ottawa itself for a fortnight, living the nomadic life of the Indians.

This blending of village life and farm life was a happy combination and I was afterwards thankful that as a boy it taught me to milk a cow, harness and drive a horse, handle an axe, make a fire and cook my own food out-of-doors if I had to for when as a student I got a job on a survey party in the untamed northwest of Canada, life in the tents was no hardship. It was a continuous picnic to gallop forward with the red and white pole that formed the foresight of the surveyor and to hunt for fresh camping grounds with woods and water convenient to pitch tents. It was the blossoming out of the practical application of all the occupations that had been the recreations of my boyhood days.

When Robbie moved from public to high school he merely moved up one storey in the stone school on Martin Street.

University of Pennsylvania Archives

R.T. McKENZIE AND JAMES NAISMITH as teenagers.

P.C. McGregor was the principal and his teacher. P.C. was famous in the Ottawa Valley of his day for his ability to recognize talent in a student and bring it out. During his tenure of over 30 years as principal of the Almonte high school he turned out a brilliant array of pupils who became well-known or outstanding in their chosen fields. Some of these were classmates of Robert Tait McKenzie. "Mac" Bell who became a noted geologist, traveller and writer; "Bob" Knowles a clergyman and novelist; James Naismith, clergyman and inventor of basketball. Another Almonte high school graduate who distinguished himself was Edward Peacock who became director of the Bank of England, Comptroller of the Duchy of Cornwall and was later knighted.

University of Pennsylvania Archives

McKENZIE FAMILY PHOTO (left to right) Tait, Bertram, William. Mrs. McKenzie (center).

Agnes McKenzie headed her class and William was an above-average student but Robert still showed little scholarship. The exasperated P.C. was often heard to remark: "McKenzie, your head is full of rats and straw."

McGregor was relentless in training students for university however and doubtless McKenzie benefitted from the discipline. Another student of the day wrote in later years:

> No pupil of his [McGregor] ever worked half as hard as he or put in longer hours. In the bleak days of winter he would come at eight in the morning and stay until five in the afternoon, devoting extra hours. His classroom had no artificial lighting so we huddled with him at one of the windows to dig out the intricacies of Greek and Latin grammar in the waning twilight.

> P.C. had apparently learned his classics the hard way and he passed the same method along to his pupils . . . he regarded the great epic poetry of Homer and Virgil as having been written for the sole purpose of being parsed and scanned word by word, and line by line, a sort of autopsy on a dead language.

> At any rate he gave us no glimpse of the poetic beauty which these immortal classics embodied, nor did we acquire any historical background of the stirring events they portrayed. Perhaps it was just as well. Those of us who went on to college found ourselves with a foundation upon which the superstructure of literary and historical interpretation could be built.

Robert Tait McKenzie went from the Almonte high school to the Lisgar Collegiate Institute in Ottawa and from there to McGill University, at age 18, in 1885.

Three years later his mother left Almonte for London where Agnes was teaching kindergarten. William McKenzie was then at Fort McLeod in Manitoba doing missionary work as a Presbyterian layman. Bertram was an engineering student at Queen's University in Kingston.

Many years would pass before Robert Tait would return to Almonte, the scene of his childhood.

CHAPTER II

McKenzie at McGill

Despite the active outdoor life of his boyhood in Almonte, Robert Tait McKenzie entered his pre-med course at McGill University as a slender, underdeveloped youth.

At McGill he discovered organized athletics in Barnjum's gymnasium, a plain red brick building at Number 19 University Street. It was a glimpse into a new world.

> Students were pouring in through the main door when I first saw it one afternoon in late September. They entered the narrow passage that separated the office with its closed door from the open dressing rooms. The principal piece of furniture in the dressing room was an upright coal stove and several wooden benches. The wall was lined with square wooden lockers, each with its ventilating auger hole exhaling the peculiar and characteristic odour of stale sweat. On raising a curtain in the corner of the room, a lead-lined cubicle was discovered in which the more daring might enjoy the fearsome pleasure of an icy shower.

The equipment in use was new to him—dumbbells, Indian clubs and bar-bells. There were horizontal and parallel bars, tumbling mats, and a vaulting bar.

> On that afternoon in 1885, I stood diffidently watching with some envy the assurance of old-timers swinging on the rings, clambering over the ladders, lifting dumbbells and manipulating the other strange appliances that I now saw for the first time. Suddenly the office door opened and out came an alert little man about five feet six inches. He was in his late forties, with moustache and side-whiskers, well set up, compactly built. He was dressed in brown velveteen jacket and breeches, black stockings and low shoes. This was Major Frederick S. Barnjum.

Major Barnjum was an independent sort of fellow who had come to Canada from England in 1859 as an artist. An enthusiastic horseman and gymnast, he had organized the Montreal Gymnastic Club the same year with fifty-six charter members. They soon needed more room to expand and arranged with the governors of McGill University to have a gym built. Barnjum visited gymnasiums throughout the U.S. and advised on the equipment needed. The gymnasium opened in 1862.

Barnjum was eccentric and refused to take any salary or expenses

---

*Unless otherwise indicated all quotations in this chapter are taken from the autobiographical notes of R. Tait McKenzie, University of Pennsylvania Archives.

out of the funds the members provided. As new members flocked to the club, surplus money accumulated and was later used to form the Montreal Amateur Athletic Association.

McGill appointed him "Drilling and Gymnastic Master" and assigned him classes for three hours weekly. For the remainder of the week, he leased the building from the university and conducted his own gymnastic classes.

He used exercises founded on those of Maclaren of Oxford University and also developed a system of his own using clubs and bar-bells in class drills of great precision.

Robert or Rob as classmates called him, joined an evening class determined to strengthen his light frame through gymnastics.

An evening class would begin with half a dozen exercises by the whole group on bridge ladders to strengthen the arms and upper part of the trunk. Then the class would divide into smaller groups called 'squads', each with a leader. Each group proceeded from ten minutes at the vaulting bar to the bar-bell exercises which brought almost every muscle of the body into play, yet by working antagonistic muscles against each other, never overstrained any. The Indian clubs came last—a marvellous combination of grace and powerful work-out for the muscles.

Acrobatics became a passion with me. The mattress of my bed, hauled out on the floor, served to deaden the shock of an uncollated neck-spring, and every new trick was seized upon and practised.

With friends equally keen on acrobatics, McKenzie attended burlesque and vaudeville shows at the Theatre Royal. For 10¢, 20¢, or 30¢ according to the show, the boys sat transfixed by juggling and trapeze acts which they later tried to imitate.

It was here I saw the peerless jugglers Cinquevallis, Leroux and Wilton on the bars, the Hanlons on the trapeze, the seven Craggs in their evening dress doing their thrilling falling pyramid: 'Gus' Hill juggling his gilded Indian clubs.

Many of these feats were difficult and required long practice but others were easy, although they required two—like the Bear Walk, and the Catherine Wheel. And so, Jim Naismith and I got together a 'brother-act' that so impressed Barnjum that he gave us a number to ourselves at the annual gymnastic show.

The next Christmas at the concert given by the high school in Almonte at the town hall, we did our act ending it with a Catherine Wheel in which each grasps the ankles of his partner, diving forward and rolling across the stage. Accustomed to a larger space than the stage afforded, we kept rolling along, bursting into the dressing room and collapsing among the girls attired for their next number.

At Barnjum's gymnasium, advanced members appeared at the Spring exhibition in special numbers. Once in a while Barnjum selected a proficient junior to join this group. McKenzie showed keenness and aptitude and was chosen for the Ladder Pyramid Team, a distinction which increased his self-confidence.

The gymnastic classes opened up new vistas for him.

The pitting of one's strength, skill and speed, agility, and enduring in formal public competition was also a new experience, divided equally between two imposters—triumph and disaster. Every contest was prefaced by a period of sickening anxiety and foreboding, the reports of uncanny speed or 'grasshopper-like' agility of one's opponents.

Football, sprinting, hurdling, high and broad jumping, were added to the program. He tried distance running but was exhausted after half a mile in 2.30. He found his own athletic distinction lay in events not requiring great strength or stamina but in which skill, coordination and assiduous practice counted, such as in jumping and hurdling.

Strange to say in tug-of-war on cleats, he found: "By devising a series of holds on the rope with the hands, arms and knees, I was able to pull with comparative ease, men much stronger and heavier than myself, much to their annoyance."

University of Pennsylvania Archives

COMPETITORS FOR THE WICKSTEED MEDALS, McGill University, 1886–87. (left to right) Tait McKenzie, G.A. Brown, Major Fred S. Barnjum (Instructor), W.A. Cameron. Reclining: James Naismith.

The development of physical skill appears to have been uppermost in Robert Tait McKenzie's mind during his college days while the academic side of his life proceeded in an uneventful way. Each summer he worked to finance the following university year. His autobiographical notes suggest that these excursions were more interesting and memorable to him than his school life.

The summer of 1886 he went with a survey party to run the Indian trails from Portage la Prairie to Lake Manitoba and up the Assinaboine and Souris Rivers, making them into government roads. The chief surveyor was a handsome, young French-Canadian with black hair, waxed moustache and fine clothes. This was Ibrahin du Fresne and also in the party was Achilles du Fresne, a cousin, and brother-in-law—Jules. Tait considered Achilles a "beau sabreur" and woodsman of great experience. "They all talked the French of Quebec and I quickly became accustomed to it" he related later.

Achilles was also a student at McGill in civil engineering. He wrote an account of this particular survey some years later:

> McKenzie was my captain and head chopper. Jules was his helper. I would go ahead along the old Indian trail, locate a curve, plant a 15-foot pole with a flag on top. I would then shout to McKenzie and we would walk toward one another and so get the direction to cut the lines which were averaging some 400 feet.

> We were a party of men locating old Indian trails on the western Prairies before the settlers would buy and occupy the lands, reserving a strip of 66 feet wide. . . . Some of the best days of our lives were spent there.

> We had plenty of good sustaining food. Breakfast was mess bacon, barrels of hard tack, blackstrap molasses, dried fruits, potato chips. One case of good Hennessy brandy and one 10-gallon keg of Jamaica rum. Besides we had birds to shoot, fish to catch, good water, lime juice, and open air day and night . . . . The cook, a good young man about 22, was with McKenzie, the only one who spoke English.

Of the cook, Robert said:

> [he] said he had the necessary accomplishment on what proved to be most slender foundations. He was from near my own home in Ontario . . . . He set bread at night but it would not rise, so we had biscuits made with baking powder and from that time on . . . his vain attempt to learn the art and the midnight excursions to pour his failures down the holes of unsuspecting gophers. He made something out of flour known as 'Christ-killers' which only the Indians seemed to manage, but that was all.

Jules and Robert were "humble" mound builders and travelled in a cart, Achilles on horseback. Years later writing from Atlanta, Ga. at the age of 73 about his old friend, McKenzie, Achilles recalled with nostalgia:

University of Pennsylvania Archives

J.I. DUFRESNE'S CAMP on the western shore of Lake Manitoba, August 1886. Water-colour sketch by Tait McKenzie.

In the evening the twilight was long being in the latitude of about 53 degrees. We would sit on the ground Indian fashion under the blue sky, observing the galaxy of stars above. The conversation would often carry us to our respective home towns. McKenzie would tell us how good and intelligent was his mother dear. He had a small travelling trunk covered with leather which had crossed the ocean with his father when he came to this country from Scotland.

McKenzie left the party in October, already two or three weeks late for University.

Next year he went on another survey party but this time the chief surveyor was a full-blooded Iroquois Indian, Tom Greene, a graduate from McGill. Robert joined the party at Calgary and they pitched their tents in the crook of the Elbow and Bow Rivers. In the party was Tom's brother, "a real Indian", and a student from Queen's University named Ross.

At Calgary McKenzie saw his first real prize-fight, an edifying experience.

The construction gang of the C.P.R. were scarcely 100 miles ahead. A coal mine had been opened at Lethbridge and in the newly built roller-skating rink and dance hall, "Denver Ed" Smith met a local bartender named Gorman. Around the ring at intervals were the Red Coats and yellow-striped breeches of the troopers from the Northwest Mounted Police Barracks, miners, and ranchers, railway men and loafers with a sprinkling of women who haunt all frontier towns.

In the background stood the blanketted Indian braves from the Sarcee Reservation nearby with some Blackfoot and Bloods who came to see how white men fought. Impassive and silent they watched the strange spectacle as it went—round after round. Gorman was tall, a clean-limbed athlete, and a fine boxer and with light gloves soon had Smith bleeding

from nose and mouth. Round after round it went till about the
30th . . . then the 40th round. About the 46th round Gorman went white
and was knocked down and out, beaten by superior stamina.

The surveyors went south on the Fort McLeod trail. It was level
prairie "for the most part with herds of half-wild cattle wandering at
will, rounded up once a year for branding calves." Settlers were buying
land, moving in and putting up fences, but the only roads were the old
Indian trails that cut across the country following the contour of the
land. These often traversed private property because the land was sold
in sections. A new owner would put up a fence, but the next traveller
would knock it down. The owner would put it back and wait with a gun
for the next trespasser on his property.

It was for this reason that the government sent survey parties to
construct government roads.

I thus had the privilege of establishing the King's highway by the use of
my pick and shovel. I would start out at daylight, cold and wretched,
catch the horses in the dew-drenched grass, and after breakfast, pack my
tin-can with salt pork, dried apples or prunes, half a loaf of bread, butter,
tea and sugar, wrapped in paper, and a bundle of sticks for a fire, for
usually there was no wood in sight on the plains.

On one occasion some Blackfoot Indians expressed their disapproval. A
party of six blanketted braves, well-armed, rode down on me and by signs
told me to be gone. I shook my head and went on digging. They
threatened but I went on. Then they rode away about 50 yards turned
their horses and came galloping on me yelling and brandishing their
rifles. I jumped up out of the pit with my spade raised and the intention of
getting one at least. The horses swerved right and left and they rode
away scowling.

After this, two of us were detailed for this work and Ross and I worked
together. This I rather regretted for when I was alone I did seven pairs of
mounds, stopped at about eleven made my tea and lay down in the shade
under the cart and read for an hour or more. And the unfortunate Jean
Valjean from Victor Hugo, George Eliott's creations and Joseph Andrews
(in cheap editions) filled my imagination. And with another present this
was not possible.

But we had our diversions. I was a good acrobat and could do a row of six
handsprings without stopping, so Ross would get into the cart, Bill [the
horse] securely harnessed, and I would start my row of handsprings
straight for him. The horse would gaze in astonishment and horror at
this whirling, revolving monster and then would bolt across the prairie,
Ross hanging on to the reins for dear life.

The survey party happened to be on the Blackfoot Reservation at
Blackfoot Crossing on "Treaty Day" when the Indians received their
blankets and treaty money. It was followed by a week of horse-racing,
gambling, and feasting, "and we got into it through Ross who was a
good sprinter and could easily beat any of them on foot."

University of Pennsylvania Archives

BESIDE THE MCLEOD TRAIL, at Blackfoot Crossing on the Bow River, Alberta, August 1887. Running Rabbit's Camp on the left, government buildings in background. Crowfoot's camp on right. Crowfoot's house extreme right. Water-colour sketch by McKenzie.

University of Pennsylvania Archives

McKENZIE FRIGHTENS "BILL" by turning handsprings (survey of McLeod Trail, 1887). Water-colour sketch by Tait McKenzie.

A favourite race was a man against a horse, 50 yards with a turn. Under ordinary circumstances, the man should win because he can start quicker and turn so much quicker than a horse that he more than makes up for the greater speed of the horse in the straightaway. But the Indian ponies, accustomed to the chase, can stop in their own length and wheel like a flash, so we made the mistake of our lives when we backed Ross.

Ross was beaten and they lost their money.

Back in Montreal that Fall, McKenzie and three other students decided to take lessons in boxing. Their instructor was a coachman who had been a lightweight champion. The lesson hour was set for 7:00 a.m. McKenzie recorded later:

> He would say: 'This morning I'm going to make everyone's nose bleed.' And he proceeded to do so with a dextrous side flip of the glove that soon had us standing in the corners wiping our faces. He was a good teacher and first showed me the pivot blow introduced by George Leblanche and afterwards barred from boxing.

In the summer of 1888 McKenzie had a complete change of pace and scene by going to Collins Inlet on Georgian Bay to work in his uncle's lumber company. His job was to measure lumber prior to its loading onto barges and schooners that came up the slip. With his characteristic enthusiasm, he undertook the mastery of the task, later recording:

> I loved to feel the board as it came running down from the high tramway between my leather-protected hands, to balance it for an instant against the apron over the thigh, then to drop it in place on the pile—a pretty feat.

His duties at the mill were varied and in the evenings the workers "yarned or pole vaulted" in front of the boarding house "with an occasional grudge to be settled by a fist fight."

That summer the man who had set him on a physical fitness path, Major Barnjum, died after an attack of meningitis followed by an ear infection. McKenzie felt a deep sense of loss when he returned to classes in the Fall. This was his final Arts year and he was just beginning his medical course.

McKenzie's devotion to gymnastics and athletics had attracted attention among the faculty but it was his friend, James Naismith who was chosen to take Barnjum's place in the gymnasium. Naismith had won the all-round senior gymnastic championship two years before and was the mainstay of McGill's football team. He was a theological student in the Presbyterian College and was urged by Sir William Dawson of the McGill Board to take over the gymn. Naismith was McKenzie's senior by five years and it was natural that he be given the position. But he needed an assistant and he turned to McKenzie.

We talked it over and he agreed to take the classes if I would help him unofficially and informally. I had never led a class before and neither had he.

After a hard football game he would come to the gymn completely exhausted for he was a relentless player who never spared himself so long as he could stand up, so I was forced into leadership in spite of a natural diffidence.

That Spring [1889] I competed for and won the coveted Wicksteed medal (gold) representing the gymnastic championship.

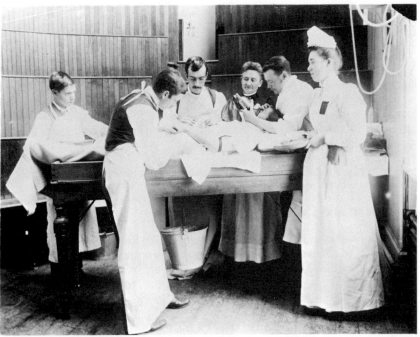

University of Pennsylvania Archives

BOGUS OPERATION STAGED IN MONTREAL GENERAL HOSPITAL for McGILL QUARTERLY. Tait McKenzie as anaesthesist.

During the summer of 1889, McKenzie worked for the Hansa steamship line at the Montreal dock. Their steamships carried merchandise from Europe to Canada and cattle on the return journey to England. Robert Tait's job was to count the stevedores, note the hour they went off duty, and arrange for their midnight supper at one of the boarding houses.

On hot summer nights one could see by the coal-oil lanterns, from twenty to eighty sweat-beguiled labourers, wolfing their supper in one of the upper rooms along the greystone-lined street that looked down on the wooden wharves of the harbour and out on the river.

The checking of cattle was the cause of many disputes. A steer would back up after it had been counted and often we had to go down to the stifling air between decks, crawl over their backs, watching for any that were lying down, and count them again, always at night—for they were loaded at the last moment and the ship sailed at daybreak.

The life of the wharves was full of emergencies. It agreed with me, however, for at the Fall games another student and I took four first places—he at shot put and hammer throw, and I at hurdles and high jump.

McKenzie and another McGill student were invited by the University of Toronto to participate in open competitions. This was one of the first approaches to intercollegiate competition. McKenzie won the high jump five times and cleared 5' 9'', a record that stood for five years. (This was within 9 inches of the world record for 1892 which was 6' 5⅝''—a remarkable achievement for a student. It is interesting to note that the 1976 Olympic high jump record was 7' 4-½'' which shows how the standard has risen in the past century)

The following year McKenzie made the football team and was a member of the tug-of-war team for two years. Football games were preceded by misgivings.

The reports of gigantic proportions and wolf-like ferocity of the team one was to meet on Saturday were all on the debit side and scarcely balanced by the short-lived triumph of victory with their tawdry medals or hard-earned cup.

James Naismith graduated from McGill in 1890 and McKenzie succeeded to his position as Instructor in Gymnastics. Uncertain of his qualifications for the task, McKenzie went off to Dr. Sargent's summer course at Harvard. Here he was introduced to Anthropometry, the science which relates the physical potential of the human body to its proportion.

The implications of this science fired his imagination. The usual drills were taught but in addition, Sargent discussed anatomy as applied to exercise and went thoroughly into the influence of proportion.

His speculation on athletic types illustrated by a large collection of photos taken by himself of heroes of the ring and the wrestling mat, the cinder-path, the field, whose names were as familiar as those of the demi-gods who fought before the walls of Troy, inflamed my imagination and began to exercise a fascination that has never left me. I resolved that I, too, would wield a spade in the work of digging up new facts in this untilled field.

The field was a comparatively new one. Dr. Dudley Allan Sargent had pioneered in physical education in the United States. As Director of the Hemenway Gymnasium at Harvard in 1879, he began to accumulate the vital statistics which, reduced to chart form, proved valuable to gymnasium directors for it showed the tendency of proportion to govern skill in athletics.

Applicants at Harvard filled out a history form showing record of muscular tests, examination of heart and lungs, weight, height, chest-girth, and other measurements, and the condition of the skin, muscles and spine. These were plotted on a chart and showed the physical condition of each student. The medical examiner could then recommend appropriate exercises for the development of any deficient organs.

Dudley Sargent said of his system: "One-half of the fight for physical training is won when the student can be induced to take a genuine interest in his bodily condition—to want to remedy his defects, and to pride himself on the purity of his skin, the firmness of his muscles, and the uprightness of his figure. . . The student is no longer compelled to compete with others in the performance of feats that are distasteful to him. He can now compete with himself (that is, his own physical condition from week to week and from month to month)."

Six months later the Harvard student underwent another examination to determine any improvement and new suggestions might be made. By requiring this examination, the Harvard faculty also exercised some control over zealous athletes whose over-exertion might injure them.

The Harvard course was intense and strenuous but on Saturday afternoons the summer school group adjourned to the beaches of Boston. McKenzie recalled in later years: "I can still see (by closing my eyes) the agile form of Francis Dohs on the hard sands of Nantucket joining our party by a series of handsprings and roundoffs that amazed the casual and untalented bathers." Several years later McKenzie returned to Harvard as lecturer at the summer school.

The Fall of 1891 found him back in Montreal with a diploma from Harvard's summer school under his arm and a head full of new ideas for gymnastics at McGill. He was now in charge as Instructor.

At McGill they played a football close to the English rugby. Tait saw his first game of American football in 1892 on a visit to Springfield as a member of the investigating committee of the Canadian Rugby Union. The match was between Harvard and Yale. He was entirely unprepared for the vindictiveness displayed and the serious way it was taken by the spectators. At this match he watched seven players being carried off the field. The Canadian group came home strongly opposed to adopting the American game but despite this opposition, Canadian football began to change:

> I became a familiar figure on the field with my little black bag with its adhesive plaster, absorbent cotton, curved needles and silk thread, bandages, perchloride of iron, iodine and aromatic spirits of ammonia, and more than one anxious night was spent with a concussion case.

In 1892 McKenzie graduated as a medical doctor but by interning at the Montreal General Hospital, he was able to carry on as Instructor at the university gymnasium. An assistant replaced him when hospital duties conflicted with classes. Often he would arrive for his gymn class reeking of ether after a three-hour stint in the operating room as anaesthetist.

The deeper he went into medical practice, the more McKenzie became convinced of the need for preventive medicine. He was appalled by the great numbers of accident cases and diseases which could have been prevented. He visualized a sound program of physical exercise playing a large part in preventing disease, physical breakdowns and accidents.

He himself was not, however, immune to disease. Typhoid fever hit him in 1893 and for some time he was excused from the hospital to recuperate. He found a way to turn the time to good use and took a position as ship's surgeon on the S.S. "Lake Superior" running between Montreal and Liverpool. At the end of each trip he had a free week in England and used it to visit hospitals and gymnasiums. This helped him to formulate plans for changes he felt necessary on the Canadian scene. Training in taking care of the body should, he felt, begin at an early age and if not before, at least at university level. He had long been disturbed by the haphazard approach to physical education at McGill. There had been no attempt to classify students up to this time, and the fit and unfit were lumped together in classes that frustrated either or both sets of students. It also placed unnecessary physical strain on those less fit as they tried to participate in exercises beyond their scope.

When he returned to McGill in the Fall of 1893, he approached the Board of Governors with a plan for the medical examination of incoming students. He stressed the superior academic performance of students who kept physically fit through regular class exercise.

"In looking over the standing of the members of McGill's football teams from 1880 to 1886," he said, "out of a total of 105 men, 21 were medalists at college, 20 took first rank standing, and 16 were in the 2nd rank honours."

He pointed out that the winners and runners-up of the Wicksteed medals since 1883 included seven medallists in scholastic work, six took first rank honours, and three had second rank standing. These statistics indicated the relationship between regular exercise and clear thinking, the former preparing the body for long hours of mental work.

Can we afford to sit by and watch in full operation the causes which inevitably tend to change the robust boy from the country or village into the lean, dyseptic or sleepless neurasthenic, incapable of doing . . . the good work that he may so well be fitted for by talent and education?

The defects of our system have merely to be mentioned to be obvious. The instructor has to work in the dark as to the physical condition of the individual student. In the limited time and with the large number of students, anything like graded work is next to impossible. Lectures, especially in the professional faculties and the Donalda department, clash with the gymnasium hour.*

He pointed out the difference under the Harvard system:

> At Harvard today record books show the names of 245 students whose
> test of general strength (of arms, legs, lungs, et cetera) surpasses the test
> of the strongest man in 1880—the year the gymnasium opened.*

His proposal for McGill included a new gymnasium. The one of
Barnjum's day was still in use with all its original drawbacks plus a
few new ones. The cold shower in the dark corner, the antiquated
lockers with no locks, the lack of ventilation and adequate heat, still
prevailed. Added to this the gas-lights let the gas escape into the area,
plaster was falling from the ceiling in dangerously large chunks, and
the roof was leaking so badly that on a rainy day the floor was covered
with pools of water.

McKenzie divided the McGill students into three groups: the
athletic, the sedentary, and the bookworm.

> The athletic man takes to athletics naturally and from choice. He is of a
> tough and hardy make-up and needs more than the ordinary gymnasium
> exercise. While not all can with advantage to themselves, turn
> handsprings, take dips, or do the grasshopper on the parallel bars, still
> there are a few who take as naturally to heavy gymnastics as ducks to
> water, and profitably so. Some men must have these hard and severe
> tests to develop and maintain their powers up to their best possibilities.
> These men should be encouraged in reasonable efforts in this direction,
> guided and watched by someone who has proven his ability and who can
> be trusted to aid them.*

By far the greatest number of students at McGill belonged to the
second group:

> . . . students who do not take exercise as an end but merely as a means to
> an end and that they may be better able to continue their studies and
> graduate at least as sound physically as they entered. For this class
> simple exercises in such forms of movement as will keep the body in the
> best working condition are required, not a system that tends to produce
> an abnormal development of muscle.*

He advised bar-bells and light clubs for this group to secure
moisture of the skin, full deep breathing, and free circulation
throughout the whole body.

For the third group—the bookworms—McKenzie thought special
exercises and special care were required. "To these men the plotting of
measurement on a chart showing their relative physical standing,
would furnish stimulus to work."

Dr. McKenzie envisaged a Physical Education Department headed
up by a medical supervisor. He suggested that assistants might be

*R. Tait McKenzie: Report on Physical Education in McGill University," printed
pamphlet, ca. 1893, McGill University Archives, McGill University Scrapbooks, Vol. 1,
pp. 168-169.

University of Pennsylvania Archives

MEMBERS OF TAIT McKENZIE'S CLASSES AT McGILL, 1891. McKenzie (center).

found among students with remuneration in the form of scholarships. The Director of the new Department, he advised, should be a university graduate preferably with medical training, a skilled athlete, and able to stimulate interest in exercise among students.

The Board of Governors accepted his proposal in principle but the university was financially handicapped and could not set up such a department at this time. As a compromise they endorsed physical examinations for incoming students and appointed McKenzie as Medical Director of Physical Training. It was the first appointment of this kind in Canada.

From 1894 to 1904, Dr. McKenzie held several positions at McGill. He was Medical Examiner, Instructor in Physical Culture and then Medical Director of Physical Training, as well as Demonstrator of Anatomy. In 1904 he also lectured in Anatomy.

During this period when attending Sargent's summer school as he frequently did, he often took McGill students with him. One of these, Carl Schroeder, recalled in later years:

I cherish with great joy our visits to the Boston Art Gallery where he literally introduced me to phases of art hitherto a closed book to me. He was keen on all sports and greatly interested in high-class performance, acrobatic or athletic. Many a time did I accompany him and Dr. Sargent to Keith's when some noted artist performed. Invariably this was followed by a visit backstage to interview the artist and more often than not resulted in having the performer strip for us to note his special development. There is no doubt of this influence on the art he created. *

Journal of Health, Physical Education and Recreation, May 1944.

CHAPTER III

Some Treasured Friendships

It is not quite clear at what point in his life, Robert Tait McKenzie ceased to be known as "Robert" and more frequently became "Tait" to friends and associates. Old friends of high school and college days tended to call him Robert all their lives, but his medical associates seem to have chosen "Tait." Perhaps it all began with his professional life both as a doctor and as a writer of medical and other articles for publications of his day. R. Tait McKenzie he eventually became known as and popularly, "Tait."

Specializing in orthopaedic surgery, McKenzie found his medical practice expanding rapidly in Montreal. In addition to his duties at the University, he was being pressured by the Y.M.C.A. to train twelve leaders out of his evening gymnastic classes for their new gymnasium anticipated the following year.

From these exacting duties he needed a change of pace and found relaxation and pleasure in water colour sketching. It was said of him that he always had a small notebook in his pocket on which he would scribble whenever something around him took his eye or fancy. He belonged to a Pen and Pencil Club and filled innumerable sketch books with life drawings, portraits, details of architecture or drapery, for later reference.

He taught at the Montreal Art Association and belonged to a social set which included art and literary figures of the day. His painting was sufficiently acceptable to show with the Royal Canadian Academy in their 1898 exhibition where his "Cathedral," "Late Afternoon in Winter," and "A Blizzard" appeared.

In the same building as his bachelor quarters at 913 Dorchester Street lived E.W. Thomson, poet and journalist, then correspondent in Montreal for the Toronto *Globe*. Arthur Stringer, later a prodigious novelist, was then a writer on the Montreal *Herald*, and with Dr. W.H. Drummond and others of like mind, used to gather at McKenzie's establishment.

We had many a merry evening at that time with the inevitable debate on the salad at dinner. Thomson was an outstanding Canadian. His series 'Cupid in Office' shows him as a sensitive poet and his 'Ode to Abraham Lincoln' goes into all collections of Lincolniana.*

---

*All quotations unless otherwise indicated are taken from the autobiographical notes of R. Tait McKenzie, University of Pennsylvania Archives.

Thomson was older than McKenzie and sometimes acted as counsellor. He was a tall, handsome man and McKenzie considered him "the best of company." Later he went to Boston to edit *The Youth's Companion* returning to Canada in 1902 to settle in Ottawa as Canadian correspondent for the *Boston Transcript*. McKenzie and he remained friends and kept up a correspondence throughout their lifetime as McKenzie also did with William Henry Drummond, the doctor and poet for whom he had a deep affection.

Drummond and he were both then struggling young doctors with much in common. At the Drummond parental home was a fine art collection and an atmosphere which drew McKenzie. Drummond was writing poetry and used to try out his French-Canadian dialect poems on his friend.

"I cannot remember my first meeting with Dr. Drummond," McKenzie wrote in later years.

We were both young and it was before his marriage, probably at some of the snow-shoe tramps in Montreal where his first poem 'Lac St. Pierre' was a favourite song in the concert that followed the tramp over the mountain. [Mount Royal]

Afterwards he wrote 'The Papineau Gun' which we all thought was not quite up to his first effort. We had some tastes in common and occasionally I would see him at athletic games for he was a weight man—hammer and shot in his day, and delighted in the stories of athletic prowess told of Rory Ivor MacLennan and other Glengarry heroes.

We sometimes went to the Caledonian gathering [Highland games] where the interest he took was more in the men and their conversation than in their deeds. Every one of them furnished good stories that were recalled with increasing delight as they were polished and elaborated in retelling.

After his marriage in 1894 he began again to write and 'Vieux Temps' written about this time was one of the best things he ever did. It became popular immediately and was recited by more than one of his confreres at the convivial gatherings that were so characteristic of Montreal at that time. . .

It was largely through the inspiration of his wife and by her efforts that his verses were collected and put in condition for publication and *The Habitant* was published as a subscription book and that with uncertainty as to its fate on account of the active opposition expected from some French-Canadian sources who, it was feared, might object to the patois in which it was written.

This was disarmed by the preface of Louis Frichette and by his own introduction. The book had immediate and widespread success and edition after edition was exhausted and he was encouraged to go on working in this unexpected vein. His next volume, *Johnnie Courteau,* had its audience waiting for it and confirmed the good opinions formed of the first.

He felt deeply and sincerely the truth and value of his work in spite of the cloak of jesting indifference with which he covered an extremely sensitive, introspective nature. He did his work at first hand seeing with his own eyes and not through those of others and he made permanent the loves and joys and sorrows of the French-Canadian voyageur and habitant.

I always felt that his best work would be done in the realm of Irish verse rather than the dialect of the French-Canadian and this seemed about to be fulfilled when I got a poem published, 'The Boy from Calabogie' which contains the essence of Drummond's personality—the true, if dim, reflection of his Celtic nature.

After McKenzie moved to Philadelphia, he corresponded with Drummond regularly, pleased with his friend's literary success. The Drummonds visited the McKenzie home not long before Drummond's untimely death.

While in Philadelphia he [Drummond] lunched at the Franklin Inn Club [of which McKenzie was a member] and members will recall with delight the rich brogue of his splendid stories for he was an artist in telling a story. I had an opportunity of bringing him and Forbes-Robertson [British Shakespearian actor] together in a small party of friends and he read one or two of his poems to the great delight of the company. This was my last glimpse of him.

Drummond went north after returning home having some business connection with mines in Cobalt, Ontario. News came to McKenzie of his death in April 1907.

Another life-long friendship formed in Montreal was with Maxime Ingres, grand-nephew of the renowned artist Ingres, and a Professor of French at McGill University.

Max was a man of great charm. He had come to Montreal as head of the Ingres School of Languages and I met him through a fortunate accident.

The Metropolitan Insurance Company of New York wished to open a branch in Montreal and offered Dr. F. Furley, an associate of McKenzie's, the position of medical examiner.

He accepted but could not undertake the examination of the Industrial Branch for which they paid only 25¢ to $1.00 according to the size of the policy. He offered it to me as we worked together in the dissecting room, so I reported to the representative at the Windsor Hotel. Among other things he asked: "Do you speak French?" to which I replied: "When do you expect to open your office?" "In about six weeks." So I replied: "Yes, I do." and got the job and sent for Max whose advertising I had seen. We at once started an intensive course at 2430 St. Catherine Street, using blank insurance forms. By question and answer, I was well equipped for the work by the time the office opened and a firm and warm friendship with Max was established which lasted the rest of his life.

In the Fall of 1894, the Marquis of Aberdeen, then Governor

General of Canada, took Sir John Abbott's house on Sherbrooke Street in Montreal, for a short social season. Lord Aberdeen was looking for a swimming instructor for his sons and consulted a doctor whom he had met socially. He was referred to McKenzie who offered to teach them himself.

It was a singular offer considering the demands on the doctor in his professional life, but it was characteristic of the man. He was always alert to opportunity and when it knocked he answered promptly, almost intuitively. He was naturally interested in people and the lives of others. One might say he took this job on for the chance it gave him to associate with a higher level of society but it is more likely that he seized the opportunity without analyzing where it might lead.

This small and seemingly casual step extended his education socially and led to contacts and friendships abroad which proved rewarding both personally and professionally far beyond anything he could have foreseen. First of all what began as a short-term casual engagement developed into a warm and valued friendship with the Aberdeens, cemented by common Scottish ancestry.

The boys got on well under his instruction and in the Spring of 1895, he was invited to sail for England with the eldest son, Lord Haddo, then a boy of 16. They sailed from Quebec and went to Scotland where McKenzie had his first glimpse into the life-style of the nobility. He was awed by the 50,000-acre estate at Haddo House with its two farms and lakes and a forest of Scottish pine. In London, he met Dudley Majoribanks, Lady Aberdeen's brother, then a light-weight champion at Harrow. The two men had a boxing match which ended in McKenzie having difficulty "chewing for a few days while Dudley was decorated with a black eye."

Back in Canada, Tait continued the swimming lessons with the boys. He recalled later:

> On hot summer afternoons [in Montreal] we would cross to the swimming club at the tail of St. Helen's Island and dive from increasingly high platforms till the most daring would get to the cross-piece nailed to the flagpoles and plunge into the water 10 feet below. Others would swim up with the swift current and come back up the eddy to the safety of the wharf.

> Osler [later Sir William] used to quote: 'He climbs best who knows not whither he is climbing' and so this swimming led me to these boys and to the beginning of a long and close friendship. They were both bright and fearless and soon learned all I could teach them.

By this time Tait McKenzie had become well known to the Aberdeens. Lady Aberdeen was a warm and motherly person who espoused worthy causes and Aberdeen was a wise and paternal gentleman. McKenzie had come to feel much at home with them and they in turn appreciated the fine sensibilities and idealistic goals of the young doctor.

The same summer the physician of the Governor General's household retired and Tait was asked to come to Ottawa with them for the winter as household physician. The new program at McGill was proceeding as scheduled and McKenzie felt confident in leaving it in care of Dr. J.J. Ross. As for his medical practice, he had gained, as he said, mostly experience.

I had been in practice a little over a year and in the first year from October 1893 to October 1894 had cleared $876.00 which with $400.00 from the gymnasium was no gold mine to leave. So I accepted the offer of $1,500.00 a year . . . and left my office at 2430 St. Catherine Street and joined the Vice-Regal party. . . .

It was an uproarious party that thronged Windsor Station. The students at McGill had unhitched the horses and drawn the sleigh themselves. The rear platform of the private car, 'Victoria', was beseiged. I was standing uncomfortably on the station platform when the signal 'All Aboard!' was given and I climbed on the car.

I was at once recognized by the crowd and persistant demands made for a speech. His Excellency, of course, thought it was for him and the embarrassing situation was only saved by the train pulling out to cheers, yells and waves. Never have I been so embarrassed and going into the car, everything was strange, the reticent A.D.Cs. whom I had scarcely met and the abysmal ignorance of court etiquette all made a combination that threatened to overwhelm me. At dinner in the car, Her Excellency turned to me and said: 'Don't you think this champagne is corked?' I could only mumble 'I don't think so.' Fortunately Dr. James Barclay was on board. At home with either Royalty or Vice-Royalty for he had been chaplain to the Queen, he had a fund of conversation and stories that kept the conversation going all the way and at last we arrived in Ottawa, climbed into the waiting sleigh and drove to Rideau Hall.

At Rideau Hall, Tait found an old friend, Charlie Gordon, better known as the novelist, Ralph Connor. Gordon was a guest at the time McKenzie arrived and Tait recalled: "I clung to him like a sailor to a floating spar. He put me right on many things, told me the relative importance of officials and servants and gave me a start."

There were about 75 of a staff and McKenzie's duties consisted of a daily inspection of house and stables and an hour of consultation with the staff. Lunch was at two, after which any official functions for the day were attended to—visiting hospitals, orphanages, and other institutions. Dinner was at nine o'clock or later.

It was not long before I realized that society was a business that had to be learned. There were discussions as to who should sit next to whom at the table. One had to aquire the small change of conversation that is so necessary. The offering of a ponderous idea is like tendering a hundred dollar bill for a ten cent article. There is neither the time nor the inclination to change it, hence the necessity of the small change of conversation. The inevitable introductory remark about the weather, the compliment about dress, the remarks about the table decoration and surroundings that keep away the inevitable embarrassment of silence. The life at Government House was a continuous series of entertainment, mostly official.

It was at Rideau Hall that he met another Canadian poet whose work he had long admired. The occasion was a garden party the following summer:

On a bright Saturday afternoon . . . I was in line watching the guests as they were presented and passed on to join the crowd that overran the gardens and broad spreading lawns.

Guest after guest was announced, made their more or less awkward bow and walked on with a feeling of relief. Senators, judges, M.Ps., strangers to the city, and society people—so-called to distinguish them from the other people . . . suddenly my ear caught the name Lampman, familiar and well-loved to me for I had read and re-read much of his verse. A smallish man stepped forward, slightly built with sloping shoulders and delicate sensitive hands. His wavy hair, dark brown in colouring to match his eyes, a full rather short beard scarcely covering his chin, he also wore a moustache. A complexion like a shell—white; and with a kindliness of glance that made men and women his friends from the first. He had a soft, modulated and rather indistinct voice.

I slipped around behind the official group and joined him, introducing myself as a brother of William P. whose verse was well known [Rev. William McKenzie was then an instructor in English literature and rhetoric at Rochester University, N.Y. and a frequent contributor of verse to the *Christian Science Monitor*]. . .

We became friends from the first and soon found a deserted path behind a hedge where we walked up and down, entirely neglectful of my duty to bring tea and cake for the dowagers and engage in airy persiflage with their daughters.

This began a friendship that became more and more intimate until his death [1899]. During my stay of six months I saw a great deal of him. . . At this time he was at a desk in the Post Office Department, Ottawa, a position got for him by friends, after having been a school teacher in Orangeville, Ontario, a work he detested and was glad to give up.

I saw him frequently for an evening, or more often a long walk in the woods and it was a delight to hear him talk. He came down to visit me several times [in Montreal] and we noticed that his health was failing and urged him to get leave of absence and take a complete rest instead of the two weeks allowed. . .

In 1898 he came down to Montreal in early summer and spent nearly a month with me. The house became a sort of salon—Drummond, Arthur Stringer, E.F. Scott [Canadian poet] and others dropping in and we had some wonderful evenings, and Sundays out in the woods sketching. He became interested in drawing and declared with great pride that he had at last learned to draw a sheep that was easily distinguishable from a rock. . . .Owing to Drummond's efforts he got the privilege of the

Laurentian Club [Quebec] and went up there in August. The long vacation did not build him up as we had hoped and we dreaded the winter. I heard from him but little after his return except for his Christmas reminder . . . on the eve of February 8th he was stricken with a sharp pain in the lungs, lingered until the 10th and thus passed away one of the most gentle, lovable and valiant souls that ever drew the breath of life.

In later years McKenzie wrote:

Whenever I go to Ottawa, Scott [E.F.] and I usually take a pilgrimage to Beechwood cemetery and if in Springtime we go through the woods he knew so well and loved so dearly.

Some years later McKenzie modelled a portrait medallion of his friend Lampman as a memorial for Trinity College, University of Toronto.

ARCHIBALD LAMPMAN (1903) Bronze bas-relief portrait. 12 inch diameter.

A PAGE FROM TAIT McKENZIE'S SKETCH BOOK kept during a bicycle trip through France in 1896.

During his winter at Rideau Hall, plans were laid for a bicycle trip through France with Haddo the following summer to improve the boy's French and extend his education. Young Haddo was already taking French lessons from McKenzie's friend, Max Ingres, who was invited to go along on the trip. Along with two other boys from Montreal, they sailed in June. McKenzie took charge of the party at Liverpool and Ingres took over when they reached France.

They met Ingres' half-brother, Theo Jongers, an interior decorator, in Paris.

They had not met for years and Theo was full on enthusiasm for his younger brother, Alphonse, then in Spain—a great genius, a second Velasquez! So they sent for him and he joined us at the Hotel Moderne, Place de la Republique. He presented a striking figure with his broad-brimmed hat, black butterfly tie, black coat and corduroy trousers, the 'real' artist at last! With him we haunted the churches, museums and galleries—an artistic orgy—discussing our experiences at night in the cafes to the disgust of boys who soon got fed up.

We decided Alphonse should get a bicycle and join us, so he learned to ride and we all streamed out of Paris by Boulogne sur Seine to Orleans via Barbison, then circled south-east and north to Rheims. By that time he had become a good rider and Max persuaded him to come to Canada with us.

We all sailed to Montreal, where he first lived with his brother, but soon came to live with us. [McKenzie and E.W. Thomson]

Alphonse Jongers had studied with the famous American portrait painter, John Singer Sargent in London and already had a reputation for his style which resembled the old masters. He was an academician in art and scorned the modern school of his day which took liberties with both the medium and the subject. Jonger's portraits were faithful likenesses painted in rich, sensual colours. Tait McKenzie predicted he would become "the Raeburn of Canada."

One of his first commissions in Canada was to paint a portrait of Lord Aberdeen. Later he painted many prominent Canadians. He was as colourful a personality as his costume suggested when McKenzie first met him. Squarely built with rugged features he looked like a prize fighter and was in fact a good athlete:

He had learned to box with Pat Rooney. . . . When he went to New York City later he took up wrestling at the New York City Athletic Club and became an expert. . . . He took one of the Sherwood studios, 57th and 6th Avenue. Every Christmas week I used to make it my headquarters and many Casanovic adventures could be told of that place. . . . Alphonse had a colourful career.

While Jongers was living in Montreal at McKenzie's quarters the Spanish-American war broke out and 913 Dorchester Street became a "camp of Spanish refugees, and Italian and French strays."

University of Pennsylvania Archives

SIR WILLIAM OSLER (1923) Bronze memorial portrait medallion, 38 inch diameter for John Hopkins Hospital. Re-studied for Medical Library, McGill University, Montreal, Canada, as gift of the sculptor.

McKenzie acquired a small collection of portraits painted by Jongers later, including one of Thomson, one of Max Ingres, and one of Mme. Ingres. He wasn't able to retain however, a favourite portrait of a "dark-haired French-Canadian friend of mine," he recalled later. "She claimed it on my marriage and it is, I fear lost forever."

Jongers did in fact fulfill the promise McKenzie saw and between 1900 and 1924 in New York City painted both the fashionable and illustrious. His work later hung in the finest galleries of the United States.

Two other friends of Tait McKenzie's Montreal period were William Osler and Andrew Macphail, both doctors and both later knighted. Both were at McGill when McKenzie first met them.

In 1894 Osler left the Faculty of McGill for Philadelphia and greater opportunity on the Faculty of Medicine at the University of Pennsylvania. He later went to England and Oxford University.

Andrew Macphail graduated from McGill in 1891 and returned to the Faculty some years later as Professor of the History of Medicine. Dr. Macphail was a talented writer and once a reporter on the Montreal *Gazette*. Essays, biography, critical pamphlets, came from his pen as well as two major works, a *History of the Medical Services,* and *History of the Great War*. He was editor of "The Canadian Medical Journal" for many years.

With many common interests, he and McKenzie became friends during their student years and remained life-long friends.

Thirty years later while preparing a medallion portrait of Sir William Osler, McKenzie wrote to Dr. Macphail (then Sir Andrew for he had been knighted for his war work) asking his advice as to inscription. The warmth of their friendship is revealed in Macphail's reply: "The remembrance of your visit is yet with me as a precious thing." Another letter following one of McKenzie's is likewise revealing: "Your letter is like a light for me. I shall keep it for use against the time this ponderous committee begins to move." Aside from their common interest in medicine, McKenzie frequently consulted Macphail when called upon to prepare parts of textbooks.

One of McKenzie's earliest portrait medallions was of Macphail's much-loved son Jeffrey.

CHAPTER IV

The Hidden Talent

The fifteen months spent with the Governor-General's household had been pleasant and enlightening and Tait McKenzie returned to private practice in Montreal with renewed vigor in 1896. The long and serious talks with "His Ex" had reinforced his convictions along several lines including the value of his work in treatment of deformity by exercise.

At McGill he moved from assistant administrator to full demonstrator in anatomy at a salary of $200.00 a year with four hours' work every day except Saturday. Still in charge of gymnastics at the university, he was given the title of Instructor of Physical Culture.

At this time a group of gymnasium directors in U.S. universities were trying to set up an organization where they might pool their knowledge and formulate a general system for college gymnasiums. Hitherto each gymnasium director had set up his own system largely along the lines of current Swedish and German practices. Many of the directors were doctors and able to discuss physical education problems from a medical standpoint.

McKenzie already knew some of these men and in October 1897 he was invited by Dr. Anderson of Yale to come to a conference in New York City. Here he met Dr. Raycroft of Chicago who like himself had been an active athlete as an undergraduate and was interested in the same problems. Raycroft was then involved in conducting medical tests for cardiac and muscular efficiency. His findings would provide background in prevention of athletic overtraining and consequent physical injury to the athlete.

Dr. Anderson later recalled: "We were iron men in wooden boats. . . . Among our leaders there was no unity, no harmony, and every man was for himself, not only in the colleges but in all other gymnasiums taught by Americans including the Y.M.C.A. and secondary schools."

The discussion at the conference proved fruitful and plans were made to form the Society of College Gymnasium Directors under the leadership of Dr. Anderson. McKenzie returned home imbued with hope for the future of physical education in colleges.

During that winter he lectured in "Artistic Anatomy" at the Montreal Art Association. In demonstration he found the work of drawing and painting from the human figure unsatisfactory for him. His natural inclination was to see masses in three dimensions and although landscape painting had been a pleasure, he wanted another media to express the figure.

Watching athletes at the university, facial changes specifically began to interest him: "Why do men make such strange contortions of the face when they run?" he asked himself. Studying facial muscles in the dissecting room, reading books, watching runners, he began to collect data to determine the difference between facial muscles under stress of physical effort as opposed to stress under emotion—such as rage, hatred, anxiety, sorrow.

> Slowly certain differences and resemblances began to form in my mind. The best way to record this seemed to be in clay. It could be pushed about, changed and worked on indefinitely.

With modelling clay, he started on a mask depicting violent effort which seemed to include the emotions of rage, hatred, and "something more." He asked George Hill, a sculptor friend home on a visit from Paris, to give him some tips. Gradually he produced three masks of expression entitled "Effort," "Breathlessness," and "Fatigue."

Next he wrote a paper, took photos of his work, and sent the package to the *Journal of Anatomy and Physiology* in London, England. The article entitled "The Facial Expression of Violent Effort, Breathlessness, and Fatigue" was accepted and published later (1900). The acceptance of the article encouraged him in his new venture and he refined the masks and had them cast in bronze.

During the Christmas vacation in 1899, the American Society of Anatomists were to meet at Yale. Dr. McKenzie had a date to attend the annual meeting of the newly formed Society of College Gymnasium Directors* at the Yale gymn. He decided to present his findings on facial muscles under stress to the American Society at the same time.

In his journal he later wrote:

> One comes in life to a fork in the road and one must go right or left.

> At the meeting of the Anatomists were papers on the variation in the cross section of the tibia in various races, the convolutions of the Polandic area by Weeder, gleanings—not even gleanings—for I thought of Oliver Wendell Holmes when he said 'after the harvest comes the gleaners, and after the gleaners, the geese.' In the anatomical field we were the geese. I thought of this as I heard the arid discussions on these trivial variations of anatomical form.

His paper read to the distinguished audience of major U.S. surgeons, was received with enthusiasm, the upshot being an offer from Piersol, Professor of Anatomy at the University of Pennsylvania for McKenzie to become his assistant. It was a tempting offer but later in the Yale gymnasium he found his true fraternity:

> In the College Directors meeting another spirit was abroad. Here were a

*Later renamed The Society of Directors of Physical Education in Colleges.

group ploughing a new field: Sargent with his dominant personality and active mind, compiling his statistics and discussing tests of strength and athletic types not yet determined; Edward Hitchcock, the benevolent pioneer in anthropometry with his New England common sense, his youthful assistant, Paul C. Phillips; Watson Savage, just appointed to a new gymnasium at Columbia; Jay Seaves with his long black beard and gentle voice; Caspar Miller from Penn; Stroud from Tufts; George Goldie from Princeton, a sturdy Scot of no formal education but with a knowledge of athletics and gymnastics derived from a lifetime of practice... In such a group, I felt the spirit of life strong. Here was a field worth tilling. I made the decision to devote myself to Physical Education rather than Anatomy.

Back in Montreal that winter, Tait McKenzie ventured into relief work in sculpture. A friend from student days, Dr. Charles Wilson, put him in touch with sculptor Philippe Hebert and in his studio Tait learned to model in relief. One of his works, *The Skater*, in plaster, was accepted by the Royal Canadian Academy for their 1901 show. He was still exhibiting in their painting shows in 1900 and 1901.

The next year at the annual meeting of the Society of College Gymnasium Directors, he presented his paper on "Strain, Breathlessness and Fatigue as Shown by the Face". Again it was received with enthusiasm.

My paper had a rather startling popular success. A telegram came from Marshall of the New York *Tribune* asking for an interview... he questioned me about the masks of expression and made a display story of it in his Sunday paper. Caspar Whitney took me home to talk over a series for *Outing* and I returned to Montreal well pleased with my excursion.

At the same meeting Dr. Phillips of Amherst College had circulated his table of measurements of 74 of the fastest American sprinters. Ruminating over this later, a bold idea formed in McKenzie's mind:

Why not model a sprinter that would represent the type as determined by these measurements?

I spoke to my sculptor friends but they were cold and uninterested, so it seemed up to me to do it myself. Phillips generously let me use his figures. To them I added many more, plotted a chart, and got the mean of this selected group. Then I started on a figure one-quarter life size in the round.

Here the lack of studio training became speedily evident. The armature or iron skeleton which supported the figure broke, or it bent, or it came out at the most unexpected places and it took two fresh starts before it could be made to stand on its feet, but during the two years it took to complete, I served in part the apprenticeship through which every craftsman must go.

Pride prevented him from consulting Hebert or other sculptors following the first rebuff. Thus he worked in isolation uncertain of whether he could produce a figure in the round that could support its own weight.

As regards a model he had an advantage over contemporary sculptors for at this time McGill boasted some crack athletes—Percy Molson, Fred Tees, O.V. Howard and J.D. Morrow. Day after day he studied the sprinters, each of whom could run 100 yards in 10 seconds flat.

The dimensions best suited to sprinting excellence had long been disputed. Of Phillips' 74 well-known athletes, some were giants and some were very short in stature. Their average age was 21 years, average height 5' 8-¾'' and average weight 145 pounds. Of these, the shortest sprinter was 5'3'' and the tallest 6'1''. The main characteristics were of a bony framework, taller but lighter than normal, narrow hips, high insteps and short feet. McKenzie's eventual statue was of such a man—small-boned, square-chested, lithe, of the race-horse type. The muscles of the back are taut, the arms and shins are stretched for the pistol shot from the "Get Set" starting position. Crouched for the start, he holds in his clenched hands, corks.

The crouching start was discovered by Charles Sherrill when he was a student at Yale in 1888. From the time of the Greek Olympics of ancient times, the standing start for sprinting had been in use. Once asked what he considered the greatest contribution to form by an athlete, McKenzie cited Sherrill's discovery:

> Sherrill, instead of standing, stepped back of the starting line, stooped forward and put his hands on it, planted his feet behind the line and made the unexpected discovery that the thrust from both feet in this position, apparently unfavourable, gave him a quicker start than the time-honoured pose. So was invented the crouching start now [1937] taken universally by athletes and giving a beautiful combination of lines and mass for the sculptor.

McKenzie's small statue *The Sprinter* was finally completed and shown to his Montreal medical friends and a few artists. They expressed admiration and full of optimism, he shipped it off to New York City as an entry to the Society of American Artists annual show. Without comment, it was accepted and included in their 1902 exhibition.

Viewing this acknowledgment as evidence of his artistic skill, McKenzie ignored the local sculptors' disdain for his work. Next he tried the Royal Academy in London where again it was accepted on its own merits without question and was shown in 1903.

> With great daring, I sent it to the Salon in Paris in 1904. I still cherish the little blue slip that recorded its acceptance. It became popular [he later wrote] and has remained my most widely circulated bronze.

Later the students of McGill presented a replica of *The Sprinter* to

Canada Post Office

Commemorative stamps issued by Canada Post Office for 1976 Olympiad held in Montreal, Canada. One dollar stamp shows THE SPRINTER (1902) Bronze statuette. 1/4 life size. Two dollar stamp shows THE PLUNGER (1925) Bronze statuette. 1/4 life size.

the Canadian Intercollegiate Athletic Union as the R. Tait McKenzie Trophy for this sport, to be competed for annually.

Although created by careful measurement and mathematically accurate according to the ideal sprinter's proportions, *The Sprinter* was also aesthetically satisfying, a fact that astonished a great many art critics. It embodied a scientific accuracy of proportion along with artistic sensitivity for line. In the world of art this was a new and unheard of phenomenon. The classical Greek athletic art though beautiful and artistically satisfying had not always been physically accurate and certainly followed the fashion of proportion of the day. McKenzie's work attracted attention because of its very novelty, as well as expression of athletic movement.

Comments appeared in the press. The Boston *Herald* reported:

> So true is the feeling of readiness, of keen and genuine vitality expressed in every fibre of the lithe and couchant figure that it seems as if one had only to say 'Go' to see it spring forward with the fleetness of the wind.

Not only was *The Sprinter* appreciated artistically, it drew the attention of the public to athletics. The Society of College Gymnasium Directors promptly commissioned McKenzie to model a statue of the ideal all-round athlete for them.

Again Tait carefully assembled measurements taking as models the fifty strongest men over a period of five years, who had excelled at Harvard in all forms of sports from rowing to jumping. He found that the proportions for the average athlete were more light and graceful than he had expected and *The Athlete* developed as a slender figure about to test himself on a grip dynamometer, an instrument used by Sargent and McKenzie in their gymnasiums. Like all of McKenzie's athletic works, this also was a small statue (¼ life size).

The first copy went to the Society and the original was later shown at the Paris Salon (1903) and the Royal Academy in London (1904). It stamped the sculptor as a genuine artist and is considered by some as McKenzie's finest work.

Items about him as a new genius in the art world began to appear in print. The Boston *Globe* illustrated his works in an article entitled "Athlete and Sculptor" in September 1903 reporting that President Roosevelt had recently purchased a copy of *The Sprinter* for the White House. Of *The Sprinter*, they said:

> There is something about the figure which makes it clear that he [McKenzie] had made a careful study of the young athlete who trained for the quick, nervous 100-yard dash and that he was in sympathy with much more than the mere muscular grace and strength of the athlete in general. It was apparent that the artist was himself imbued with the entire modern spirit of what might be termed college athletics. And such is the fact for Dr. McKenzie is himself an amateur athlete of some considerable standing; is medical director of the Department of Physical Training in McGill University, Montreal, the greatest university in Canada and ranking with the best in America. . .
>
> He combines to a rare and exceptional degree his love for art with his love for science and athletics. He has primarily a scientific mind which is, however, very materially imbued with this deep artistic instinct and the latter finds direct expression through the former since Dr. McKenzie took up sculpture and modelling. . .
>
> He is perhaps the only living exponent in sculpture of the great athletic spirit which has swept over the world within the past decade and which has become such a conspicuous feature of college education. . .

The reporter had found McKenzie in the studio of Henry H. Kitson, a Boston sculptor, where McKenzie was spending some of his vacation.

> He was busy brushing up the bronze cast of another statuette *The Athlete*. . . . There is a strong feeling of the Greek in the pose and lines of the figure with just a touch of the modern in the face and general expression which gives it character and distinction. . . . There is no doubt that Dr. McKenzie has a splendid future in the field of sculpture. He has the genius and the capacity as have few . . . and that rare scientific training he has had will stand him in good stead in this field of his endeavours.
>
> He is a student and he maintains the attitude of a student toward everything he does which is what all successful artists and sculptors have ever done. Angelo was a student up to his death as was Leonardo de Vinci.*

Later in England, Professor Percy Gardner of Oxford University, an authority on classical sculpture, was to place *The Athlete* on a level with the work of the great sculptors of ancient Greece, comparing it to the *Apoxyomenos*.

*Quotation courtesy of the Boston *Globe*.

University of Pennsylvania Archives

THE ATHLETE (testing his strength on a grip dynamometer) (1903) Bronze statuette. 1/4 life size. Modelled from the average proportions of 400 Harvard students and the fifty strongest over a period of eight years.

With the success of *The Athlete*, Tait now felt sufficiently competent to abandon the use of anthropometry in sculpture and rely upon his intuition.

The year 1904 was an important one for him.

In 1904 the University of Pennsylvania completed a new gymnasium and Franklin Field, a beautiful architectural unit to provide for exercise both indoor and out and a letter came offering the directorship to me. I had to decide quickly. My practice in Montreal was good. I had been appointed lecturer in anatomy. The work in physical education at the moment was interesting but hopelessly handicapped. At McGill there seemed to be no prospect of change. The old gymn got older. Plans were made for a new one but nothing was done. . .

I had been preaching what should be done for a long time. Here seemed the chance to put into practice what I had preached. I met a committee in Philadelphia at lunch in the old red brick Bellevue Hotel. Champagne flowed and I said to myself with Scottish caution—'they want to see how I carry my liquor.' And I remembered Osler's [Sir William] remark about American university methods of choosing a professor: 'At Harvard they ask you who you know; at Columbia what you've got; and at the University of Pennsylvania they invite you to dinner, set before you a cherry pie and watch what you do with the stones.'

McKenzie passed the test and was accepted on these terms—"a full professorship in the Medical faculty, payment of a reasonable but not large salary direct by the University and *not* through or by the athletic association, responsibility to the university alone and *not* a committee or association," and the continuing of his private medical practice.

The tensions involved in making the momentous decision over, Tait McKenzie sailed in a joyful mood bent on spending the summer in the artist's colony of Paris. Here he would unwind and give himself over to learning more of the sculptor's craft.

A life-long admirer of women, his autobiographical notes and diaries astutely avoided recording any romances. However, on this journey to Europe the name of one woman keeps reappearing in his journal with great enthusiasm. The woman was Carrie Jacobs-Bond, a widow who evoked his sympathy in her efforts to establish herself in the music world.

Met Mrs. Carrie Jacobs-Bond from Chicago—a most charming, plucky little woman, a doctor's widow, left to fight her own way with a young son and invalid mother. Has a gift for song writing and has written several books of songs in sets of music of her own. These she has published herself and they are popular in America. She is going over to try her luck in England. She has no singing voice but half talks and half sings them most exquisitely with the most beautiful and original accompaniment. She sings like a bird. They are children's songs . . . exquisite works of art which she sings like an artist. She has letters to wealthy Americans in London and intends giving drawing-room recitals and arranging her own copyright and publishing affairs. She ought to succeed for they are the

best things I have ever heard and if ever there was an artist she is one . . .
She certainly is a brick and deserves all the rewards that come after
years of near poverty and toil. . . .

May 24:   Heard the concert last night—a weird affair redeemed from
utter banality by the work of Miss McCabe and Mrs. Jacobs-Bond who is
certainly an artist.

He saw his statuette of *The Athlete* at the Royal Academy in
London and was much struck by Watts' equestrian statue in the
Academy courtyard.

If England had not done anything else in sculpture but produce this
work, she would have earned her place. It shows a man nude sitting on
his horse as if part of it . . . the modelling is in great simple planes with
masses of light and shade without being cut up by trivial forms. The
movement of the group is overwhelming and there is no point of view
from which the arrangement is not good. The exaggeration of some forms
and the suppression of others gets the effect that would otherwise be
impossible, of power and dignity. The whole conception of combining the
two most graceful exponents of power—man and horse, the wielding of
them into a single unit and the grandeur of line and mass, its simplicity
and the overriding force of expression all convince me that here is a
masterpiece that alone would suffice to redeem British art from the
slough into which the flood of banal memorial statues has cast it. Watts
is a man that the nation should honour and cherish for it will be long
before another such is likely to arise in the atmosphere of England which
is certainly not conducive to the highest form of imaginative creative
work.

So much for McKenzie's opinions on the English art scene of the day.
He takes a further swipe at the English:

Went to the Wallace Collection, Hertford House in Manchester Street.
This is the finest thing for its size in the world, I fancy. It is too big a
thing to describe here but the arms and armor are in many cases, unique,
the metal working of hilts and shields is a revelation. The pictures are
arranged with a taste that surely cannot be English. The hanging is
perfect. Sir Joshua stands out a bigger man than ever. Vandyke goes
down a little in comparison. Rembrandt is there in his strength, also
Murillo, Velasquez and Rubens. Such a magnificent and well-arranged
collection leaves one stunned for awhile. . . . Went into the Press Club
and got to bed early, rather tired.

On May 28th, he again heard Mrs. Bond sing—this time at Beckstem
Hall and the next day he had dinner with Mrs. Bond, Mr. and Mrs.
Wareham, and Mr. and Mrs. Robert Barr. They adjourned to the
Warehams.

This is the first time I have heard Mrs. Bond sing and recite under good
conditions. She is certainly an artist and ought to do very well here I am
sure.

McKenzie had been invited out to Cambridge to lecture at one of the colleges but found upon arrival that the students were in the midst of exams and only one hundred and fifty men showed up.

> I had just begun my talk when a bugler in a neighbouring court began practising which was very disconcerting but it served to stir me up and I was going strong when he stopped. The lecture went well. I spoke without notes after I got started and the pictures [Masks of Expression] were well received. The audience was most responsive and enthusiastic and I spoke for nearly one and a half hours. After the affair there was a sort of reception at Shipley's [Sir Arthur Shipley, Master of Christ College] rooms where I met many of the prominent Cambridge men.

McKenzie had not visited Cambridge before and the next day saw the famed King's College chapel for the first time.

> Of King's College chapel I cannot say enough. The best example of perpendicular or late Gothic architecture, it stands a wonderful creation, long slender columns and spreading out on the roof in intricate grouting. Stained glass windows so large that the whole building seems barely supporting the great expanse of glass, so frail and delicate is the stone work. The lawn and bridges at Clare and Kings are of marvellous beauty. This is the finest thing I have yet seen in Cambridge and I think anywhere in the world.

Back in London he visited the Aberdeens and found Lady Aberdeen happily busy founding societies and running meetings. In his journal he commented: "She makes quite a whirlpool in the social and political pond."

He also visited some political friends and went to see a painter and sculptor named Swan at St. John's Wood.

> He is a big, stout, gray-haired man with ruddy good-natured face and thick neck. He took me directly to his studio and showed me his sketches in clay, pencil and oils. Tigers, lions and leopards mostly, some done in wax direct. Others worked up in the plaster. His plan is to carry the modelling as far as it can be done in each medium through which it passes and he is skilled in working in them all even bronze, the hardest of all. Has pickle vats for finishing the bronze and giving them their colour and surface. He keeps a plaster moulder at work all the time at three pounds a week and has two studios and a workshop and store-room, all with special lighting. He liked the *Dorothy B.* medallion and *The Sprinter*. Gave me some useful hints about the technique of work and the way of going about it and carrying it on, the measurement points, et cetera. He has a most extraordinary feeling for line and gets the character of an outline with unfailing accuracy. I have never seen anyone yet who had this so highly developed. His colour not quite so good though far from ordinary. . . . He has industry, enthusiasm and genius and consequently is one of the great men in the modern art world. I stayed so long discussing and learning that I did not get away until after 7 o'clock and kept Jimmie Barr waiting for dinner.

On June 4th, he again met Mrs. Bond and went with her and

Robert Barr, the journalist, to Forbes-Robertson's house to hear her sing for him and his wife.

> They can advise her better than I could. . . . They were greatly delighted with her singing and predict a good reception for her.*

Not long after this, McKenzie prepared to leave for Paris, having completed arrangements for the Leicester Galleries to handle his sculpture in London. In his journal there appeared no further reference to Mrs. Bond although McKenzie modelled a bas-relief portrait of her playing the piano, some years later.

On June 10th he sailed for France. Arriving in Paris he first called on Paul Bartlett, an American sculptor whose work he had greatly admired. Bartlett was a virtuoso who had exhibited at the Paris Salon when only 15 years old. He was about McKenzie's own age and a hard worker. He had already produced a colossal statue of Michaelangelo for the Congressional Library in Washington, D.C. and had a reputation for excellence in equestrian figures and animal studies. Bartlett welcomed him and made suggestions for finding a studio.

McKenzie finally selected one at 9 rue Fulguerie opening onto a courtyard. It was large with a small bedroom and a sort of kitchen attached, one of a group of studios lining both sides of the courtyard. There was a large skylight and one side was all glass covered with thick curtains that could be arranged at will to separate the direction and amount of light. About 30 artists—sculptors, painters and illustrators—were living and working in this court alone and the atmosphere was exhilarating.

Dining with Bartlett at the Chat Blanc, Tait soon became part of a group who dined there nightly, among them Wilson Morrice Canadian painter, and R.E. Brookes, American sculptor. They were a congenial group. Of Brookes, McKenzie said:

> He is one of the best fellows here ... happy, good-natured and cosmopolitan. He knows all the people in this quarter by their first name, has a fund of good stories, sings darkey songs, and yet works seriously. He is in the same court and is good to me in advising and helping me in my work. He is well-known in Boston by his bust of Oliver Wendell Holmes.

McKenzie found a model—a Spaniard about 5' 8'' who spoke a little French and no English at all but who proved intelligent. Tait was soon hard at work modelling from 8 a.m. until 12:30 when he lunched. In the afternoon he would assess the work of the morning and make a call or look up a friend. Every day or two he dined with Theo Jongers, brother of his friend Alphonse of Montreal.

He found the streets of Paris full of interest and colour. At the Paris Salon he found his statue *The Sprinter* but was disappointed that

---

*Carrie Jacobs-Bond composed ballads still sung today, e.g. "A Perfect Day," "I Love You Truly," "Just A-Wearyin' for You."

it was not better placed. His medallion portrait of a Montreal girl, *Dorothy B.*, was also there.

His friend, the novelist and journalist Robert Barr, came over from England during the summer and interviewed him for an article to appear in *The Outlook*. Barr wrote:

I found him . . . arrayed in the clay-smeared blouse of a sculptor, putting the finishing touches on his statue of *The Boxer*, a wonderful representation of a prize-fighter in a state of activity, with the right arm extended to ward off a blow, while the left is ready to deliver the impact of the clenched fist where it will be most effective. It is a striking figure in every sense of the word. . .

Last year he boxed up *The Sprinter* and sent it to the Committee of the Royal Academy in England. There was nothing to show that the sender was a doctor or anything else but simply an unknown artist who sent his work in the usual way for the annual exhibition.

The Sprinter was given a prominent place in the sculpture rotunda of Burlington House, the palace on Piccadilly where the Royal Academy holds its exhibition.

At the same time he invited criticism from a body known to be much more severe than even the authorities of the Royal Academy. He forwarded *The Athlete* to the judges of the Salon in France. It was accepted and exhibited. This year he had one statue in the Royal Academy and three in the Paris Salon.

Such a thing has probably never happened in this world before; that a man who has received no artistic training should produce work which not once, but on four occasions has received the seal of commendation from artistic experts of two European countries seems incredible to people over here. I have quit telling French artists about it, because they so evidently don't believe it, and being too polite to say so, I feel that I am taking an unfair advantage of them. . . . You cannot persuade a Frenchman that any untrained artistic amateur from the West ever got into the Salon except by paying his franc and going in with the general public.

When I was searching the rue Fulguerie for his studio, I asked an artist who was coming out of the courtyard if he knew where Dr. Tait McKenzie might be found. He said: 'There is no doctor of that name in this neighbourhood but there is a young sculptor named McKenzie at No. 9.'

Late in the summer McKenzie visited Rodin's studio but found him surrounded by people, mostly women. Tait presented him with his card but "he took it in a distraught sort of way and went on talking with the lady at his side." McKenzie seemed to have mixed feelings about Rodin and his work. Later he wrote of him:

He is not much occupied in naming his figures that being done usually at the suggestion of others. He has an inspiration, an arrangement of lines and masses which seem to him good and puts it down careless of what it may be called which is after all, the true artist's point of view. Everything is to him a form, mass, and interlacing of lines. Along comes the literary man and sees the beautiful form and says "To me it is like Adam weary with the weight of grief that has come upon him.' 'Tres bien,' says Rodin, 'We will call him Adam.' His figure in the Luxemburg called *The Bronze Ape* is merely the portrait statue of a young Belgian posed in the most advantageous position to show his best points and so with many others. Rodin is a sort of inspired faun . . . incomparably the greatest sculptor of our age. . . . [In his studio] . . in one corner is an enormous hand jutting out of a block of marble holding a mass in which are partly disengaged two figures. This had a marvellous bit of modelling. I believe that at Meulon, his other studio, he has drawers full of hands modelled in all sizes and poses. While I was there he was modelling a hand for which one of the ladies was posing . . . much of his work [McKenzie wrote later] we now see was done twenty years ago for the old man is said to be very commercial and never to lose an occasion for turning an honest penny. From this I suspect he must have a strain of Scotch blood in him which would doubtless account for his greatness.

The most of his work at Meulon which we hope to see for there he has his museum and lives. The Balzac about which such a furious controversy raged is there, so I did not see it. I went away disappointed that the chance for speaking to him was so poor but impressed with the work. In appearance he is short and stout, rosy-faced with grizzled beard and bright eye and chubby hands. His brow is prominent and projects over his eyes in two bosses while his hair is kept close-cropped and pompadour. He is not a good talker and among most people is considered stupid to a degree. He is an inspired modeller but little more.

The summer with its instruction and associations had been a great stimulant for McKenzie and he returned to Montreal, rested and in fine fettle for his move to Philadelphia.

He also had to participate in a physical education program to be held in conjunction with the World's Fair at St. Louis in August. Commemorating the United States purchase of Louisiana, the American Association of Physical Education had arranged with the officials of the fair to set up a complete program including lectures and track and field events. Authorities in the field of physical education were to come from all over the world. McKenzie was to lecture on "Artistic Anatomy in Relation to Physical Training."

While the games were in progress, Drs. Gulick, Raycroft and McKenzie set up a series of tests to find out what took place in the physiology of a man who has run the Marathon distance, or as much of it as he could before he gave out. They tested the runners before the start for heart and kidney functions but testing them after they finished was another matter. Men who failed to finish the course could not be found for examination afterwards and those who were successful were quickly surrounded by friends and borne off triumphantly for celebrations. The doctors also acted as rescue squad from time to time, searching for drop-outs along the course. In one case they found the last member of the group lying in a field several miles from the finish with a gastric hemorrhage.

No scientific knowledge was gathered but a lasting friendship developed among the three men. Dr. Raycroft spoke of McKenzie in later years as "possessed of remarkable powers of concentration and uncanny ability to turn out a good job on the first attempt."*

McKenzie left Montreal for Philadelphia in August. The Montreal *Witness* reported his departure from McGill:

> Mr. McKenzie will be greatly missed from Montreal where he has a host of friends. . . . Along with other interests, Dr. McKenzie has travelled through Europe picking up curios and interesting sketches and ornaments, illustrative of a catholic taste as well as a love of the beautiful which makes him choose as his life work the proper development of the human body. Dr. McKenzie expresses great regret at leaving Montreal friends including the McGill boys, a regret which is mutual, only tempered by the hope that in the future the Doctor will return to his native land.

The Journal of Health and Physical Education: R. Tait McKenzie Memorial Issue, Vol. 15, No. 2, February 1944.

CHAPTER V

Breaking New Ground

Philadelphia heralded Tait McKenzie's arrival as a "boon for athletics". "Dr. Robert Tait McKenzie, physician, athlete and sculptor," one newspaper reported, "will shortly begin the work of developing the University of Pennsylvania students in a more thorough and complete manner physically than has ever been attempted at any institution of training in this country. . . . It is expected that when sufficient time has elapsed to allow Dr. McKenzie to demonstrate the value of his theories and the materials at his command, he will turn out some of the greatest athletes ever known in amateur or professional sport."

"The university authorities made no special effort to conceal the fact that they expect great things from Dr. McKenzie's supervision of athletics here," ran another press report. "The present gymnasium which is regarded as one of the best in the world is the first that Penn has ever had. . . . Many candidates were considered [for director] and at last the position was offered to Dr. R. Tait McKenzie of McGill University, Montreal, Canada. Dr. McKenzie had made a most enviable reputation at McGill and his department was a model in every respect. Because of his expert knowledge of medicine and athletics, he is believed to be the best man fitted for the position at Pennsylvania," and they added: "Dr. McKenzie is a young man with a pleasing personality and a typical Scotchman in appearance."

Assuredly great things were expected of McKenzie in his new and unique role. As Director of Physical Education he would have the opportunity to establish basic standards for other universities to follow. At Penn the old department had struggled along for years under limited accommodation and part-time directors. Physical education had remained outside the faculty. Now it was to be accepted on equal footing with other departments, sharing their rights, privileges and penalties. Under the new rules the most rigid supervision of athletics in force in any American university was to be inaugurated.

> The Board of Trustees passed a resolution requiring all under-graduates to undergo a medical examination upon entrance, and to take a minimum of two periods of exercise a week under the direction of the department for all four years, with credits and penalties the same as in all academic subjects—a radical policy. . .*

*R.Tait McKenzie: "Physical Education at the University of Pennsylvania from 1904 to 1931—and the Gates Plan," Pamphlet. Reprinted from *The Research Quarterly*, Vol. III, No. 2, May 1932.

McKenzie arrived in Philadelphia while Weightman Hall, home of the new department, was being completed. He moved into the building, even sleeping there, and began the exciting work of assembling staff, supervising equipment, and attending to the other details for the forthcoming term. By October the new gymnasium, Weightman Hall, and the stands about Franklin Field to accommodate 19,000 people had been completed and Physical Education was admitted to the academic family.

To save time and energy, Dr. McKenzie retained both office and studio in Weightman Hall. From his windows he could look down on Franklin Field (the first horse-shoe shaped playing field in the U.S.) and study the athletes in action.

The first students to be examined were the football men. Eyes, ears, lungs, heart and throat were tested and a complete measurement of the muscles of the body made. Also on their chart went physical features and habits along with any specific disease or tendency in ancestry. The athlete was asked to give ages of parents and tell whether they or any other member of the family had been afflicted at any time with, or died from, tuberculosis, rheumatism, or diseases of kidneys or nerves. Habits relating to use of tobacco and alcohol were recorded. Unless the students passed their tests to McKenzie's satisfaction, they were not allowed on the football field. It is assumed that initially there must have been much opposition among students to such rigid screening.

Examining incoming students, McKenzie found them in all sorts of physical shape. "What was to be done for the physical education of this heterogeneous mass? Obviously they couldn't be sorted out according to academic standing."

The sound and energetic ones took care of themselves for the most part. They played football and rowed in the Fall, spent their spare time in basketball, swimming, soccer, boxing or fencing in winter. "But these were only about 20% of the whole . . . At the other end were the cripples and defectives who could, at least, be given prescriptions to strengthen such weaknesses as could be affected by exercise."

Between these two classes were the main portion of the students with no special ability. Progressive gymn exercises were set up for these and they "learned the simple things that every well-educated man should know about handling of the body." The swimming pool of the new gymnasium was filled with beginners.

The football players in strict training during autumn received credit only while engaged in that sport. In the next term they had to work out in the gymn. "In this way," McKenzie explained, "it is hoped to give every man an opportunity of educating himself in all forms of activity to which his body will lend itself."

At the formal opening of the gymnasium in December, Dr. McKenzie addressed the assembly and said in part:

The students of the university may be compared to its life blood, always on the move, circulating from classroom to lab, each one like a blood cell, gradually accumulating his burden of carbon dioxide. Up to the present time he has had the most inadequate means of becoming oxygenated.

What has been supplied to the university by the Alumni tonight may be said to represent a new heart and by all the laws of regional anatomy, Franklin Field must then be its lungs and students can now come, jaded and worn out by a day's work, sluggish as the venous stream that creeps back to the heart, and in the exercise hall, swim pool, and on the campus they will find new life and energy and exhilaration that will make light the heaviest task.

Tonight . . . Penn has shown herself to be in the vanguard of educational progress . . . Already the larger cities, realizing the necessity, are insisting upon medical supervision and physical training in their public school systems, and we hope to have Penn supply this need by giving courses on the theory of exercise and on personal hygiene that will enable medical graduates to establish and supervise such work in public schools of any community in which their work is placed.

It is hard to realize the possibilities for good contained in such a course to the man himself, to the community in which he may live and to the nation at large.

In his address, McKenzie elaborated on the new facilities at Penn to give his audience, many Philadelphians who had contributed financially to the new gymnasium, a clear picture of how it would be used.

Already 500 men have been examined in preparation for this work [he said] . . . as soon as our apparatus is in place, the actual work will begin, starting with the lightest exercises, gradually increasing in difficulty and extending through the entire range of gymnastics so that drooping shoulders may be squared, the flat chest deepened, and that erect and fearless carriage acquired that will enable every man to look the world in the face.

But what of the man, all too common, who cannot keep up with the procession, who from a sensitive realization of his physical inferiority shrinks from open competition with his fellows? For him also a place has been given . . . showing in full detail exercises directed toward his particular weakness. These exercises will be explained and demonstrated to him . . . and he will report his progress from time to time. As he gains in confidence, strength and skill, he will naturally pass into the regular class. He will work off his physical "condition" and become an undergraduate in full physical standing. . .

The policy of the department may thus be said to contain something of the hospital clinic, a great deal of classroom and laboratory, and a little of the arena.

. . . By the system it is hoped that a young man coming to Penn will improve in health and strength from year to year.

The entire program was idealistic and full of promise and

reassurance to the many parents, teachers, and medical people assembled. And it appeared to be off to a good start.

That Christmas, McKenzie's mother joined him in Philadelphia at his new living quarters on 18th street. His brother William with his wife, Daisy, came over from Boston, and Agnes from London for a happy family reunion. Among the many congratulatory and warm wishes from friends in their Christmas greetings, came a letter from his dear friend, W.H. Drummond in true Drummond style:

> An' Oh, but the corner's lonely, Mac,
> since you left for the south. Little Mai
> went down to the Glasgow boat this morning
> and when she seen there was ne'er a glint
> o' the McKenzie tartan on board, only a
> drove of sheep from Mull and maybe an
> Englishman or two, the lassie wept as
> your great grandam wept after young
> Kintail was hanged, only because he kept
> the head of the Exiseman too long below
> the waters of the loch O'shone! O'shone!
>
> I'm awa' to Boston next Tuesday evening
> to 'dine' as they ca' it wi' the Beacon
> Society. . . . .
>
> Here's to ye, Mac. Slainte to ye, Slainte.
> Drink deeply and heavily and go home with
> the watch in the morning.
>
>   Ever thine,
>
> P.S.   My wife's best wishes and success to you again and again
>
>   W.H. Drummond

Gymnastic classes began at the university in February. The Department of Physical Education had two divisions: one theoretical, one practical. The theoretical division gave third and fourth year medical students courses on the application of anatomy and physiology to exercise and to the many questions with which it was allied such as blood-pressure, strain, fatigue, exhaustion, anthropometry as applied to the growth and development of children, tests for efficiency and demonstrations relating to problems affecting a child's health in school were to be given.

This training was to equip the medical graduate with the ability to instal and supervise a system of physical training in public schools and colleges of any community where he might set up practice.

The practical division of the department was set up for the general student body. Following initial examinations, they were delegated to class exercises and sports suited to their physical efficiency.

The winter progressed without many hitches. In April an outdoor show was held on Franklin Field demonstrating the class gymnastics, boxing and wrestling, swimming with life-saving, diving and other feats.

In these early days such entertainments were well attended. [McKenzie wrote] This form of propaganda is, I believe, invaluable. It dispells ignorance and excites interest in our subject. We carried it on systematically for a number of years, and pictures of our annual pageant became part of the world news service. I came across one long afterwards at a movie theatre in Amsterdam which it had reached in touring Europe along with the other instructive films that keep an audience quiet till the melodrama comes on.

All this stir made its impression on the faculty. They at first were inclined to consider physical education as a sort of bastard child left on their doorstep, diverting the time and nourishment destined only for legitimately begotten members of the academic family. This attitude was overcome, in part at least, by discussions at Faculty meetings which the director assiduously attended, papers read before medical and educational societies, and demonstrations of the work done which spoke for itself, and now one does not hear its place at the educational table seriously questioned.

The students were at first enthusiastic; they enjoyed it. When the penalties began to obtrude themselves, however, that was another question. Some had taken lightly the regulation. They liked the added credits but forgot that they also involved penalties; but when they found themselves conditioned as a result of neglect they 'troubled deaf Heaven with their bootless cries' and led the Director to the stake with howls and execration while he burned to a cinder, fortunately in effigy.*

Dr. McKenzie was, in fact, burned in effigy by a mob of "disgruntled slackers but the provost, Dr. Harrison, stood behind me like a rock till the flames died down," he later wrote.

A small percentage of students opposed all forms of games and often it corresponded to the percentage who failed in other subjects. To win these over was not easy.

By the end of the first school year for the new Department, 1,000 students had been examined, 594 had been found defective in some part of their body exclusive of eyesight and assigned corrective exercises. Interviewed by the press and asked if any change in the state of the latter took place during the year, Dr. McKenzie replied:

Yes, indeed. A quick cure was the result in many cases. Why some men when they first came into the gymn were unable to lift their own weight! These were found later, after instruction, to be climbing ladders and ropes with the greatest freedom. . . . Often we find men who do not wish to engage in physical class work but after the first objection has worn off they take the greatest interest in the work. After a student has spent

*Ibid.

three hours in a lecture room or in a lab, his brain is tired. Let this man go to the gymn, take some exercise, and then get a shower and a rub-down and he is like a new man. Soon . . . athletic exercise becomes a pleasure.

A record of defects was kept as well as a complete set of measurements. Periodically special investigations were undertaken on the occurrences and stability of reflexes, presence and meaning of heart murmurs, and other subjects later published as papers. The heart and lung cases were kept under observation and sometimes put on special diets and rest. Exercises for postural defects were written on cards and prescriptions given to instructors.

During the year, Tait McKenzie had settled into the social and cultural environment of Philadelphia as time permitted. He joined the Franklin Inn Club for professional men, and frequently lunched at their clubhouse on Camac Street. He also joined the Philadelphia Sketch Club. He began attending orchestral concerts, the theatre, the art shows. Although he exhibited no new work in the year, his name was not absent from the art world. *Success Magazine* in an article entitled "Sculpture and the Athlete" commented:

> Realism in sculpture is always an interesting thing although not always synonymous with beauty. We attribute considerable importance to modern French sculpture because of its accurate depiction of life as seen by such men as Rodin and Meunier, and recently an American sculptor of considerable merit has come forward and placed himself in the ranks of the realist. The work of Dr. R. Tait McKenzie, Physical Director of the University of Pennsylvania. . .

The next school year [1905] soon arrived and brought a new crop of students to be examined, segregated, scheduled for exercise, and soon the football men were back on the playing field preparing for the season.

McKenzie had set up some work in sculpture in his studio overlooking Franklin Field and here he worked until it was time for the game to begin below. Then he would amble down the stairs, cross the field and sit with the substitutes on the bench, studying the figures in action.

He spent hours watching professional wrestling matches, not caring who won or lost, interested in the play of muscles and the strenuous poses of the contestants. Interested in boxers and pugilists, he welcomed an opportunity that came to him at this time to do a death mask of John L. Sullivan.

John L. had come to Philadelphia to appear at the Variety Theatre. McKenzie attended the show and later visited the pugilist backstage to request permission to take a mask of his features in plaster.

He had first seen John L. about 1890 in Montreal when he posed as a living statue in a minstrel show "not an impressive sight as he was slightly knock-kneed with sloping shoulders and wide hips and his muscle form not accented."

I next saw him after he lost the championship as a very stout man boxing exhibitions with Jake Kilrain and jeered by the crowd. This was about 1894.

Dr. McKenzie made an appointment at that time to take Sullivan's measurements to assist Dr. Dudley Sargent in recording such statistics for anthropometric records.

When I called at the St. James hotel his keeper, McVey I think, said he was not at home but a deep rumbling voice from the room said 'let the young fella come in.' He was very drunk but genial . . . they were trying desperately to get him in shape for the evening's performance. He swayed about a good deal and I made such examination as I could and then he insisted on showing me how to box. I put up my hands and he made uncertain lunges at me which I parried and clinched. He was pleased to say that I would go far if I practised and did not hurt my eyes which he termed 'a damned bad habit.'

It was John L., the philosopher, I saw in 1905 in Philadelphia. We went up to the studio in Weightman Hall and I vaselined his face, eyebrows and moustache, poured the plaster carefully to interfere as little as possible with breathing and he very patiently submitted. I promised him a copy and he said artists always did promise copies of their work but never kept their promise. I sent him one which has doubtless disappeared. Another copy went to the collection at Princeton.

The mask shows his ears which are untouched by deformity, his nose but slightly thickened and a scar low on the forehead made by Corbett in their fight when he took the championship from him.

His narrow forehead was accentuated by his thick neck which went up in a continuous line with his skull to the top of his head so that he seemed to taper to a point. A very low type. On asking visitors what the profession of the original mask might be, they, not knowing who it was, frequently replied, 'a politician.' . . . Not so far wrong at that! Some asked if it was Taft which was rather hard on the President!

John was perhaps the last of the old pugilists who fought with bare hands. . . . He was a brute and a bully, quite ruthless and quite fearless and in his drunken moods a maniac. . .

The death mask of John L. became part of the Department's collection of Tait McKenzie's work.

Again the McKenzies congregated in Philadelphia for the Christmas festivities, this time joined by Bert and his family from Ottawa. Again, among the many greetings from old friends, came a long and heart-warming letter from his friend Drummond.

December 27, 1905

My dear Mac,

Man, but you're an awfu' curse!
The curse of the dark hilt! Wow! Wow!
I heert o' the curse of the thrawn piper,
the curse o' the empty herrin'—creel,
the curse o' Grummil, the curse o' the
sober fiddler (and that's a maist unnatural
curse) but the hilt of the dirk!

On the 26th January I hope to attend
at the Athletic Club Rooms, New York, the
annual dinner of our Laurentian Club.
The 26th falls on a Friday. Would a nearby
date, either side, suit your Philadelphia
friends? If so, I'm your man. Mrs. D.
will accompany her liege-lord to the field
disguised as a page. You are hereby authorized
to 'fire away Flanagan' (as they say in
Galway) report progress and if a retainer
is concerned, anything you say 'goes.'

. . . Mac, I'm afraid we've struck it in
Cobalt. 'Drummond Mines, Limited.' It's
averaging about a ton daily . . . I'm up there
most of the time . . .

Happiest of New Years to you and yours
and thanks a thousand times for kind interest,
but sure you always have a great heart.

Faithfully thine,

W.H. Drummond

(The above mentioned visit was the last time McKenzie saw
Drummond who died in the Spring of that year)

The Physical Education program proceeded more smoothly the
second year, and McKenzie became involved in physical education
beyond the university campus. His attention since his arrival in
Philadelphia had been drawn to lack of facilities in the city for summer
holiday recreation and examing the situation he invited Dr. Stecher,
Superintendent of Schools, and Dr. Martin Brumbaugh to attend a
conference held by the Public School Athletic League in New York
City. He hoped that a similar organization might be set up for
Philadelphia. The result of the conference was the formation of the
Playgrounds Association of Philadelphia. McKenzie sat on the first
Board of Directors, Brumbaugh was first president, and Stecher first
secretary.

Following this, 60 schools yards were acquired to provide safe places for children to play during the summer vacation within the city. The children looked after the playground—clearing it, raking it, preparing baseball diamonds and running tracks, and generally taking care of it which McKenzie believed, enhanced its value to them. He and Stecher later devised exercises for public schools. Both principals and teachers showed little interest at first but at the end of the first year in practice, the two men held a field day and invited the parents. McKenzie obtained the university stadium for the occasion and they set up a program of relays and track events. It was a successful event and helped to put physical education on a firmer footing in public schools.

During the summer vacation of 1906, McKenzie joined a group of American artists who annually congregated at "The Holy House", a picturesque New England mansion turned into a boarding house and run by Florence Griswold, herself a painter. It was at Lynne, Connecticut, near Long Island Sound and here by the sea Tait sketched and painted with his friend Alphonse Jongers, and another Canadian artist, Arthur Heming.

Back in Philadelphia in August, he made preparations for an exhibition of his sculpture which Doll & Richards Galleries were holding in Boston in November. The show included his *Athlete* and *Sprinter, The Boxer,* and a number of portrait medallions, as well as a medal completed for the Public Schools Athletic League. The press mentioned the show commenting on the athletic works "these statuettes have attracted much attention both by their realistic adherence to types of American athletes and their intrinsic beauty of form." They were not as impressed with the portrait work commenting "most of them are wanting in the last fine degrees of subtlety and distinction."

The effect of his work in physical education, however, was applauded by the press in the Spring of the next year when outdoor exercises were held at Franklin Field:

> The gymnastic and athletic exhibition on Franklin Field yesterday by hundreds of men engaged during all the past year in regular exercise is worth 10 years of inter-collegiate competition by a few picked teams that monopolize athletic fields and shut out the average student from common privileges while the team practices in secret [they said].

> Under the systematic and far-sighted leadership of Dr. R. Tait McKenzie for the past year, the students at the University in all departments have been trained in athletic exercise just as they have been trained in other studies. Instead of lavishing all athletic privileges, expenditures and opportunity on a few men on the team . . . the general body of university men have been trained.

That summer Dr. McKenzie was invited to speak at the 2nd International Congress on School Hygiene to be held in London in August.

The ocean voyage brought him an unexpected reward and another

major change to his life—close friends suggested later that it provided
him with a new incentive to succeed in his chosen fields. On board ship
he met Ethel O'Neil, eldest daughter of John O'Neil of the Hamilton
Spectator, Hamilton, Ontario. On a sabbatical with a view to becoming
a concert pianist, she was on her way to Berlin to continue her musical
studies.

At the age of 24 she had been offered the chair of Music at the
Science Hill School in Shelbyville, Kentucky, one of the oldest schools
for girls in the United States. Successful as Head of the Music
Department, in 1907 she was granted leave of absence for further
studies abroad.

Ethel O'Neil was pretty with large expressive dark eyes and fine
features. She had a winsome manner and vivacious personality with
yet an elusive quality. She was a talented musician. She was 27 and
he was 40. They discovered that they shared not only artistic ideals but
a deeper understanding of life. McKenzie forsook his Scottish caution
and was swept off his feet.

Perhaps the subject of marriage had been on his mind for some
time for his future in Philadelphia seemed assured and he was now
financially better situated. But the haste with which he at long last
married, seems quite unlike him. Before August ended, his bachelor
days were over.

They parted in London and Ethel went on to Berlin. McKenzie
presented his paper on "Systematic Physical Exercise for College
Students" at the Hygiene Congress but his mind was elsewhere.
Ethel's family knew the Aberdeens, now in Ireland, and Tait phoned
Lady Aberdeen. In his journal he wrote:

> I told Lady Aberdeen how I had met on the steamer the one woman who
> was necessary to complete my life and how I was going to Berlin to marry
> her before the British Consul, if it could be done in no other way. Lady
> Aberdeen called His Ex. and we talked well into the morning hours. She
> thought my plan ridiculous and suggested that we consider it for a few
> days during which she consulted the Dean of the Chapel Royal and
> others and found that a two-weeks residence in Ireland was necessary
> before a legal marriage could be performed. She then insisted on taking
> charge of the whole affair. I was to go to Berlin as planned, Ethel was to
> come to her in Dublin and we were to stay the necessary time and be
> married from their house. His Ex. approved and entered into the scheme.
> In due time it all took place as planned.

On Sunday morning, August 18, 1907, the marriage of Dr. R. Tait
McKenzie of Philadelphia and Miss Ethel O'Neil of Hamilton took
place at the Chapel Royal, Dublin Castle, in the presence of their
Excellencies, The Earl and Countess of Aberdeen. Lord Aberdeen took
great pleasure in giving the bride away for the Aberdeens themselves
enjoyed a life of domestic happiness and expected similar good fortune
for their two young friends. Captain, the Honourable A. Hore Ruthven,
acted as best man, and Honourable Grace Ridley was maid of honour.
A few friends were present. Vera Lichenstein of the McGill faculty of

music transposed a reel played on the piano by Max Heinrith, to the accompaniment of pipers. Dr. Andrew Macphail named it "The Tait McKenzie Reel."

Later Tait wrote in his diary:

> I remember driving back from the Castle along Sackville Street . . . just the two of us in the Vice-Regal carriage. . . . The shrill whistle of the police as they recognized the Vice-Royal equippage and stopped the cross-town traffic, coming to the Salute as we passed. Feeling as I did, it was easy for me to lift my borrowed top hat and murmur "Bless you, my people" while Ethel bowed and smiled to the astonished populace. Our triumphant progress ended at the Vice-Royal Lodge where we had a gay lunch and Lady Aberdeen announced that as the Secretary, Lord Haskell, was away, the Secretary's Lodge was vacant and at our disposal for a few days after which accommodation had been reserved at the Shean Dormast Hotel. After lunch we went out through the grounds to it, set in its trees, the drawing room looking out on the garden, a grand piano, and the place to ourselves, a butler and maid to serve us . . . from there we went to County Down and raced together on the sands of the beach and sketched the rich landscape where the mountains of Mourne come down to the sea. We visited with friends of Ethel's at Baltz Castle, then home to our new life together.

Returning to Philadelphia in September, the bridal couple took up residence at 26 South 21st Street. They were warmly welcomed into social and university circles and Tait was soon involved with his next school year. Ethel soon found her place in the music milieu and began a series of musicales for the winter. Dr. McKenzie's mother moved back to Toronto to live with her cousin, Mrs. Pitt.

Searching around for a more suitable home for his bride, he purchased a semi-detached four-storey house that had belonged to the symphony conductor, Leopold Stokowski. Located at 2014 Pine Street, an older part of the city, it was within walking distance of the university. The kitchen and servants quarters were on the ground floor, dining room, drawing room and McKenzie's studio on the next floor, Mrs. McKenzie's music room and bedrooms on the third floor, and an attic bedroom at the top of the house. A dumb-waiter brought food from kitchen to dining room above.

On Sunday mornings young college athletes came to pose for McKenzie and later to stay for lunch. Often during the sitting the strains of Bach or Beethoven would drift down into the studio from the music room where Ethel was practising on her grand piano. McKenzie loved to entertain his friends and the house welcomed guests from far and near. Ethel was a charming hostess creating an atmosphere which one guest remarked "made one want to settle down in front of the log fire and stay."

Ethel lectured on music history, in particular ancient musical instruments, and became a well-known figure in the music world of Philadelphia. She continued her piano study with Robert and Gaby Casadesus and had the distinction of being the first pianist to present

University of Pennsylvania Archives

MRS. TAIT McKENZIE (1912) Bronze bas-relief portrait. 12 × 17 inches.

Rachmaninoff's later well-known Prelude in C Sharp Minor on the North American Continent.

She adored McKenzie and this adulation proved an inspiration to him as a journalistic friend, E.W. Thomson wrote in a little poem entitled "On First Beholding Blighty" (a small statue completed by McKenzie during the Great War).

> Before God gave him Ethel, Rab had skill
> Industry, energy, persistent will
> But not that charm of charms whereby his art
> Now subtley happifies the gazer's heart.
>
> That touch of love his fingers and his brain
> Transfer from her fond soul, to shape again
> In bronze benignant as the Heavenly plan
> Which made 'oor Rab, the Genius, Ethel's man.

McKenzie's bas-relief portrait of his wife completed in 1912 revealed his response to this adulation. The inscription lettered in ancient Gaelic translates:

> To Ethel,
> The thousand times beloved
> Daughter of Neil, the royal hearted,
> The dark-haired, the precious
> Joy of my youth, pride of my life
> Darling of my heart,
> With my soul's devotion.

CHAPTER VI

A Text for Physical Education

Up until World War I, Dr. McKenzie's program proceeded more or less as he had planned despite periodic friction with the Athletic Association who hired and fired coaches, arranged games and generally, "sailed the stormy seas of intercollegiate politics." In his autobiographical notes he described the routine:

The Director's day in October was a busy one. The examination of freshmen from 10 to 12:30 p.m., 2:30 to 4:00 and 4:30 to 6:00 with letters dictated and signed often in between. This continued until the thousand or more had been examined. . .

Into the Director's office they came in a continuous stream—freshmen, athletes, thin, fat, tall, short, lean, some richly bronzed by the sun of a summer camp or a seashore, some pasty-white from the city. He stands on two footprints marked on the floor; before him is a mirror with two wings, the examiner standing behind and slightly to the side so that he can view his back, front, both sides without changing position; the examiner dictates to the clerk his findings—a lowered right shoulder or slight curvature, a flat chest or flabby abdomen, knock-knees, a flat foot, all the diversions from the normal pattern of man. Now and then the flat-bottomed, deep chested, straight legged athlete comes to relieve the eye and encourage the examiner's mind.

. . . And so the procession passes day after day. The husky country boy is advised to report for football or the crew, and the thin, highly strung neurotic is cautioned and prevented from burning up his limited stock of vitality.

30,000 or more thus passed before me. In my mind's eye I see the gradual improvement of the student's physique. More come in trained by outdoor life. Fewer have the city pallor and the statistics show an increase in height and weight of the college student of today over that of 30 years ago. Today [1936] he leads a normal, muscular life with the freedom of the outdoors and less restrained by clothes. Even on the farm they now work stripped to the waist and on the beaches one wonders at the ingenuity with what is still kept in place. . .

And so a course developed that could be graded like academic work, members of the teams being considered justly as honor men . . . the work went on steadily progressing, broadening, becoming more accurately adopted to our conditions, the number of students doubling until 1914 and the Great War.

During this period, he often came to grips with the athletic coach but his word was law. In 1908 he made news headlines in Philadelphia by ordering two of Penn's best middle-distance runners, Boyle and Quigley, off the track for three weeks to rest their hearts "which he declared were strained by too much training." Such decisions did not sit well with the athletic coach pressed for time in preparing athletes for competition.

The most prominent coach in the U.S., Mike Murphy, was then at Penn.

Dr. C. Ward Crampton, a medical associate, wrote in later years:

McKenzie showed us how a college physical training man could get along happily and constructively with an athletic coach . . . The beginning of the century marked a clash of various opinion, precedent, and faith in the practice and theory of physical training. . . McKenzie seemed somewhat calmly aloof from the field of strife. . . He was quiet, wise, and helpful as the decades unfolded their progress . . . in the physical fitness field. He would question rather than criticize or correct. He imposed no self-made theory of salvation upon others. His gods were . . . the concrete, reliable, unfailing, trustworthy gods that have nursed the human race, while he allowed the gods of the market place to lead who would to gusty heights of glory. . . . The dust raised by windy argument would settle and disclose McKenzie unperturbed, plodding ahead—and quite a bit ahead. He helped us all and graced the national scene with a healthy serenity.*

It was McKenzie's practice to make friends and not enemies and he made a friend of Mike Murphy, later writing an introduction to Murphy's book *Athletic Training* published posthumously by Scribner's in 1913. "This compact little volume," he wrote, "contains the expert advice of the most successful trainer that ever lived, upon every phase of track and field athletics."

McKenzie gradually won over the students who had opposed his rigid disciplines in the beginning. The first graduates of his 4-year course dedicated the Class Record to him, the highest honour they could give, referring to him as "Physician, Artist and Friend, a True Pennsylvanian."

Since his arrival at Penn he had come to view American sport in a new light. In 1913 McGill University finally built a new gymn and invited him to the opening. He was reported in the press in response to some queries on sport that he considered sport in the U.S. as quite clean "although many people profess to believe otherwise. . . There is not a school in the country that does not encourage athletics and the colleges further this." His views on American football too had changed. At this time there had been efforts to change Canadian football and this interested him. He agreed that a reduction in the team would improve the game.

The less men on the team the greater the opportunity for scientific

The Journal of Health and Physical Education: R. Tait McKenzie Memorial Issue, Vol. 15, No. 2, February 1944.

development. That is the secret of the American game. It is thoroughly scientific and nothing is left to haphazard. Every man has his place in the play and the coaches have the system down so fine that they can immediately point out the reason for the failure of any play to advance the ball. The English game will never go in the U.S.; it is illogical. The heel-out, the scrimmage with its practically off-side formation, do not appeal to the American mind. . .

At this time when formal physical training courses were being set up in many American colleges, McKenzie came in for criticism from some quarters which he deftly fielded. One such occasion involved a doctor at another university who publicly complained that the college system of physical training resulted in lop-sided athletes. McKenzie responded and was reported by the press as saying:

Baseball is one of the best all-round developers that can be found for the young undergraduate. . . Swimming is another splendid exercise. Football is excellent, track work is good, wrestling has been for almost the entire history of the world recognized for its worth and rowing will surely pass muster. I could name many other varieties of athletics all excellent developers.

. . .gymn work at Penn falls to every undergraduate unless he is a member of a Varsity team. . . I examine the football men at the start of every season and so with all the other teams. If they are not up to muster they go to the gymn until they are fit. . .

We go a little farther at Old Penn. Every graduate must be able to swim. He does not get his diploma until he learns. We have never failed to teach an undergraduate to swim and that credit goes to George Kistler, of the swimming team. . . . Penn has been foremost in building up the entire undergraduate body as well as athletic teams. Each year an outdoor exhibition is held that rivals anything seen in Russia, Germany, or Sweden among college students. . .

The day of the athletic freak is over . . . the all-round collegian is coming. The chap who can excel in one sport, as a rule, is better at another sport because he has had the advantage of being trained on the first sport. The all-round collegian will play football or soccer in the Fall, wrestle, fence or play basketball in winter, baseball, lacrosse or turn out for the track team or crew in Spring. The undergraduates have plenty of time to keep up athletically all year and they will be a lot better for it.

Dr. McKenzie's department did not run itself however and required that he keep in close touch with the actual practices. The same fall [1914] he surprised the rowing candidates with a new order that no man would be permitted on the Schuylkill in a Penn shell unless he had first presented coach, Vivien Nicholls, with a certificate signed by Kistler, that the bearer could swim twice the length of the gymn pool or 200 feet and that he had seen him do it. There had been drownings on the Schuylkill when shells capsized in midriver.

For some time McKenzie had been collecting material for a book, begun before his marriage:

Living in Philadelphia, the home of the leading medical publishers and with a seat on the medical faculty, each man of which had written a textbook of his subject, it was natural that the question of writing should come up early.

I had made it a habit to write a paper on some aspect of my work at least once a year. These were accumulating. I was meeting with many new and stimulating experiences and when the representative of a leading publishing house proposed that I write a text book on Physical Education, I welcomed the suggestion.

An outline of the contents was made and references bearing on each chapter were collected from book and magazine. I haunted the fine library of the College of Physicians. As president of the College Physical Education Directors Society, I arranged the winter meetings so as to include invitations to view the methods used for the blind at the excellent institution at Overbrook, Pa., the Deaf and Dumb at Elwyn, the incorrigibles at Glen Mills and these visits formed the basis for chapters.

At that time there were no textbooks on the subject. Fernand LeGrange's fascinating book on the *Physiology of Exercise* occupied the field practically alone. A few articles on certain effects of exercise could be culled from the foreign magazines at the College of Physicians and were requisitioned. There were the old German books on Gymnastics by Gutsmith to draw on and the writings of Ivy and his followers among the Swedes. Sveboda had his widely advertised Ling method of exercise distributed by mail at one-half price to customers sworn to secrecy. Checkly had published his book illustrated with pictures of his muscular physique advocating free exercises by contracting muscle group against muscle group and pointing to his own person as a demonstration of efficiency neglecting to state in the intervals of these exercises he had practised the far from sedentary trade of boiler maker.

. . . In the realm of medicine, the application of physical medicine was in the hands of the masseurs . . . electricity was looked on with suspicion by the profession . . . and the use of radiant light and heat was just beginning to attract attention. Hydro-therapy was confined to the spas and turkish baths. No attempt had been made to give a comprehensive view of the whole subject giving the possibilities and especially the limitations of these apparently new but really old and fundamental methods of medical treatment.

In 1907 I received the additional title of Professor of Physical Therapy at the University of Pennsylvania and in my lectures to the second year students covered these fields and established application of these methods. In this I was greatly assisted by Joseph Nylen, a trained masseur who graduated from the University of Pennsylvania and became my assistant and succeeded me at the hospital when I retired. . .

In the summer of 1908 I went to Noank with my trunkful of material, spread it on the floor of Captain Fletcher's barn and every morning dictated a chapter to my secretary. . . . By the end of September the manuscript was ready enough and during the winter references were verified, new material was uncovered and by Spring the first edition of *Exercise in Education and Medicine* was ready for the press.

It was published in 1909 by W.B. Saunders Company of Philadelphia, simultaneously in England and America, revised and reprinted in 1915, and again in 1924.

It became the physical education bible for those engaged in the field and was later used as a textbook. In the preface of the first edition, McKenzie wrote:

> Exercise and massage have been used as remedial agencies since the days of Aesculapius but definite instruction in their use has seldom been given to medical students. Perhaps a cerain laziness which is inherent in both patient and physician attempts through the administration of a pill or draught to purge the system of what should be used in normal muscular activity but there is a wide dearth of knowledge among the profession of the scope and application of exercise in pathologic conditions and the necessity of care in the choice and accuracy of the dosage will be emphasized throughout the second part of this book.

In the first half of his book he related his experience and that of others concerning the effects of exercise on vital organs of the body, the various physical education systems then in existence in Europe and in independent bodies such as the Y.M.C.A. in North America, and the kind of physical education available at American schools and colleges, as well as municipal playgrounds. In the second part of his book he thoroughly covered the use of exercise to correct or reclaim defects in the human body all the way from scoliosis to chorea and infantile paralysis.

He defined exercise as including massage and mechanical devices used in physiotherapy—in fact all movement designed to act on the muscles, the blood vessels, the nervous system, the skin, and the abdominal organs. For even the simplest exercise such as lifting a dumbell, he thought "education should be directed to teaching skill in performance—skill that tends to economize the amount of effort required—for it is the common experience of shot-putters to find that every record performance is accomplished with the greatest ease owing to the smooth, accurate application of group after group of muscles at the proper time and the perfection of balance and speed of the body's movement."

In his opinion, the whole man must participate bringing into play all the muscles. "Exercises of strength and skill should be employed to train coordination . . . alertness of mind so necessary in ordinary life" he wrote. "This shortens the period between thought and action and gives that condition known as 'presence of mind' ".

He outlined exercise programs for all ages starting with the infant whom he thought should have several hours daily of free exercises unencumbered by clothing. "Give him something to kick against—the wall or footboard," he advised, "and a ring or handkerchief to pull on with his hands . . . the amount of muscular work done by an infant in the course of the day is quite as great as that done by the active adult, weight for weight, as proved by Schlossman's tables . . . and any curtailment of this necessary activity must be harmful."

His book included an ideal program for public schools going so far as to allot so much space for each pupil, light arranged to fall over the left shoulder and at least one-fifth of the floor space for windows. He thought children in the senior grades should have two 5-minute periods of corrective exercise in addition to participation in games at recess. To him physical training in public schools was not just a matter of health but necessary to educate the nerve centers and to build character.

> During the whole of childhood these centers are developing and their growth is not completed until adult life. . . . For this reason, not less than one hour in five should be devoted to training the motor area of the brain, in addition to time allotted to free play. This should take the form of both gymnastics and athletics.

Public playgrounds were included. Discussing the importance of the whole playground movement in the United States at the time, he said:

> On the playground the child lives. In the school he only prepares to live. Watch how a child plays and you will know how he will work later on. That is why supervision by a director who will cultivate all that is fair and honest and courageous in children is imperative for every playground. . . . It is the unsupervised playground that becomes a nuisance where the bully holds sway and the worst accidents and injuries occur. Without supervision the stronger boys take possession of the equipment and give no opportunity to the smaller ones, and the whole value of these laboratories for character building is destroyed and their use perverted.

For mature people and those leading a sedentary life, he advocated exercises directed principally to the muscles of the arms and trunk, taking care not to overtax the circulation. "Ball games combined with simple apparatus work are usually effective and interesting. If combined with the leg work and fresh air obtained in a game of golf, tennis, or a brisk walk in the country once or twice a week, the result would be increased efficiency in business and a general feeling of well being."

McKenzie had been an enthusiastic supporter of the Boy Scout movement founded by Sir Robert Baden-Powell and he included such groups in his survey:

> His [Baden-Powell] experience in the Boer War made him realize the helplessness of the average city dweller when called upon to take care of himself in the woods or on the plain. He started to train boys in the art of scouting, woodcraft, teaching them observations of the birds and beasts, the management of boats, canoes, camping outfit, ropes and arms. In America Ernest Thompson Seton had his band of *Seton Indians* to whom he taught the art of scouting and the signs of the woods and with Dan Beard and a committee of sympathizers the modern Boy Scout movement began. . . . The movement has been popular throughout Europe as well as America and has done much to build up the physique of its members.

He also approved of the Campfire Girls started by Dr. and Mrs. Luther Gulick. To him this organization's training was ideal for girls.

The dominant idea is to keep alive the fire of the hearth and dignify the activities that surround it. Not only is the outdoor habit cultivated but the state of mind that makes for simplicity of life, physical accomplishments, self-reliance, and cooperation. She learns to take long walks and to sleep in the open. The conquest of the water is accomplished by canoeing and the art of swimming. The care of the body is the central part of 'Wohelo' (work, health, and love)—their call—and just as friendship which boys in their teens form in the team work of their games leads to cooperation based on personal trust and knowledge in men, so girls are forming groups in which the spirit of team work and cooperation will appear later in women who understand each other, and are able to do team work for the home, the country, and the nation.

Such a picture fitted into the traditions of the day. Tait McKenzie did not believe in track and field for women. Instead he advocated eurhythmic gymnastics, dancing, archery and swimming.

McKenzie's book was widely acclaimed. The New York Medical Journal said: "We are very glad to see this book. The physicians of Europe, especially of France, Germany and Sweden have made a specialty in the treatment of certain diseases by exercise for a considerable time and good books have appeared in their languages on the subject. But there are few good works in the English tongue."

The New York Times outlined the book and commented that the parts on playgrounds, physical education in public schools and the physical education of mental and moral defectives should be read by all municipalities. "As a result [of it] . . . the City of New York has taken over the responsibility of providing recreation, baths, et cetera for the children of the streets. . . . Juvenile crime has decreased in each district where playgrounds are in use."

The British *Lancet* reviewed it in 1910 declaring it an excellent book and remarking that it was easy to read despite the technical details. "Some of the best parts of the book are those on exercise as applied to pathological conditions." They placed great confidence in the author for "well-informed as Professor McKenzie is, he is careful to insist on the limitations of exercise and massage in medicine and to avoid the common quackery of claiming that these methods can cure every mortal ill."

The Boston Medical Journal reviewed it and said in part: "McKenzie is neither pedant nor radical. He has an interesting chapter for the blind and deaf and we see a picture of blind children playing Blind Man's Bluff. The medical part of McKenzie's book is quite as interesting as the educational part and should prove of great value to practitioners . . . it is a capital book."

One of the first letters of commendation came to McKenzie in December 1909 from Dr. Osler, then Regius Professor of Medicine at Oxford.

Dear McKenzie,

Your book came and is most interesting. It is full of good stuff and should become an important manual on the subject. Your models are splendid.

I have already had an opportunity to say a good word for it in one or two places. I wish you could come here and straighten out what is called the Eton slouch.

I am sure the work will have the great success it deserves. I am greatly pleased to see a quotation from my old friend, Fuller; I wonder from which book does it come.

To this McKenzie replied in January:

The quotation from Fuller that you speak of is from his work *Medicina Gymnastica*.

I am much pleased to know that you think well of my book and feel more encouraged to go on. I have been wondering if in your travels about Oxford you have come across any traces of Archibald McLaren. He wrote a brilliant essay on training which is a classic in the matter and in style. He had a gymnasium at Oxford which I once visited; and I also have found references to him in the memoirs of Sir Edmund Burne-Jones from which I gather that he was very closely associated with that group of young enthusiasts of which Morris and Rosetti were leaders. I am under the impression that his son, Wallace McLaren, is still living in Oxford but I do not know anything about him.*

Visiting Oxford and Osler later the same year, McKenzie spent some time searching for information on Archibald McLaren who had written the first books on physical training. He was fortunate in finding a very old man who was a cousin of McLaren's and spent some time talking with him.

McKenzie's book soon sold out in both England and America and for the second edition he made some revisions.

Jiu Jitsu was left out of the second edition and also Glima—Glima is belt wrestling of Iceland. An exhibition of it was shown at Stockholm in 1912 and several years after a group of wrestlers came to Keith's. I had them give a show in the gymn. . . . I found that sooner or later every Glima wrestler had his elbow dislocated from the force of the throws they had to take so I abandoned all thought of using it to enrich our program of exercise. Continually we were on the lookout for such contributions from foreign countries and I remember with pleasure the demonstration given by some Chinese students of the shuttlecock kept in the air by dextrous kicks with the side of the heel.

As late as 1944, McKenzie's book was still considered a standard work on the subject of exercise. John L. Griffiths, Commissioner of the Intercollegiate Conference in the United States remarked then:

*Osler Library, McGill University, Montreal. Manuscript collection.

His book . . . published many years ago, I read over and over again. In fact I think that book, more than any other, served as my athletic and physical training Bible. The present generation of men and women who are conducting as best they can the physical training activities for the youth of the nation, as well as those that follow, will always be indebted to men like Dr. McKenzie who pioneered the way.*

*The Journal of Health and Physical Education: R. Tait McKenzie Memorial Issue, Vol. 14, No. 2, February 1944.

CHAPTER VII

Three Months Abroad

In 1907 Augustus Saint-Gaudens died at his home in Cornish, New Hampshire. This was the American sculptor whose style and technique McKenzie had been studying for some time and to whom his bas-relief work was most closely related. McKenzie never met Saint-Gaudens although later their work appeared in the same group shows.

Saint-Gaudens had been apprenticed in youth to a cameo-cutter in New York, later studying in Paris. He rose to fame in 1880 with his *Farragut* statue which stands in Madison Square in New York. He was founder of the Society of American Artists and one of a group of American artists involved in revolt against the academic sculpture of the period. But it was his mastery of delicate line and sensitive modelling in bas-relief that attracted McKenzie who worked more and more in this medium.

A high degree of movement can be expressed in relief but it requires stringent discipline to produce an illusion of depth when working with one-quarter to one-half inch of clay. Bas-relief always remained McKenzie's favourite form of sculpture and here his skillful surgeon's hands served him well.

Most of his work was portrait, often of friends and often not commissioned. A face, an expression, a talent inspired him and led to asking the subject to sit for him. The subsequent portrait frequently became a gift to the sitter. Reproductions might be ordered and sold to friends, individuals or groups interested. Sometimes McKenzie kept the original and copies were cast in bronze for sale.

His athletic plaques and commemorative medals demanded more of him and if commissioned work, had to satisfy a committee but in portraiture he had a free hand. It gave him greater pleasure especially when he felt he had captured the personality and "spirit" of the model.

Christopher Hussey, an early biographer, considered McKenzie's early work in relief, in particular "the exquisite modelling of children" equal to his later work. Wrote Hussey: "Of McKenzie's relief work as a whole it may be said that it shows an adroit and effective management of planes with a degree of salience that is astonishing. The portrait . . . clearly displays a shrewd but kindly insight into personality."*

Tait McKenzie's list of bas-relief portraiture eventually totalled

---

*Christopher Hussey: *Tait McKenzie: A Sculptor of Youth,* Country Life Publishers, London, England, 1929.

over 90 works and included poets, writers, actors, actresses, doctors, musicians, statesmen, and a few children.

McKenzie's first portrait in relief was completed in Montreal before he left McGill, entitled *The Mother*—a profile of his own mother. His next work was a sensitive portrait of poet Archibald Lampman. Next came one of a young boy, Jeffrey Macphail, and *Dorothy B. at Sixteen*.

After he moved to Philadelphia and had a home of his own with a studio, regardless of work in athletic or other statues in the round, Tait McKenzie always kept a relief work set up in one corner of the studio to be worked on at leisure.

Some critics considered his bas-relief portraits "mere likenesses," or "academic." Others praised them highly. Charles Wharton Stork, a Philadelphia journalist, called them "his most perfect achievements."

It is hard to see how some of them could have been done better. His technical affiliation is with such realists as Dalou and Meunier, men who tried to interpret modern life as intimately in bronze as Millet did on canvas. . . Each person has been studied and rendered individually . . . the clean-cut profile of Dr. Keen, or the nervous intellectual features of Forbes-Robertson as Julius Caesar. There are the vigorous modern types such as Robert Barr and Dr. Sargent; and again odd, anomalous faces such as those of painters Dougherty and Ullman. Equal success in so many attempts could hardly be expected of any artist except Lenbach.

In January and February 1908, Tait McKenzie and Philadelphia artist, Eugene Ullman, held a joint exhibition of their work at the McClees Galleries in Philadelphia. From there it went to New York, Pittsburg, Indianapolis. It included some of McKenzie's athletic statues and quite a number of the portraits in bas-relief. The one of William Henry Drummond, Canadian poet, was considered by some critics as the best of the group. Pittsburg called McKenzie's sculpture "the most interesting and important of its kind seen here for a long time."

Although doing more portrait work, he did not let up on athletic studies. During the summers, the McKenzies took a cottage by the sea at Noank, Conn. and their house was often filled with students. Here came such athletes as Carl Periera, Mifflin Armstrong and Hector McDonald. In the mornings they would work out, or swim, or pose for the sculptor and in the afternoon McKenzie would re-study the morning's work, or they might picnic on the sand. During this time he developed *The Competitor, The Supple Juggler,* and *The Relay*.

The Competitor depicts an athlete tying his shoe. It was McKenzie's first athletic work completed without the use of measurements and indicates his innate sense of harmony and feeling for design. Commenting on this work among others in a lengthy magazine article, Charles Wharton Stork wrote:

McKenzie has said no surface must be left unaccounted for. Anatomy

The Metropolitan Museum of Art, Rogers Fund, 1909.

THE COMPETITOR (1906) Bronze statuette. 1/2 life size.

must underlie every pose, every bulge of muscle, but this anatomy should not intrude upon the general effect.

I recollect a statue at the Salon where every attachment of the pectoralis muscles to the ribs were sharply brought out. The result was only a little less painful than the . . . Saint at Milan who carries his skin over his shoulder like a cloak. Of course the lay observer is unable to pronounce on the finer points but there is a firmness about Dr. McKenzie's work which assure him that the technique is right. Again every statue must stand another difficult test . . . its lines must be harmonious when looked at from every angle. . . Let us take Dr. McKenzie's *Competitor* in this respect. The more one scrutinizes, the more one enjoys following the shifting contour of the legs, the straightforward left arm and the sloping back. Line flows easily into line so that the observer never imagines what infinite experiment and care were necessary to produce this effect of repose. And in that word 'repose' is concentrated the highest praise that can be given to such a work.

The pose of *The Supple Juggler* is that of an old test for suppleness, possibly originating in Scotland. It consists of picking something off the ground beside the left foot by bringing the right arm over the left thigh and between the shins. The completed quarter life-size statue was Rodin-like but with McKenzie's deft, refining touch. The originals of these two were purchased by the Metropolitan Museum of Art in New York City.

The annual Penn Relays held in Franklin Field became famed events during McKenzie's tenure. To these came school boys from public, grammar, high, parochial and prep schools and academies "scurrying around the cinder track in races varying with the age of the competitors." The carnival culminated in the intercollegiate championship races in which each contestant covered anywhere from 100 yards to one mile. Teams from English and French universities as well as America "have made athletic history on Franklin Field," McKenzie wrote. "In England as a result of visits to Penn, the Achilles Club was formed by Oxford and Cambridge graduates to cultivate and celebrate in London relay races of the same kind."

Tait habitually recorded the annual meets in pencil sketches and eventually completed the athletic figure entitled *The Relay* in 1909, working out the final version during the summer vacation at Noank with Maurice Husek, an undergraduate as the model.

These pleasant summers by the sea were restful but much in demand as a lecturer, McKenzie's vacation was frequently broken by commitments abroad. Such was the summer of 1910.

McKenzie was appointed by the Secretary of State to represent the United States at the Third International Congress on School Hygiene convening in Paris, August 1st. He had already been invited to address the British Medical Association in July and the McKenzies decided to spend the entire summer abroad.

In June they went to Montreal to visit friends and then on to Ottawa where despite rain, Tait helped put up the monolith to Dr. Fletcher* in the Experimental Farm. "The contractor knows his

*Dr. James Fletcher, F.R.S.C., bronze medallion in high relief set in memorial stele of granite, Dominion Experimental Farm, Ottawa, Canada.

University of Pennsylvania Archives

THE RELAY (1909) Bronze statuette 1/2 life size.

business," Tait wrote in his journal. "And by 5 o'clock we had the stone in place with the hose and cap and I had a plaster cast of the portrait trimmed and fixed to fit the place for it."

Returning to Montreal, they sailed from there for England. Ethel suffered from migraine headaches at this time and McKenzie noted in his journal: "Ethel is laid out like a fish on a plate," but later recorded: "Ethel has been in fine condition after her first day when she was laid out with her old enemy."

During the 11-day voyage, McKenzie prepared his Paris speech in both French and English and also drafted a paper on amateurism. The major incident of the trip was his being called upon to operate on a doctor with a gland infection. They docked at Liverpool on June 19th and went to Chester where Tait would like to have stayed a week wandering around the "quaint old streets" but a busy schedule lay ahead.

In London at the Bank of Montreal he met Henry Bovey formerly of McGill but recently Rector of the Imperial College. Bovey had been promised a knighthood but had not yet received it.

Tait visited the Royal Academy where he found his bronzes being shown under the name of "Miss R. McKenzie" and threatened "I will call and wring the secretary's neck when I get time," but he was soon caught up in the social whirl and forgot the incident. Visits to art galleries, luncheons with friends, trips to the theatre, social and business occasions of various sorts filled the days to overflowing. Ethel unaccustomed to the busy round on which Tait thrived when abroad, found it all exhausting. The migraine headaches occurred more frequently and she was glad to escape to the country and visit quietly with friends occasionally while her popular husband moved from one meeting or engagement to another.

Here is a typical example of the pace:

25th June:

Business in morning with a look at the Grafton gallery to a collection of portraits of fair women. Sargent holds his own. Two good portraits by Gerald Kelly whom I used to know in Paris. In the afternoon to Tate Gallery. Took a bus for the Japanese-British Exposition and met Sir Lauder Brunton with whom we dined. After dinner we made the rounds of sights. The most interesting to me being the wrestling for they had 35 picked men including the champion of all Japan. . . . He had a fine corporation and seemed proud of it. The wrestling consists in trying to shove or throw the opponent off the raised platform by a series of arm and belt holds and is very clever but does not call for much endurance. The ceremonial is quite interesting and elaborate, however.

26th June: (Sunday) Spent day at Noldringham Surrey with Robert and Mrs. Barr. I was sorry to find my old friend in poor health.

27th June:

Lunch with Viscount and Lady Ridley . . . discussion was lively on the political situation and the plans of the landowners to invest their money in Canada or elsewhere so as to avoid the enormous increase in taxes. At the table was Ivor Maxie, M.P., a cousin of Winston Churchill . . . and brother-in-law of the Earl of Leconfield who owns the 'Leconfield Aphrodite' undoubtedly the work of Praxiteles. He has promised to take me to see it before we go. A most amusing fellow . . . they all unite in hating Lloyd George, but differ on every other political question. Ridleys much interested in my work and asked me to send *The Competitor* and *The Relay* to their house with a view to purchasing them. R.E. Mathews came in later and we had a long talk over political situations. . .

June 28th:

Lunch with Sir Malcolm Fox, just knighted for his work in introducing physical education into the army, and had a charming time. . . .

June 30th:

Spent the morning at the Abbey [Westminster] looking over the memorials to the illustrious dead . . . stayed so long we missed our train but took one later to Burley Heath where after a 3-mile drive we arrived at Hartsborne Manor, the residence of Forbes-Robertson and his family, and of Maxime Elliott to whose taste and wealth the improvements are due. It is a long house of two storeys high but beautifully furnished and decorated. There are about 250 acres of grounds surrounding it and plenty of room for the children, three little girls, to play about. Miss Elliott is devoted to the children and they seem to have a very happy time of it. . .

July 1:

Ridley called for us at 11:00 a.m. and we went to the Japanese exhibition again. In the sculpture there were but few things that made me feel I had much to learn from them . . . after lunch we went to a matinee given for the cause of Physical Education and heard Barrie's new skit on the modern tendencies of the drama called "A Slice of Life." It was admirably acted by Gerald du Maurier, Irene Vanbrugh and Cecilia Forbes. Ellen Terry recited *The Daffodils* by Wordsworth. Her voice is gone and she looks old at last. Her reception was most cordial showing how loyal the English people are to their old favourites . . . in the evening, Dominion Day reception at the Queen's Hall to which we went with Jimmy Barr who dined with us. He is as gay as ever although now he has become an ardent socialist while his daughter is a suffragist. . . . The reception was a great crush and we met a number of old friends, the Boveys, Honourable Sidney Fisher, and many others.

Invariably on visits to London, Tait McKenzie met his old friend, Edward Peacock, who had become Governor of the Bank of England and financial advisor to the King and moved in a rarified financial atmosphere. Being of modest means, Tait was always glad to get some tips on handling his investments.

Ed Peacock came in for tea . . . He is going to fix me up with his best advice. He is remarkably wise and sure of his position and inspires one with confidence. . . . Ethel posed for Mathews [R.E.] who got quite an interesting portrait in profile. . . . After he left we went to 16 Cambridge Square to dine with Lord and Lady Haddo and meet their Excellencies. Lady Aberdeen is as generous and kindly as ever and we had a long talk about a portrait of Lady Tweedmouth over which she had had so much difficulty. . .

A week later after a visit to Fitzwilliam Museum at Cambridge to see the early work of Burne-Jones, Rosetti and Morris, the McKenzies left for Dublin where a "warm welcome and supper" awaited them at the Aberdeens. Archie Gordon, Lady Aberdeen's son, had been tragically killed in a motor-cycle accident the previous year and she wanted Tait to make a memorial bust of him. They further discussed the relief portraits of her parents and made arrangements for McKenzie to go to the Highlands to have a look at the setting and do the modelling.

Back in London, Tait lectured at the British Medical Association meeting held in Queen's Hall, July 26th.

The opening ceremony with the brilliant, gorgeous gowns of the officers making the scene look quite gay. After the president's address, the guests were brought up on the platform and presented to Sir Henry Butler, the president. The meetings of the following days were full of interest especially some work of Leonard Hills on the inhalation of oxygen and its relation to endurance he claiming that by preliminary inhalation of oxygen the breath can be retained for 7-8 minutes without discomfort and that it has a marked effect in postponing the onset of fatigue.

July 28th:

The dinner was the greatest I have ever seen and the speeches were lost in the great hall. . . Lord Aberdeen spoke . . . and I went home with him after to his hotel. And we went out for a walk later talking about the dinner and the relation of the medical men to health movements.

July 29th:

Had dinner at Sir Lauder Brunton's and met some distinguished men from Rome and Russia, Germany and Spain, and among them Dr. Crile of Cleveland who was most interesting in his account of his experiments showing the influence of fear on structural change. Dr. Brock of Rome had some amusing anecdotes of Dr. Osler and his young daughter who are great friends, Osler leaving the chair at an important meeting to keep a tea engagement with her.

July 30th:

Ethel being out at Windsor I had lunch with E. Norman Gardiner who has just published a most interesting work on the Greek Athletic Festivals which will give me some ammunition for my article.* He has

*Article later published in pamphlet entitled "The Chronicle of the Amateur Spirit."

certainly killed his subject most thoroughly and it should long remain the authority on Greek athletic sports .... Left for Brownsgrove, Worchestershire, the same evening to get full particulars for the two portraits of Lord and Lady Tweedmouth which I want to start in Paris or Brussels ... got back to London just in time to pack up and leave for Paris.

In Paris McKenzie attended the School Hygiene Congress. Two things which impressed him most were the confusion in the conduct of the Congress and the fact that they seemed to know little or nothing about what was happening in America "partly our own fault, it is true." At the opening ceremony, representatives of various governments were introduced to the assembly but the proper papers had not arrived for Drs. McKenzie and Harrington of the U.S. until the middle of the week. The result was Tait spoke at the end of the week of meetings on Friday night and Harrington on Saturday night at the closing exercises. Harrington spoke in English but McKenzie in French. It was disappointing for the two men to have their contributions expressed so late in the proceedings leaving no time for discussions or questions from the floor. The next congress was scheduled to take place in Buffalo, N.Y. in 1913 and McKenzie commented "it will then be our turn to show them what we can do."

During the week he managed to get to the Luxemburg Gallery and have a look at some medalists' work. "St. Sanders loomed up bigger than ever, both from originality and beauty of design and also from interest in technical achievement. He has always got impeccable taste and when he does use decoration he never oversteps ... it is always quite exquisite and just right," he wrote in his journal.

On August 8th they left for Brussels to attend the Universal Exposition and further meetings on physical education. McKenzie representing the U.S., spoke in French again, "which was well received."

The meetings began at once and were remarkable only for the controversy between George Daning of Paris and the Swedes who took umbrage at his statements of ideas that movements should be curvilinear and never straight back and forth, that the nearer natural they become the better. It developed into a personal dispute which ended in them calling one another liars and imposters but no blood was spilt. ... On Friday we got together [Drs. Harrington, I.A. Cabot, and McKenzie] and outlined our report which is to go to the Department of State and on Saturday I met a Mr. Paul Otley who is the Secretary of the International Institute of Bibliography who came to explain the difficulties of starting an International Journal on physical education. He was charming and cultured.

He told me how Belgium was deeply concerned over physical education on account of her precarious position between France and Germany. They feel that their safety lies in a strong, vigorous, alert people able and willing to care for themselves. . . . In the afternoon we went to the Palais de Cinquantinaire where the modern art is housed and we saw a most bewildering collection of modern pictures from all over the world. I was especially interested in three rooms of medals and looked at my own modest case. . . . It is a liberal education to see the collected work of so many masters of this delicate art and I took many notes and sketches. So far as I can see America had not done anything better than St. Sanders who has added a new note to the art of the medal, a modern and individual touch, and it remains for his successors to impress this on the art and Frazer [Earl Frazer, New York sculptor] is doing this, I think, in his own way, and I will try to do it in mine.

McKenzie visited Van der Stappen, an aged and ill sculptor, whose "Mort d'Ompdrailles", a group of wrestlers, he had seen and admired. In his journal he recorded:

August 14:

This was a great day. First I went to see Van der Stappen, the sculptor. He lives in a beautiful house and has two studios. His assistant was working on a high relief portrait from a model, took my card and reported that he was ill but that Madame would come down. She was a gray-haired, distinguished lady, most kindly and courteous. I explained that I merely came to express my admiration of the 'Ompdrailles' group and to ask where I could purchase a photo of it. She took me into the dining room and showed me the sketch about two feet high which she had cast in bronze; it was his favourite work. Then she showed me his great work, the monument to Labour, which I fear he will never finish—a shaft before which rises Pegasus and the youth 'Ambition' or 'Effort' trying to catch his head on either side. At the other, the ox and driver and behind a dynamo with allegorical figures surrounding the shaft, has three designs . . . finally she took me upstairs for a word with the master who was in an easy chair. A little shrunken man whose effort to speak and rise made the red of his cheek and lip turn blue. He is just fluttering on the brink and may die at any moment.

He was much pleased at my visit and told me there was no photo of the 'Ompdrailles' but that he would have one made 'surement' and send it to me. . . . He looked at the football group pictures and liked them very much. Strongly advised against trying to keep them nude at all, saying any action would bring into relief the parts over which the clinging drapery was stretched and that the rest did not count so much as the fact that one should record the costume of one's time just as the Greeks did or as did Velazquez. He is right. I bade farewell to him with a lump in my throat. He said: 'Goodbye, we will not meet again. Je suis fontu.' (I am done for) 'but I am glad you came.' Madame bade me farewell at the door with tears in her eyes. And so I went ruminating on the injustice of this fine mind, clear and active, crippled and thwarted by the breaking up of a body that was until last year, robust and healthy.

I went out and had another look at the group. One Herculian wrestler, lifting a limp form of another and showing him to the crowd who are collected to see them wrestle and his arms lifted to form a Cross and his feet trailing off the front of the pedestal. The contrast of life and death, of vigor and relaxation, is tremendous, and the composition has distinction rarely seen in sculpture.

McKenzie also visited Van Gelder, art critic and collector, who had a chateau at Zee Crabbe and a large collection of sculpture and paintings. From Brussels they went to Antwerp and sailed from Harwich, entraining next day for Edinburgh and a rest "ensconced at Miss Knox's comfortable house on Great King Street."

Tait looked up Sidney Mitchell, architect for the Tweedmouth memorial, then bought some plasticine and made a start on the portraits of Baron and Baroness Tweedmouth. "It is a great pleasure to get my fingers into the clay once more," he wrote in his journal.

During a three-day stay in Edinburgh he visited and viewed with delight a collection of fine medallion miniatures at the Scottish National Portrait Gallery. Some of these were done in a Wedgewood-like process developed by James Tassie, a Scottish artist of the 18th Century.

> Saturday we called on Aunt Janet at Ashley Terrace [he wrote] and found her looking very well. . . . Asked her to come over next year and I believe it might be possible. Mother and she would make a great pair together. She is alert and interested in everything. . . . On Sunday it being rainy I put on an old coat and went to Greyfriars. Walked about the churchyard and through the Grassmarket and around about the Castle and down to High Street and through the Gardens [Princes Street Gardens]. Edinburgh is the most wonderful place. On the Hill I counted houses of nine storeys facing on Leith Road and the skyline of the ridge going up and ending in the Castle is one of the greatest sights of the world. When the windows are lighted, it looks like a dreaming city. . . .

On August 22nd, they left for Inverness and Tomich.

> This is my first glimpse of highland scenery and the impression made by the great rounded heather-clad hills with the changing lights of red and purple and green is profound. Every little while we come to a cultivated part just like Canada and then again the rocky barren hills with occasional black-headed sheep half lost among the heather which is at its best.

They stayed at the Tomich Hotel not far from the setting of the memorial fountain for which he was to design bas-relief portraits. The tiny village lay in a valley at the head of Strath Glass surrounded by beautiful heathered hills and the McKenzie's two-week stay was a pleasant and refreshing holiday. The Guisachan ("Place of Fir") estate now belonged to the third Baron Tweedmouth who rarely came to Tomich except to fish in the Glass river.

Lady Aberdeen's father had purchased Guisachan with its fir trees as a hunting lodge but became interested in the countryside and the people who lived there and introduced better methods of farming. He built roads and houses of granite, a school, an inn, a mill and brewery, and raised the standard of living for the Scottish people roundabout.

As a young girl at Guisachan Ishbel [later Lady Aberdeen] had been accustomed to taking her pony and going on messages to the village, delivering medicines and diets which her mother prepared for those on the sick list, and meeting the villagers on equal footing without any class distinction, a custom "that belongs especially to Scotland."

McKenzie found the fountain which had already been built a disappointing structure which seemed to have no real design with lines and planes leading nowhere but he hoped to persuade the architect to alter it and made sketches suggesting changes.

The portraits were to be placed on either side of the drinking fountains. There was a large basin for horses and near ground level, two small ones for dogs.

> The village is just a row of houses along the road .... Old Duncan McLennan, the Stalker of the Guisachan estate, is a character full of anecdotes and reminiscences of the Tweedmouths who are near to the hearts of the people here on account of their lavish generosity. He has been most helpful in coming in and criticizing the portraits. His son-in-law is now Head Stalker and Duncan has retired to his cottage to rest on his laurels.

An Indian Prince came to the hotel during the McKenzies' stay, for deer and grouse hunting, and Dr. McKenzie had some good talks with him on physical education and sculpture.

> A delightful man, tremendously interested in all kinds of questions relating to the welfare of his people... he invited us to visit his Court at Baroda and promised to give an entertainment of wrestling for me... he has 50 wrestlers under pay at his Court and says in the old days they used to have two hundred.

> The whole country here is redolent of Prince Charlie but his personality does not improve with acquaintance [Tait wrote later in his journal] and I fear the songs and poems cannot cover the fact that he was useless and a good deal of a blackguard.

At the end of the two weeks, the McKenzies left for Drumnadrochit on Loch Ness and from there down the Caledonian canal to Oban and on to Glasgow where, having completed the portraits, Tait had the medallions cast in bronze. In mid-September they sailed for home.

Today the memorial fountain at Tomich stands beside the main road, a curio and an eyesore for McKenzie's suggested changes in architecture were never made. The fountain was for some strange reason never connected to a water main and no water has ever flowed to refresh and slake the thirst of humans, horses or dogs. A "white elephant" to the village for the Guisachan estate now belongs to strangers and the memorial fountain to nobody being outside the entrance to the estate. Tourists sometimes stop their cars and inspect it, reading the inscription:

BARON AND BARONESS TWEEDMOUTH (1910) Bronze portrait panels
with life size heads set in memorial fountain at Tomich, Ross-shire, Scotland.

To the memory of
Sir Dudley Coutts Majoribanks, Bart.
1st Lord Tweedmouth
Born December 29, 1820, Died March 4, 1894.
Whose home was at Guisachan 1854-1894
Who built the village of Tomich and whose chief
delight was to work for the improvement
and development of the district
and also
To the memory of Isabel Lady Tweedmouth
Who was the mother of the people
on the Guisachan property
from 1854 to 1905.
This fountain is erected
by their children
Edward 2nd Lord Tweedmouth
and
Ishbel Countess of Aberdeen.

CHAPTER VIII

The Amateur Spirit

In 1911, Tait McKenzie finished the life-size bust of Archie Gordon in plaster and sent it to Haddo House in Scotland. Following the suggestions of Van der Stappen, he completed *The Onslaught*, his football group, in full dress.

The pose depicts a blocked line play which was later legislated out of the game because of its danger to players.

Mike Murphy was the coach at Penn when it was modelled. McKenzie used to bring him up to the studio to watch the statue in progress and criticize. Murphy repeatedly put the scrum through the play on the field so that McKenzie could study the spirit of this characteristic movement of the American game. Almost every one of the figures was modelled after one of the "Red and Blue" (Penn) gridiron stars. Dr. Robert G. Torrey and "Big Bill" Hollenbach, well-known Penn men, posed a number of times. Like most of his athletic works, the figures were one-quarter life size.

It was exhibited in the International Art Society show in Rome and at the Royal Academy in London, the following year. Later [1926] he worked the group into a football frieze banking a relief portrait of the famous Harvard player and coach, Percy Haughton, as a memorial at the Harvard stadium.

The Onslaught was one of McKenzie's works which drew considerable comment. Writing in *Town and Country* magazine* in January 1912, Edward Carpenter discussed the Greek Olympic athletes and compared McKenzie's work to theirs:

The modern note has been sounded most happily and sincerely in the work of a Canadian-American sculptor, R. Tait McKenzie who has epitomized in clay the spirit of the college athlete. He has probably advanced further than any living sculptor in interpreting the vivid intensity of muscular youth on the crest of action. All the optimism and vitality and the thrill of sport assert themselves with splendid enthusiasm in Dr. McKenzie's subjects. . . .There is nothing academic or pedantic about Dr. McKenzie's Olympians except their perfection, for the sculptor has made science serve, not rule his art . . . . . *The Onslaught* . . there is a sweep, a buoyancy, a bigness, a tremendous ruggedness about this group which is nothing short of breathless.

---

* Edward Carpenter: "Studies from Life: Dr. R. Tait McKenzie", *Town and Country*, January 1912.

University of Pennsylvania Archives

THE ONSLAUGHT (football group) (1904–1911) Bronze. 1/4 life size.

Another commentary on the work followed its appearance in a New York exhibition:

> Dr. McKenzie's group is as likely to achieve and retain distinction as anything he has done. Here you have a cluster of college football men, full of vitality and eager movement, tense with the onrush of unconquerable spirit, yet harmonious with the unity of purpose which animates a team, and above all, idealized with a sense of beauty. The push, the energy and fight, concentrated so symmetrically and at the same time so like the accidential posing of nature, the well-suggested scuffling, the implied breathing, as well as the expressed exclamation, all make a sort of truth which in itself, has been said, is beauty.

A lengthy newspaper editorial* appeared applauding *The Onslaught* for the influence it might wield:

> A certain statuary group executed by the great Canadian sculptor, Dr. Tait McKenzie and pictured in a current number of *Century Magazine* is likely to have more effect upon the attitude of the people of this continent toward football than reams of editorial eloquence or thunderbolts of professorial dununciation. It does for football what some of McKenzie's

---

*Scrapbook clipping, name of publication unknown, McKenzie Papers, University of Pennsylvania Archives, Philadelphia, Pa.

earlier figures did for the ancient Greek games. . .(and) to the renewal of
interest in the Olympic Games among Americans. It shows the spirit of
the contest, its heroic element in a beautiful and convincing form. It has
been said that Dr. McKenzie was never trained for a sculptor and that his
modelling came as a mere epilogue to a series of studies of the action of
the human muscles in violent exertion. If the statement implies that
there is any chartered institution or fixed curriculum for the turning out
of sculptors, most people will be inclined to congratulate the Canadian
medical man that he has escaped it. The best sculptor may be like a poet,
born and not made. Much more probable it is, however, that he
instinctively gave himself the exact training for his particular kind of
sculpture. And that particular kind happens to be the sculpture most
expressive on this continent—the sculpture of struggle and contest, of
violent effort after a definite scrim, of power and self-mastery and the
perfect ordering and control of all resources.

The Onslaught pictures the full glory of the real game of football. . .the
attacking side is one crested wave of human energy and determination,
the defence a stern, heroic, but over-borne pier of resistance, and not one
man in the group is working for self, or withholding one iota of self that is
needed for the common good of his side, and not one man has aught of
feeling against his opponent, except that his opponent is 'the other side',
It is a vivid lesson in the truest heroism and it will aid to re-establish
football—ideal football as one of the noblest games of men.

Such a eulogy must have surprised even Dr. McKenzie and
delighted him for it is doubtful if he considered the group anywhere
nearly as effective as his written or spoken words on amateur sport.

He had been interested in the Olympics from the time of their
revival in 1896 and attended whenever possible. He felt keenly the
value of amateur contest in developing both physique and character of
youth. The professionalism growing steadily stronger in America
disturbed him and he began to prepare a paper which would present
his arguments in a forceful manner. It was entitled "The Chronicle of
the Amateur Spirit" and appeared in the *American Physical Education
Review*, February 1911. In it he drew heavily on E. Norman Gardiner's
essay on "Greek Athletic Sports and Festivals" for historical detail
citing parallels of amateur sport in Ancient Greece with the modern
U.S. trends.

It was the amateur spirit which Tait McKenzie hoped to keep alive
using his voice and his pen and even his work in sculpture. He likened
the spirit of amateurism to the Greek word *Aidos* "for which the exact
English equivalent is hard to find" he wrote:

[it] is opposed to both insolence and servility, that while it puts into a
man's heart the thrill and joy of the fight, restrains him from using his
strength like a brute or from cringing to a superior force, that wins for
him honour and respect, in victory or defeat, instead of terror from the
weak and contempt from the strong. It includes that scrupulous respect
for personal honor and fairness that would make a team elect to risk a
probable defeat rather than win through the services of those who do not
come within the spirit of a gentleman's agreement. It is that spirit of

modesty and dignity that obeys the law even if the decision seems unjust, instead of piercing the air with protestation.

Aidos is stolen away by secret gains, says Pindar; and so in our own day is the spirit of amateurism in constant danger from the insidious commercialism that threatens it by making appear plausible and right the most flagrant forms of lying and deceit. With *Aidos* in the hearts of the competitors, a sport that at first sight seems rough and brutal becomes a school for those manly virtues of self-control, courage, and generosity.

It is this spirit of honorable and manly competition that we want to see pervading our whole national life, for it is on the two great Anglo-Saxon races that the spirit of competitive sport has descended from the Greeks.

He presented the paper at a meeting of the National Collegiate Athletic Association in 1911 with the intention that they would act upon some of his ideas and suggestions. This body had been formed in 1904 to save intercollegiate football in which abuses "had reached the limit of academic endurance."*

It was only by calling together a Council by Chancellor McCracken of New York University and rallying together of its few remaining friends that averted the prohibition of the game as a college sport.

From the meeting sprang the National Collegiate Association. Delegates from all the leading universities in rank from president or dean to the director or coach met to devise ways and means to make the game safer physically and cleaner ethically . . . rules were changed and a drive made to improve conditions under which it and other games were played in colleges.

Its platform was faculty control, coaches and teacher of faculty calibre and standing, and insistence on the scholastic and amateur eligibility of the members of the competing teams, It is safe to say that through the Rules Committee and through local conferences this Association has done more to keep inter-collegiate sports clean when this was possible and to draw attention to the fact when it could not be done any other way.

It was before that body that I read 'The Chronicle of the Amateur Spirit' . . . and every year this convention served as a clearing house for ideas and stimulus for better work.*

In his paper, McKenzie warned against the intense training undergone in the latter part of Greek Olympics paralleled in recent American sport most particularly in football. Here coaches were sought who could coach teams to place the ball behind a certain line as quickly as possible and as frequently as possible by fair means or foul, the deliberate beating of the law becoming "an inestimable virtue."

New rules had been made but, he said referring to them,

*R. Tait McKenzie Papers, Biographical Notes, University of Pennsylvania Archives.

complexity not only for football but also baseball and track, made "a post-graduate course in higher mathematics necessary to permit one to dispute about them intelligently."

Again and again he urged the preservation of the amateur motive—the thrill of the contest as against the professional motive—gain.

The Greeks had gone through the same stages in their Olympiads stretching over 1200 years until they entered a period "where too much competition begat specialization, specialization begat professionalism, and that in itself was death to true sport."

In America specialization was the trend. McKenzie urged the National Collegiate body to work toward keeping the standards within reach of most students, diminishing the class distinction between athlete and student by removing the privileges the athlete enjoyed, considering the player first and not the spectator "for the spectacle should be an incident of the game rather than its sole object." (He had already experienced the power of the box office.)

The paper expounded once again Tait McKenzie's concern for the development of the whole man. He saw the playing field and cinder track as arenas for testing both muscle and mettle.

To commemorate the next Olympic Games scheduled for Stockholm in 1912, the American Olympic Committee had commissioned him to produce a sports medallion. The result was his famous *The Joy of Effort*, one of his most lyrical athletic works. It eloquently expresses the *Aidos,* the amateur spirit which he upheld so fervently.

It shows three hurdlers clearing a bar. It was first exhibited in plaster at the Games and later cast in bronze and set in the wall of the stadium in Stockholm. In honour of the occasion Dr. and Mrs. McKenzie were invited to the Royal Palace where Tait was presented with a silver medal by King Gustav of Sweden. Ethel McKenzie delighted in such honoured occasions invariably appearing in an elaborate gown and wearing a jewel-studded tiara. McKenzie, however, though always correctly dressed, preferred to remain unnoticed among the celebrities. What interested him in this meeting with the Royal family, was bringing a note from Princess Patricia of Connaught to her sister, Mary, the Crown Princess, and discovering they were both artists. "I spent a pleasant afternoon," he recorded in his journal: "going over the landscapes of Princess Mary."

Reproduced as a medallion, *The Joy of Effort* began to appear in exhibitions of McKenzie's work and received exuberant reviews. E. Norman Gardiner in an article entitled "The Revival of Athletic Sculpture: Dr. R. Tait McKenzie's Work"* (December 1920) wrote in part of *The Joy of Effort*:

Side by side they fly the hurdles with their long clean limbs outstretched and eager, clean-cut faces, each one straining for mastery. Underneath them are the words 'The Joy of Effort'.

---

*E. Norman Gardiner: "The Revival of Athletic Sculpture: Dr. R. Tait McKenzie's Work", *The International Studio*, December 1920.

University of Pennsylvania Archives

THE JOY OF EFFORT (1912) Bronze medallion. Original 46 inch diameter set in the wall of stadium, Stockholm, Sweden, after the Fifth Olympiad held there in 1912. 20 inch and 3 inch reductions used as awards.

In this relief and its title we have the keynote of Tait McKenzie's work. The joy of effort inspires his work and gives to it the freshness and vitality of perpetual youth. To this joy he owes his own success in many spheres.

Richard Elmore in another article in *The International Studio* entitled "Sports in American Sculpture"* included this work in his discussion:

. . . To put even scant apparel on a figure and to make the observer feel that there is a real body under the clothing is an undertaking that challenges all the skill and knowledge of the 20th Century sculptor. Dr. R. Tait McKenzie who handles the scalpel of the atelier and of the

*Richard Elmore: "Sports in American Sculpture", *The International Studio*, November 1925.

operating room equally well, succeeds admirably in doing that because of his skill both as an anatomist and as a Director of Physical Education. . . it may be that owing to the purpose which actuated Dr. McKenzie which was first an anatomical rather than an artistic one that his athletic figures are lacking in action. That surmise does not hold good however in the sight of his *Supple Juggler*. It is absolutely groundless before that splendidly virile medal of his so aptly called *The Joy of Effort* which represents three youths in a hurdle race . . . their technique, their garb and everything about this medallic masterpiece reveals a thorough understanding of the spirit of track athletics. It is more convincing in a way than *The Sprinters* by Charles A. Lopez."

The original 46-inch medallion was reduced and used by the Philadelphia public schools as an award. Later it was further reduced to a medal size of four inches diameter and through the years to the present time has been used as an honour award or gift to staff members in universities. Today the Canadian Association for Health, Physical Education and Recreation use it as their official logo. So impressed with the spirit of this work were the Far Eastern Athletic Association that in 1915 they obtained Tait McKenzie's permission to adapt it as an athletic award by painting Chinese faces on the athletes. It was used for track events in Shanghai where the Games were held at that time.

Following the Olympic Games in Stockholm in 1912, Tait McKenzie was in London when he saw a letter in the *Morning Post* written by Guy Nicholls, a well-known English oarsman. Nicholls advised English amateurs to have nothing more to do with the Olympic Games.

The nation with the longest purse must win. I should have thought that the lesson our athletes got at the London Olympic Games in 1908 on foul running would have been quite sufficient to choke them off from making any further attempts at competing in such company. The American idea of sport on the track is so entirely different from our own as to be irreconcilable and we are told that every unsportsmanlike trick has its contrary trick which our runners should study. Heaven forbid!

Although McKenzie had deplored the trend in American standards he could not let this go unchallenged. Responding in a letter to the editor he pointed out that the American team at Stockholm was largely composed of college students and young men in business with "an occasional school boy and policeman, many of whom paid their own expenses." He attributed the success of the Americans to the fact that almost all American schools and colleges had systematic physical education. "Far from being specialists only," he added, "Most of the members of the team could show creditable performances in half a dozen branches of sport. Success is not a matter of money only, although travelling expenses must be met because boys and men of athletic age have not usually independent means. But in America at least, the honour of wearing their country's badge is considered reward enough."

In 1913 boxing was added to physical education at Penn and McKenzie reported:

> In order to prevent the usual abuses, such as professional coaching and other methods, I have required that there be only one second for each contestant who must be an undergraduate of the university, in good standing, and that he shall at no time be allowed to enter the ring or coach the boxer he is seconding during the rounds. We do not allow anything but soft bandages for the hands. With these precautions and a good referee who will be firm in enforcing the rules and who would have the nerve to disqualify any boxer if he runs foul of the rules, I see no reason why intercollegiate boxing should not be a great deal more popular than basketball.

Up until this time, McKenzie's sculpture in the round had been solely athletic works and small—one-quarter or one-half life size. But in 1910 the University of Pennsylvania commissioned him to do a study of Benjamin Franklin for the university campus. This demanded a large work, a place having been reserved for it in front of Weightman Hall on the main thoroughfare.

A long and prominent citizen of Philadelphia, Franklin in 1749 had written a pamphlet which led to the founding of an academy for young men, later expanded to become the University of Pennsylvania. Franklin with his advanced ideas on education had advocated sports and exercise as part of the school program. It was thus fitting that McKenzie be the sculptor for this commission.

McKenzie had not modelled the draped figure in the round prior to this time and this plus the size of the statue expected, added to the preliminary work involved. He delved into literature about Franklin including his autobiography and Philadelphia history of the period. He finally chose a pose depicting young Franklin setting out from his parental home to make his way in the world. We are accustomed to seeing an aging, long-haired Franklin in bust and statue and McKenzie's version is a refreshing change.

Much research was done to determine the costume of a boy of that period and old newspapers were combed to find a description of a runaway servant as Franklin had said he was suspected of being on more than one occasion during his journey which eventually brought him to Philadelphia.

There was no portrait or illustration of Franklin as a young man available, but in the face McKenzie tried to include the personality he had discovered in Franklin's autobiography showing curiosity, alertness, vigour and self-possession.

Most of the work was done in the summer of 1911 in Tait's studio in Marion, Mass. In a well-lighted barn he worked out his problems, working first from a nude figure, later draped.

The statue was brought in plaster form to Philadelphia, then enlarged in clay, restudied, recast in plaster, and finally cast in bronze. It was unveiled in June 1914.

An eight-foot high alert, beautifully poised figure, the bronze

Franklin stands today looking above the heads of passersby away from the stadium and the playing field, out into the world. The way in which the folds and lines of Franklin's clothing harmonize in design and enhance the eager, poised figure surely marks McKenzie as adroit in handling the draped as the nude figure. He himself was very pleased with the final statue of Franklin and at finding he could create drapery that hung like velvet though made of bronze.

Harold Eberlein of the Penn class of '96 writing on McKenzie's work said:

> It is characteristic of McKenzie's conscientious devotion to anatomical accuracy that his clothed figures are just as carefully studied for physical composition as are the nudes. The Franklin statue was first modelled in the nude and then actually dressed. . .

> Despite the archaeological scrupulousness which some might think would spoil the spontaneity of the composition, the heroic figure of Franklin is full of movement and vigor, and the expression of the face is exceptionally satisfying. . .

> McKenzie's realism is altogether different from the realism of Rodin for instance whose frequent emotional tension is strongly dramatic, stimulates the imagination by its implied psychological message and faithfully conveys the stormy surgings or the spirit of anguish, or the working of some powerful and subtle passion. McKenzie's athletes are expressions of bodily comeliness, they are not spiritual expositions . . . they are satisfying and convincing maybe because of their *physical* veracity which is one of their strongest claims to permanent value.

Paul Cret, Professor of Design at the University of Pennsylvania, was the architect for the Franklin statue.

About this time Tait McKenzie and Paul Cret were commissioned by Mrs. Thomas Robbins of Philadelphia to design and create a monument for the city of San Jose, California. Some years previously a group of San Jose naturalists had set aside a park area overlooking the famous fruit-growing Santa Clara Valley. Here they began planting oak trees in honour of civic-minded men of bygone days. One such honoured was General Henry Morris Naglee, the father of Mrs. Robbins, who had developed grape culture in the Valley, served in the Mexican and Civil Wars, and done much for the city's beautification. Mrs. Robbins on learning of the oak tree planting ceremony in honour of her father's service to the community, resolved to have a suitable memorial erected in the park to his memory.

Tait McKenzie and Paul Cret were both serving in the Army overseas when the monument was unveiled in St. James Park, San Jose, in November 1915.

McKenzie's bas-relief portrait of General Naglee is set in Cret's pillar of Tennessee marble. This is the only known memorial of McKenzie's on the West Coast.

CHAPTER IX

War Work

In October 1914, Dr. McKenzie's mother died in Toronto and he returned to attend the funeral. Mrs. McKenzie was buried beside her husband in the Auld Kirk cemetery on the eighth line of Ramsay close to the manse where she had come as a bride over 50 years before.

It was Tait's first look at the scenes of his childhood in many a year and he prowled the backroads and concession lines adjacent to the early manse site ruminating on the beauties of the neighbourhood he had almost forgotten.

Canada was full of war talk and speculation. McKenzie had not, nor ever did, take out American citizenship papers. A friend and associate sculptor said that McKenzie used to say: "I'm not an American, I'm not an Englishman. I'm a Scot."

Britain was at war and McKenzie was keenly conscious of his British heritage. He returned to Philadelphia determined to join the forces and serve in some capacity. He asked for leave of absence from Penn and it was granted. Early in 1915 the McKenzies closed their Philadelphia home and sailed for England.

Tait hoped to join the Canadian Army in England but on arrival discovered he would have to apply for service through the Canadian government in Canada to get a commission. Impatient of such red tape, he joined the British Royal Army Medical Corps as a surgeon and was given a lieutenant's commission. He arrived at Aldershot and reported to the Director General "a fine old Irishman" Sir Thomas Galway who assigned him to the Department of Physical Training under the Inspector of Gymnastics, Colonel Wright.

The McKenzies were fortunate in finding a palatial old mansion called Deersted House in nearby St. John and Mrs. McKenzie took up residence. Old friends from London welcomed them. Tait enrolled in an instructors training course to become familiar with the system of physical training in use and found that they were using his book *Exercise in Education and Medicine* as their text. It was not long before his identity as the author was discovered and the commanding officer arranged for McKenzie to accompany him on a tour of inspection of the South Coast training camps and hospitals.

During the Spring of 1915 it was my privilege to visit the great camps scattered throughout England and Scotland in which Kitchener's armies were feverishly preparing for the fight in France and Flanders. . . We found large numbers of men who had broken down under the intense strain they had had to undergo. The regimental depots were choked by them and by the men who were otherwise unfit and were awaiting discharge from the terribly congested hospitals. The latter were sending their patients as soon as they could be moved to the Red Cross hospitals scattered throughout the land. These were usually country houses given for the purpose by their owners, the lady of the house frequently taking charge, assisted by her friends and neighbours. The already over-worked doctor was supposed to treat these patients but too often hero worship and lax discipline were followed by physical and moral degeneration and recovery was retarded or prevented.

The solution of this grave state of affairs was found in the establishment of command depots under military discipline and medical direction in which men reported for treatment instead of drill.*

They discovered that many men in the camps were unfit for both physical training and army service. In the case of men unfit for service, McKenzie recommended a special course in exercise. His suggestions were accepted by Sir Alfred Keogh, the Director of Medical Services, and McKenzie was put on his staff at the War Office. Here Dr. McKenzie proceeded to set up a plan in detail in cooperation with Sir Robert Jones, K.C.B., Inspector of Military Orthopaedics.

Each of the Home Commands was to have a depot equipped with electrical and hydrotherapeutic equipment, masseurs, and instructors for a special course of physical training. A disabled Colonel was to be given command of each depot with a staff of invalided officers under him.

The first step was a workshop established at Tipperary under Lieut. Col. Woodhead, R.A.M.C., to give treatment and occupational therapy.

The first depot was set up as a pilot project at Heaton Park, Manchester, with huts for 5,000 men. McKenzie was given the rank of Major and put in charge. As Medical Officer of such a unit he had the daily opportunity to see his principles put into practice and observe the results.

The hospitals and camps sent daily their pathetic contribution of maimed and crippled to the masseuse and the physiotherapist for restoration of lost function in turn and shattered nerves and the re-education of coordination lost or weakened by war. New and simple devices for muscular re-education. . .proved their value in the great hospitals of the Army and Navy.

The Swedish gymnastics. . .were used in disciplining great masses of slow, awkward men in speed, accuracy and alertness and showed how quickly improvement could be obtained.**

* R. Tait McKenzie, M.D., Major, R.A.M.C. "Functional Re-Education of the British Soldier". Pamphlet reprinted from the *Medical Record*, New York, 1919.

** R. Tait McKenzie, M.D., Major R.A.M.C., *Reclaiming the Maimed: A Handbook of Physical Therapy.* Preface to the Third Edition. (1924) The Macmillan Company, New York.

His program also included methods to raise the standard of physical fitness for all enlisted men.

Mrs. McKenzie moved to Manchester to provide a home life for Tait and related her participation in war work writing to a Philadelphia friend:

> I have been visiting the hospital and working with the Red Cross where crowds of women assemble every morning at 10:00 a.m. waiting in line for the bell, like factory girls—countesses and chorus maidens alike, chatting in the greatest fraternity. The white aprons and veil make all women sisters. We work all day making bandages, splints, large slippers for wounded feet, and all kinds of sleeping garments. Just now we are making pockets for respirators.

The McKenzies also welcomed convalescent men to their home. McKenzie reported on his work during the winter of 1916:

> We had about 4,000 men under treatment at Heaton Park . . . eight others depots were soon established.

> On arrival each man is carefully examined, and a diagnosis taken of his ailment. Massage, electricity, heat (both wet and dry) and courses in physical exercises and training all form part of the treatment. The physical training is progressive in character starting with the lightest possible movement and leading step by step to greater exertions until full physical training is attained about a fortnight after becoming able to run and jump the convalescent is considered fit for active service again. The route marching too is progressive . . .*

In a letter to Philadelphia later in May 1916, he added:

> The staff [available] here cannot cover the work. One must do the best one can with the tools at hand. I am supplementing the equipment by appliances home-made, paid for by interested friends. I will soon have a model institution for giving treatment by water, heat, electricity, massage and exercise.

Although no closer to the action than being in London for a short time when German Zeppelins were flying overhead dropping bombs, Dr. McKenzie was deeply affected by the war. The gassed, maimed, broken young men—the cream of Britain's youth—coming to hospitals or his convalescent units caused him great personal anguish. The uselessness, the futility of war—the destruction of young minds and bodies was a devastating experience for a physical education man. The courage and stamina of the men who came to be rehabilitated in his units touched him deeply. His compassion took practical expression. Working long, hard and often frustrating hours, he succeeded in devising mechanical aids to help restore the disabled.

One of the worthwhile discoveries he made was that men blinded

---

* R. Tait McKenzie, "Functional Re-Education of the British Soldier."

by war might become skillful masseurs. This gave such men once more
a useful place in society.

> In many of his tens of thousands of cases of shell-shocked, paralyzed and
> battered soldiers, the problems of restoring nervous contact had to be
> solved individually and for the first time. In paralysis from shell shock,
> particularly, rhythmic movement of the affected limbs was made the
> means of reawakening the nerve centre. McKenzie's extraordinary blend
> of anatomical knowledge and athletic stimuli made him a healer of great
> power.*

Hydrotherapy had been established at Heaton Park with the
assistance of Dr. R. Fortesque Fox who later wrote a book entitled
Physical Remedies for Disabled Soldiers (1917) to which McKenzie
contributed a chapter entitled "Mechanical Treatment and Remedial
Exercises." McKenzie designed equipment as required to rehabilitate
certain types of injuries and such apparatus as the arm table, finger
machines, finger-tread mill, wrist circumductor, wrist mill for flexion
and extension, creeping board for shoulder abduction and others were
later accepted by medical circles as standard equipment in restoring
both soldiers and civilians. Some of these were invented on the basis of
reduction studies already made by Prof. E.A. Bott and his staff at Hart
House, University of Toronto, for the reduction of disabled muscles.
McKenzie used dry heat (diathermy) for deep tissues and joints, the
galvanic electric current to bring certain metals such as iodine and
zinc directly into the body as antiseptics or regenerators, infra-red and
ultra-violet lamps, circulating baths (whirlpools of running water),
douches, continuous baths, massage and active movements.

He explained the various methods in his book *Reclaiming the
Maimed.*

In August 1916 Dr. McKenzie inspected all the convalescent
camps and after making a complete report returned to Philadelphia
since university regulations required him to put in an appearance after
an absence of 18 months.

Many American newspapers had carried reports on his work with
convalescents in the British Army, his methods and success and on his
return to Philadelphia he was interviewed repeatedly and asked to
speak on his work to various groups.

Meanwhile the United States had joined the war and he was put in
charge of the Walter Reed Hospital where his apparatus was then in
use. At the request of the Canadian government he toured Canadian
hospitals advising on the treatment and equipment, and setting up
classes for masseurs, physical instructors and medical officers. He
spent much time with those whose faces had been disfigured by war,
working with the plastic surgeon, Dr. William L. Clark. He developed
a kind of thin copper mask for the use of those beyond the help of
plastic surgery. His knowledge as a sculptor enabled him to make the
mask match the original features and even the complexion of the

---

* Hussey: *Tait McKenzie: A Sculptor of Youth*

patient as closely as possible. The mask was held in place by a pair of heavy-rimmed spectacles, the nose-piece being rivetted to the mask. This work publicized, inspired other sculptors to assist in restoring the disfigured to normal life. "Often there were tears in his eyes after a happy man left his studio, fortified to face life again with dignity by near-normal features."*

During his service in England, Tait had carried small sketch books about with him and registered tiny scenes and figures for later reference. In a little leisure that had been available, he had begun the figure called *Blighty*, a statuette later part of the collection of the Royal Family at Balmoral. It was modelled after a Seaforth Highlander, McKenzie's own clan.

With the publication of his book *Reclaiming the Maimed*, his ideas were taken up by other countries. In France where fantastic losses had been suffered, military leaders were searching for the best system of physical education to regenerate the nation, and found what they needed in McKenzie's earlier book, *Exercise in Education and Medicine*. Dr. Maurice Boigey, their medical Director, wrote a similar book in the French language and it was circulated widely throughout France and Latin America where it was put into use.

In 1920 the George P. Pilling & Company of Philadelphia, manufacturers of clinical equipment, listed in their catalogue a new device for measuring the mobility of joints called an "Arthrometer" which they called "The Tait McKenzie muscular re-educational apparatus for the maimed". They also listed other equipment which McKenzie had developed for use in orthopaedics. A clinic using such equipment was set up in New York City for soldiers and civilians in conjunction with Cornell Medical College.

Thus did Dr. Tait McKenzie put all his resources into service in helping to restore and rehabilitate the injured. His methods and inventions later provided a sound basis for modern physiotherapy.

***Journal of Health and Physical Education*, V. 15, No. 2, Feb 1944.

CHAPTER X

Memorial Sculpture

Early in 1919 Sir Wilfrid Laurier, former Prime Minister of Canada, died at Ottawa. Discussion arose in government circles over a memorial to one of Canada's few great statesmen. The Member of Parliament for Montreal-Cartier, S.W. Jacobs, wrote to Tait McKenzie in Philadelphia suggesting he should compete for the commission. Tait did not approve of competition being held for such works and apprised Jacobs indicating, in any case he already had a full year's work ahead of him.

He believed that any memorial to Sir Wilfrid should be modelled by a French-Canadian "if a dignified design can be got." He suggested that Jacobs consult with J.A. Pearson, architect at the Parliament Buildings in Ottawa, who would be in charge of the memorial's architecture. (The eventual statue of Sir Wilfrid was completed by a French-Canadian sculptor, G.E. Brunet, and unveiled later in 1927.)

Also in 1919 Mackenzie King was elected leader of the Liberal Party. McKenzie wrote to him "congratulating Canada on finding the man who can fill the difficult place." The two men had met years before at the Vice-Regal Lodge in Dublin when visiting the Aberdeens and the acquaintanceship developed into a friendship which remained through the years. King in writing to McKenzie expressed similar admiration for *his* work recalling a pleasant visit to the studio in Weightman Hall, and commenting that if he had been free to choose a profession other than a political one, one in art would have been his choice.

A gifted Canadian poet and mutual friend, Wilfred Campbell had died and Mackenzie King consulted Tait on a monument in his memory. Campbell had been buried in a beautiful spot in Beechwood cemetery at Ottawa and King considered the location ideal for a memorial bench perhaps with an inset of a portrait in relief which McKenzie had already modelled for Mrs. Campbell.

Tait had lectured on Campbell's poetry before literary clubs, had collected his works, and had been a friend and admirer of the poet for many years. But because of other memorial commitments at the time, he wrote with regret:

> I wish it were possible for me to undertake this, and I am tempted to do it in any case. The only thing that comes to my mind is a stele of rough stone with a medallion set in and perhaps a verse of eight lines by himself under it. You may remember that such a memorial exists for

John Ruskin near Keswick in the Lake country. It is made of slate. Opposite this there could be a bench arranged as you suggested. It would be well to provide for the spacing of this so that people sitting on the bench could read his words at leisure.

I have just seen a sketch of a very beautiful memorial suggested for Theodore Roosevelt. There is a recumbent lion on a low pedestal . . . . This idea of isolation and of having the spectators sit and rest awhile while contemplating and reading the works of the artist seems to me important.*

McKenzie had given up his medical practice after the War as commissions for sculpture became more frequent and more demanding. He further sought relief from some of the burden of work by taking a young sculptor, Boris Blai, into his studio as an assistant.

Boris Blai had attended art academies in Russia and the Ecole des Beaux Arts in Paris, after which he entered Rodin's studio as an apprentice. When the first World War broke out he left to enlist and during this period met McKenzie whom he took to Rodin's studio. After Rodin had examined some of McKenzie's work, he suggested that Blai emigrate to America when hostilities ended and work with McKenzie.

One of the first commissions with which Blai assisted was the statue of George Whitefield which stands in the Dormitory Triangle at Penn. McKenzie had been commissioned to do the Whitefield statue in 1914 but the war intervened. Preliminary sketches were made while he was awaiting his army commission in London, using John Singer Sargent's studio in Fulham where he draped one of Sargent's models with a suitable gown.

Whitefield, a graduate of Oxford in 1736, had been an advocate of higher education in the American colonies. His Charity School of 1740 in Pennsylvania was a forerunner of the University of Pennsylvania. This statue is the most dramatic of any work of Tait McKenzie's.

Whitefield is shown as the great preacher "reaching forth a Jove-like hand with which to pulverize his theocratic enemies in the Episcopal trenches."

McKenzie's handling of the statue is a departure from his usual style, bordering on the baroque and his rendering of the billowing drapery is itself a remarkable achievement.

Another work of this year was McKenzie's first Canadian commission for a memorial statue—that of Capt. Guy Drummond, son of Sir George A. Drummond and Lady Drummond of Montreal. In 1915 at Langemarck, where the Germans first used poison gas, the Algerians whom the Canadians were supporting fled. Drummond and his men were slaughtered as they tried to stop the fleeing Algerians. The work was commissioned by Lady Drummond.

Of the Members of the Canadian Parliament who had enlisted only one had been killed, Lt-Col. G.H. Baker, Commander of the 5th

*Unless otherwise indicated all letters quoted are from the McKenzie Papers.

Canadian Mounted Rifles. He was killed with most of his men at the Battle of Sanctuary Wood in 1916.

Both the Senate and the House of Commons passed an Order-in-Council for a memorial statue to be commissioned and the secretary of the Committee wrote to Tait McKenzie asking him if he would undertake it. He accepted and met John Pearson, the architect, in New York. Early in 1920 McKenzie began sketches for the memorial and a meeting with the art jury and Pearson was scheduled for the end of January in Ottawa. At that time, Tait hoped to discuss the Campbell memorial further with Mackenzie King. Writing to King he commented:

> I have been so loaded with work that it is difficult for me to get at these sketches but as it is the first olive branch extended to me from Canada, I feel like seizing it. It is curious how one yearns for recognition among one's own people.

Up until this time only individual Canadians had taken much notice of McKenzie's skill as a sculptor; he had had commissions for portraits in relief; his work had been exhibited in Canada with good press coverage. He was, however, much better known to Canadians as a physical education man than as a sculptor.

On the other hand, his adopted city gave him plenty of recognition which says something for the American culture and attitude. Most of his commissions, portraits and statues, came from Philadelphia over the years, despite the fact that the city was a cultural centre with much talent to draw upon, with one of the finest art academies in the United States and many professional artists. Though McKenzie's style did not follow the fashion of the day, it drew him commissions from his own university where four major memorial statues of his stand today.

In 1920 he had several memorial works in process and his assistant went to work from McKenzie's designs and sketches, setting up the basic structure for McKenzie to work on later.

Today Boris Blai recalls his five years spent with Tait McKenzie as some of the most valuable in his life. In McKenzie's studio he learned how a master approaches his craft and how achieves. "There were no rough edges in the Doctor's work," said Blai in a recent interview. "Look how his drapery falls softly though made of bronze."

When Blai first came to Philadelphia some of Dr. McKenzie's society friends supposed him to be a Russian count and for a time he was entertained royally. Tait found this amusing and urged him: "Keep it up! Keep it up!"

McKenzie was a hard driver—himself first, and also whoever worked with him. Dr. Blai recalls they often worked all day on some demanding statue not stopping until perhaps 2 a.m. Then when his assistant seemed about to collapse, McKenzie would take him to a nearby steam bath, probably following that with a plunge in the pool, and they'd be ready to go again. Such a pace took its toll on McKenzie. Few knew that he had heart trouble and Blai feared he might collapse in the studio at any time. McKenzie's cheerful demeanour and industrious drive, deceived most people; few, says Blai, knew that underneath the well-tailored and meticulous suit was a body often on the point of exhaustion.

When Blai first went to work with McKenzie, he could speak very little English but McKenzie spoke excellent French and so they conversed in French, and this worked very well.

1920 was an exceptionally crowded year and in a letter to Mackenzie King, Tait reported:

> I have also been doing a considerable number of medals and other similar things so that when you come down, I will have plenty to show you in my new studio on Pine Street. I will put you on my exchange list and send you things from time to time. The most important lately has been the Whitefield statue.

In April the McKenzies went to Ottawa and the Baker memorial was discussed with the Senate Committee. Tait also met with Mrs. Campbell, Mackenzie King, Pearson and a few of the late poet's friends. They went out to Beechwood cemetery to visit Campbell's grave. Mackenzie King was then a practicing Spiritualist convinced that one could communicate with departed souls. Tait later wrote to him: "It was a very remarkable experience that we had on that afternoon."

McKenzie agreed to plan a bench to commemorate Campbell. In the back of it would be set a replica of his relief portrait of the poet. Mackenzie King undertook to raise money for the project privately. Tait considered the main expense would be the stone cutting, the setting of the medallion, and the lettering to be inscribed. For himself, he asked only expense money involved in modelling and working out the inscriptions and for casting the medallion portrait of Campbell in bronze. Back in Philadelphia he made a small model and mailed it to King in May 1920 with instructions for John Pearson to carry on from there. Regarding the Baker memorial for the House of Commons, he wrote:

> I have just heard from the Committee that they have not been able to have any meeting to decide on starting the work so I have given up all thought of doing anything on it this spring and summer. When a project of this kind gets into the hands of a parliament one may as well give up hope of any reasonably speedy action. I regret this especially as I could work on it to a great advantage this summer and it is not likely that I can get much free time again until next year. . . . We are sailing for England Saturday next [June 5] and my address for the summer will be: c/o Brown, Shipley & Co., Pall Mall, London.

As if he had not already enough on his plate, that Spring Tait launched a campaign for the Art Alliance of Philadelphia to hold an outdoor art show in Rittenhouse Square. Blai served on his committee. He recalls a prime asset of McKenzie was his organizing ability. In this instance, he carried the campaign including fund-raising through to a successful conclusion. Thirty-five of the best-known American sculptors participated in the exhibition, the first of its kind in Rittenhouse Square, May 13.

Tait's first exhibition of sculpture since World War I opened at the Fine Art Society Galleries, New Bond Street, London and was a great success. The Westminster *Gazette* reported:

> There is true Greek detachment in Dr. McKenzie's studies of young manhood. . . . He accepts the human form, accepts the traditional modes of representing it, acclaims its beauty . . . one might almost say he makes his models pagan gods.

The *Graphic* commented:

> The wonderful point about Dr. McKenzie is the way in which he made static art sculpture express dynamic force.

They devoted a whole page to illustrations of McKenzie's work.

> His best efforts . . . are decidedly those in which he emulates old Greek sculptors in themes which they made peculiarly their own. In these, unlike Flaxman and Gibson, he did not imitate the classic models so much as reincarnate the spirit in which they were produced, realizing the forms and movements of modern athletes with the same discriminating and artistic fidelity to nature that the Greeks applied to athletes of their day.

Writing to King later, Tait said:

> It [the exhibition] will lead to other things as well so we are both delighted. Next week we go north and will see the Aberdeens and other friends and on the 15th September sail for Montreal on the S.S. Victoria and will run up to Ottawa on arrival. . . . We could then talk over the Campbell memorial.

Present at the London show was Sir Arthur Shipley, Master of Christ Church College, Cambridge. The university town had set up a War Memorial Committee who at the time were not pleased with a design submitted to them featuring an angel. Shipley apprised the Chairman of McKenzie's work and the result was his first major commission in war memorial sculpture.

He went out from London to the East Anglian town to make studies of the university students, searching for the right Anglo-Saxon face for the figure:

> The first year of the War made me familiar with the youth of England as I went from camp to camp inspecting the physical training and bayonet fighting of Kitchener's army, then in the making.

> One saw the great blond yeomen of Somerset contrasted with the swarthy Cornishmen, the small black-haired men of Wales and Lancashire, changing to the young giants of the Lake country,

Yorkshire, and Northumberland, the long-headed Highlanders of Perth and Ross, and the round-headed Lowlanders of the South with their admixture of Saxon blood, but nowhere could one see a more distinct type than in the blond-haired, round-faced and round-headed youths of East Anglia.

It is this type that I have tried to put in bronze for the memorial to the men of Cambridgeshire. It is of them, as children, that St. Augustine might truly have said 'Non Angli sed Angeli,' for to him these fair-skinned, curly-headed youth must have seemed angelic indeed.

The predatory Danes have left their trace on the descendents of Hereward and Alfred and his men, and one sees continually in East Anglia the type of face that recalls the youths of Denmark and Sweden.

The East Anglian differs from the Greek of antique sculpture in certain important respects. His nose is shorter and forms an angle with the plane of the forehead—the bosses above his eyebrows, so lovingly dwelt upon by the Greek sculptors as a sign of beauty, are not so prominent. His brow is higher and his mouth larger. But he has the round head and oval contour that gives the Greek and the English youth a certain suavity of form that is in contrast with the squarer and more angular face of the young American college student who is the closest type that one can quote for comparison.*

During the Cambridge holiday called "the long", Dr. and Mrs. McKenzie were guests of Shipley. From the Master's Lodge, Tait was able to study English youths passing continuously in and out of the library and stately gardens and here he modelled the head for his figure. Upon return to Philadelphia, he began work on the figure in his studio.

1921 included many commissions for portraits in relief including one of Lord Aberdeen for Haddo House in Scotland and one of a distant clansman, Lord Seaforth, who lived at Brahan Castle in Rossshire, Scotland. The Canadian government did not finalize his contract for the Baker memorial until well on in the year but by December, McKenzie writing congratulations to Mackenzie King for winning the federal election and succeeding Arthur Meighen as Prime Minister, reported: "I am hard at work on the Baker memorial and have it almost completed. . .Mrs. McKenzie joins me in all good wishes for a successful administration."

Boris Blai assisted with the Baker memorial. Dr. Blai recalled recently:

When the Canadian war memorial was finished a number of bills had to be paid for bronze casting and other expenses that had been incurred. Dr. McKenzie had left a cheque for several thousand dollars and asked me to take charge of the bills. I paid the bills and with the amount that was left over I remodelled his studio by enlarging it and ordering a wrought iron

*Hussey: *Tait McKenzie: A Sculptor of Youth*

balcony for it. When Dr. McKenzie came back he was surprised to see the changes. 'That looks more like a studio of yours than mine,' was his remark, but he really didn't mind. After a short while he liked it and was very pleased that the change had been made. He never asked how I spent the cheque—such confidence he had in collaborators.

The Cambridge memorial, after much re-working, was finally completed in March 1922 and Tait wrote to Sir Arthur Shipley:

The great strain is now at an end and the figure has been cast and shipped so that the fortunes of *The Homecomer* are now in the lap of Neptune.

The last three months have been a time of increasing tension, with alternating waves of apprehension and exaltation, as try after try just missed getting what I could but hazily see in my own consciousness at first but which gradually took definite form.

It was not until the last two or three weeks, during which time I almost lived in the studio, having my lunch sent up to me like a hermit, that the final form of the face slowly emerged in my mind, but which refused to come out of the stubborn medium.

During the last week I had relays of my artistic friends in to criticize and discuss it, and I got much from their disputes. Even then I worked on it daily during the casting process itself.

On Monday, January 30th, Santi and a fellow-Roman appeared and proceeded to build little fences of thin brass along the ridges and across the planes while I worked furiously on the yet unfenced pastures. Next day the clay disappeared under a blue veil of plaster.*

Three streets converge where the memorial was placed and today it serves as a landmark for residents and visitors to the university city of Cambridge. Hubbard, the architect, had completed the pedestal which on two sides shows the arms of the borough and county of Cambridge, and on the ends those of Ely and Cambridge University. The unveiling was fixed for July 3rd. The captain of the ship on which the plaster cast had been loaded announced that he had not sufficient cargo and would have to visit other ports than those originally scheduled. This would not leave enough time for the bronze to be cast and in the end McKenzie had to bronze the plaster cast for the unveiling for "I will not fail the Committee," he wrote.

The Duke of York arrived for the unveiling. Rain came down in torrents on the multitude assembled. Bits of the bronze covering the plaster washed off with the rain, yet it was not as disastrous as seemed at first for by seeing the plaster statue in the open air and in place on its pedestal, McKenzie was able to make some slight modifications on the column and the features of the bronze itself when it arrived ten

*Ibid

Norman Mason-Smith, City of Cambridge

THE HOME-COMING (1920–22) Bronze monument to men of Cambridge, England who fought in World War I. Situated at the junction of Station and Hill Roads, Cambridge.

days later, altogether giving the whole memorial a better appearance. McKenzie described it thus:

> The statue shows a private soldier in full kit on his triumphal return after the War. With discipline relaxed, he is striding along bare-headed, helmet in hand, a German helmet as a trophy slung on his back and partly concealed by a laurel wreath, carelessly flung over the rifle barrel. In his hand he holds a rose. Another rose thrown to him has fallen to the ground. His head is turned to the side, his expression is alert, happy and slightly quizzical, and his lips are slightly parted as if he has recognized an old friend in the welcoming crowd and is about to call to him. In this face I have tried to express the type on whom the future of England must depend.*

Other war memorial commissions followed this successful and much publicized one. One of these came from his home town in Canada.

Alec R. Rosamond, head of the Rosamond Woollen Mills, of Almonte, Ontario had been one of the first volunteers in 1914. He was killed at Courcellette. In his Will he specified that a memorial statue be erected in the town for those townsmen killed in action. Present at McKenzie's 1920 exhibition in London were two Canadians from Almonte seeking a suitable sculptor. McKenzie's work showed the qualities they were looking for and they were happy to offer him the commission and he was happy to accept, an excuse to return to the scenes of his childhood.

Tait had not been back to Almonte since his mother's funeral in 1914 but he returned now to study the site and talk to the Rosamond family about the memorial. He chose a pose of a youth seated on a low pedestal in the centre of a wall. The face is not a portrait—it might be that of any volunteer. A bench of Indiana limestone ending in panels is embellished with a carved branch of white pine encircling a helmet. *The Volunteer* wears a uniform of a junior officer with a soft service cap and he is armed only with a revolver. The head is raised, gazing eagerly forward. On the wall is a list of 46 names and the inscription "To the men of Almonte who fell for freedom 1914-1919."

A journalist, Cullen Cain, who came to visit Tait while he was at work on the memorial in Almonte gives us a capsuled picture of the sculptor's meticulous craftsmanship. When he arrived McKenzie had just put a right hand on the statue but professed not to like it and although the journalist tried to stop him, he smiled "and clawed that noble hand and fingers and wrist all into a puddle of clay."

> And he moved the mass up an inch or two along the edge of the bench and started to fashion a new hand in a new grip. . .For an hour he worked there in the gray light of a rainy morning and I watched him in silence. Over and over he shaped the wrist and molded that hand and pressed that clay into fingers. And over and over again he blotted them out and shaped them anew. . .

*Ibid

THE VOLUNTEER (1923) Bronze statue 8 feet high. Rosamond War Memorial, Almonte, Canada.

Another hour passed and lo and behold the new hand was done. Yes, it was better than the other one, a little more natural, a little more reposeful. Not so much of an effort here to force the latent action of the eager volunteer upon you and yet the flaming purpose of the figure was none the less apparent.

My point? The finished figure did seem to be perfection. It did not merely compel admiration; it thrilled you. A master sculptor had spent months to make it. And yet he demolished a hand and moved it an inch just to make his best a little better . . . the difference between a statue and a great statue.*

Other comments on *The Volunteer* were not as complimentary. The New York *American* suggested the figure was "prettified" and "commercial." Henry McBride in the New York *Sun* covering an exhibition of McKenzie's work said in part: "The athletic works are meeting a long-felt want and enjoying popular success". But of *The Volunteer:* "it is a capable production though not inspired. . . Dr. McKenzie is much better when he clings to his college impressions and the group of football players, cleverly massed and modelled, is much the best thing he has done."

The Volunteer was unveiled in Almonte in 1923.

Just after McKenzie and Boris Blai completed the Baker memorial for the House of Commons in Ottawa, one of the best-known of McKenzie's memorial commissions came to him. This was the one he loved best and considered as his finest work. It was also his most ambitious memorial work having a main figure and an extensive frieze of many figures and much detail.

It was commissioned by the St. Andrew's Society of Philadelphia as a tribute from Scottish-Americans to Scottish soldiers who died in battle in the Great War. McKenzie was president of the Society when this commission was offered him.

A Scottish advisory committee was set up to secure a suitable site in Edinburgh, and McKenzie sailed for Scotland in the summer of 1924. The Scottish National Memorial was then under construction at Castle Hill and the Duke of Atholl suggested that the St. Andrew's memorial be made part of this national shrine but the rest of the committee were against it. They wanted something distinctive and separate. Finally Tait chose the site in Princess Gardens facing the Castle, along the promenade where strollers would pass and repass his statue.

Much red tape was involved. Permission had to be granted by the Lord Provost of Edinburgh and he also had to approve the design. He agreed on the site and Tait then engaged a rising young architect, Reginald Fairlie, to take levels, make drawings and act as architect. The two men became good friends during the trials and tribulations of erecting the monument over a three-year period.

*Newspaper clipping from scrapbook, date and publication unknown, McKenzie Papers, University of Pennsylvania Archives.

McKenzie returned to Philadelphia in October and set up a model of this sector of Princess Gardens. With this before him he designed the memorial practically as it eventually was constructed.

McKenzie's method of working with his assistant was to design the memorial, make sketches and perhaps a small working model, then set up the base for the actual statue and put his assistant to work on it. Blai worked on two large statues with McKenzie during the years in his studio. The Scottish-American War Memorial was one of these.

Granville Carrel, a member of the Penn football team, was chosen as model for the central figure. McKenzie also used Carrel's figure for the mural frieze, but the heads were modelled from Scots in Scotland. Twenty years later, Carrel, then a Major in the U.S. Army, was in Edinburgh and saw the statue for the first time. A reporter from *The Scotsman* related: "When we met Major Carrell he had just been inspecting the memorial and had been much moved by the memorial itself and by what he described as its perfect setting. It has been his ambition, ever since he came over to fight this war [1939-45] to see the figure symbolising young Scottish manhood of the Great War, for which he posed."

The memorial was supported by Scots all over the United States. Branches of the St. Andrew's Society throughout the country set up subscription committees. Virginia was the first to complete its "drive." Norval Scrymgeour, of Dundee, reporting "The Story of *The Call*" in *The Scots Magazine* (July 1932) related: "If it were possible to print in full the bulletins issued, Scottish folk at home would be moved mightily by the details of the contributions of clan societies and individuals. These bulletins comprehend a unique directory of Scots and Scottish sympathisers in the United States." Subscriptions also came in from Hawaii and London.

In the Spring of 1925, Dr. McKenzie sailed again for Edinburgh with his plans and models. The City Council and the Lord Provost approved both; formal application was made and the site in Princess Gardens formally granted.

"I spent the summer of 1925," Tait recalled later, "at Ipswich, Mass. at work on the figure and frieze—half the final size—working out details of dress and composition all that summer and following winter."

He corresponded with Field Marshal Haig concerning the dress of Highlanders and was invited to visit him when he and Mrs. McKenzie came over next. The McKenzies sailed for Scotland early in the summer of 1926 and took up residence at Darnick Tower from where Tait could "sally forth to Edinburgh to work with the architect on the setting for the memorial."

Darnick Tower had been built and owned by the Heiton family since 1425. (It is still in the Heiton family today: Miss Juliet Heiton of Callander is the present owner.) A sturdy little fortress guarding the ford of the Tweed, in turbulent times of Scottish history when invaders threatened the village, the villagers' cattle were driven behind the high surrounding stone wall and the Heiton's cattle went inside the castle, occupying the lower floor. The villagers were sheltered upstairs and the great iron gate barricading the entrance was securely fastened against the enemy. There was also a dovecote in the tower so that should the inhabitants be beseiged, a method of feeding was at hand.

Clustered around the Tower was a small village and a short walk along a footpath lay Melrose with its 12th Century Abbey where it is said, the heart of King Robert the Bruce was buried. Near also was the town of Kelso where McKenzie's father had been born. Darnick Tower, situated on the Borders, was also near Abbotsford, the luxurious mansion where Sir Walter Scott had lived and written his lucrative historical novels. As a child, Tait had dreamed the romance of *Ivanhoe* and the *Waverley Novels* and to be in the romantic land of their creation was itself an inspiration. The land including the brooding, richly historical city of Edinburgh provided a wonderful atmosphere for McKenzie's creative talent to thrive in.

The Tower itself furnished with rare treasures and antiques collected by the Heiton family, extended the atmosphere of a land steeped in history. A spiral staircase led to the studio in the Tower where McKenzie worked surrounded by coats of mail from a bygone era.

Guests came to the Tower that summer, curious and fascinated by the Tower and McKenzie at work in such a setting. One was Leo Tolstoi. Another Dr. Elizabeth Burchenal, a prominent physical educator of New York City who recalled: "I slept in the room occupied by Mary Queen of Scots when she visited there (three centuries earlier) and there still hung the portrait of the Queen presented as was her custom as a souvenir of her visit. . . . In his studio here Dr. McKenzie told me he found peace and happiness in his creative work as never before."

The historial aura of the castle also influenced Mrs. McKenzie and some of her best poetry was written during that summer. Published years later in a collection called *Secret Snow* was a whimsical ballad to Darnick Tower, part of a series which she wrote on old Scottish towers.

Darnick Tower

Ghosts do not walk at Darnick Tower
'Tis said. No gruesome shadows cower
Behind its ancient wall.
It stands, a shaft of rose-grey stone
Where quiet gentlefolk unknown
Dwell in its panelled hall.
Here Heiton, for 500 years
Lived, loved, knew life, its joys and fears.
Where other Border towers fell
They held their land, and here still dwell.
Still watch from deeply-seated sills
The moon rise o'er the Eildon Hills;
Still climb the stony winding stair
To reach the little turret where

The gentry pace. Look o'er the edge,
See lavender, beyond a hedge
Delphinium and gilliflower
Scenting the air of Darnick Tower.

Sir Walter wished to own the deed
Of this small peel-tower near the Tweed,
Close to his Rhymer's Glen.
He argued long with Darnick's laird
To sell, well knowing that he fared
With debts but poorly there.
So scribe and notary one day
Came here. Would Heiton sign away
The land of his forebears held so long
Against marauders among more strong
Than tailor's bills, or gambling stakes?
(There's still his lady's dower)
He will not sign! Then stormy words
And argument the hall disturbs;
Sir Walter his departure takes,
Drops spectacles, forgets his cane,
Vowing he ne'er will come again
A friend, to Darnick Tower.

So here they are. He kept his word.
He never came from Abbotsford
For spectacles or cane.
He never asked for their return;
The laird maintained his unconcern;
So here they still remain!

No longer now can Darnick boast
For sometimes you may see a ghost
Steal on a stealthy, creaking toe,
When dawn comes creeping, still and slow
A genial presence, kind, beneign,
Carrying documents to sign.
In every corner peers and looks—
Between the bindings of old books—
Sir Walter Scott has come again
Searching for spectacles and cane.

Beware! for a shivering hour,
You'll startle, wake, and find some morn
That cane and spectacles are gone
From dauntless Darnick Tower.

It was natural that Tait should feel at home in Scotland, the land of his ancestors, for despite his American affiliations and residence for some 25 years, his habits and characteristics were those of a Scot. He was spare, self-disciplined, thrifty, warm-hearted, and without class consciousness.

He roamed about the Scottish countryside considerably although his summer was an extremely busy one. Half-size models of types of heads for the frieze had been mounted in the Municipal Chambers on High Street in Edinburgh and a book was kept for criticisms and comments by the many visitors who viewed them for McKenzie had a great respect for the opinions of ordinary people.

He went out to see Field-Marshal Haig at Bemersyde one afternoon and discussed with him, Highland dress. Bemersyde was in the same rolling sheep-pastured land as Darnick.

> The approach was through an inconspicuous gateway, up a short shaded winding road to the old square tower of Bemersyde with its gabled roof rising above the castled keep and its three extensions of modern construction. It faces a wide lawn with sundial and well and is screened from the road by tall elms and wide-spreading beaches. Just below winds the murmuring Tweed and hard by is old Melrose and the loop of the river beloved of Sir Walter Scott and the Haunted Pool of Holywell famed for its salmon and its midnight ghosts.

> I was shown into the sitting room and soon the laird himself entered. Of medium height, broad-shouldered with eyes of startling blue, blonde hair, carefully waxed moustache and clear complexion, he gave me a cordial welcome and we went up to his study through the modern drawing room. His study was in the tower and had a fine fireplace with a secret shelf in it which was supposed to communicate with a secret room.*

Haig wrote McKenzie a letter of introduction to the Colonel commanding the King's Own Scottish Borderers at Redfield Barracks "which later opened the gates for me and insured a warm welcome at the Officers Mess," McKenzie reported.

> I later chose 12 types from them of pure Border blood on both sides and made half-hour studies in clay of their heads and incorporated them into the frieze. After tea we went down and met Lady Haig who had just come in, and saw the children on the lawn with their governess. He came out to see me off and, as the car started, he said goodbye with a friendly wave of his hand. I never saw him again.*

During the summer McKenzie worked out the intricacies of Highland dress with sergeant-majors "the most exacting and expert of critics" and others expert in the field. Having finalized the details of the figures for the frieze, on September 2nd, McKenzie sent a telegram from Edinburgh to his assistant in Philadelphia, Boris Blai.

> Please start at once on the frieze three sections exactly twice size in studio. Set up central Scottish figure exactly twice size, upstairs studio

*R. Tait McKenzie, "An Address on the Death of the Right Honourable Field-Marshal the Earl Haig of Bemersyde." Pamphlet.

* Ibid

Pine Street. Call Samuel F. Houston real estate trust for $300. expenses. All well. Sail 11th.**

When the McKenzies returned to Philadelphia, the two men went to work and spent the winter on the detailed frieze. Dr. Blai recalls today occasionally having to work to the sound of Scottish pipes and drums, no doubt intended as inspiration by McKenzie but which actually hurt his assistant's ears. Harry Lauder, the famed Scottish comedian and singer, arrived in the city on tour, and used to drop in occasionally to see how the work was progressing. He and McKenzie would break forth into Scottish duets—further atmosphere for the work in progress.

The memorial was completed in May, cast by the Roman Bronze Works in Brooklyn, and shipped to Scotland in June 1927. The McKenzies sailed for England and Tait wrote to his assistant from London on the 19th of June, in part:

My dear Blai:

We arrived safely. . . I am going to model the two decorative panels about the middle of July and have them set in place. Next week I start on the London Exhibition which opens July 1st. . . Next Tuesday we go to Court. They tell me it is a great show. I will look like this [drawing showing a tailored figure in cut-away coat] but Mrs. McKenzie will be like the Queen of Sheba and Marie Antoinette combined.

I hope the house is going well and that you will soon have your new studio completed.

Yours

(sgd) R. Tait McKenzie

The stone chosen for the architecture of the monument was Craig Leith stone characteristic of Edinburgh—a warm buff colour. McKenzie worked at setting the bronzes in place and finishing the memorial during July and August and it was unveiled September 7th.

Situated along a pedestrian path in Princess Gardens, facing Edinburgh Castle, the "Heart of Scotland" (as the Castle has been called), it is sheltered from the bustle of Princess Street. "The site and its surroundings are unequalled for beauty and historic interest in the whole world," McKenzie himself said of it. Certainly it has a scenic location and is part of the life of Edinburgh for the bench beneath the frieze conveniently located to the much-travelled pathway of strollers through the Gardens is much used.

The memorial consists of a seated figure of a kilted youth, symbolic of Scotland, with his rifle on his knees, starting up as if in answer to "The Call." The inscription reads:

** Letters quoted unless otherwise indicated are from Dr. Blai's collection of correspondence, and other memorabilia related to R. Tait McKenzie.

THE CALL (1923–27) Bronze. Main figures 8 foot high. Recruiting frieze 25 feet long. Scottish-American War Memorial, Princess St. Gardens, Edinburgh, Scotland.

The Call
1914
A Tribute
from men and women of Scottish blood and sympathies
in the United States of
America
to
Scotland
*A people that jeoparded their lives until the
death in the high places of the field.*

Judges V.18

Behind the pedestal is a bench and a wall rising about 14 feet. The wall frames a frieze 25 feet in length illustrating the response to the call to arms:

> It shows a scene that had burned itself into memory of the sculptor in the dark days of 1915. It is in three sections: the first shows a pipe band with twelve pipers, four side drums, two tenor drums, and the bass drum. The second shows a recruiting party headed by a captain, two ranks of four men in uniform, and one of four men armed but in mufti. Immediately following them in the third section come the recruits: miners, farmers, shepherds, clerks, fishermen, gamekeepers, representing all sorts and conditions of men volunteering for active service, a cross section of the manhood of Scotland in 1914 and 1915. The discipline varies from the pride and precision of the band to the disorderly rabble of the untrained but eager recruit.*

In the stone underneath the frieze an inscription in 16th Century Scottish lettering reads:

> If it be life that waits,
> I shall live forever unconquered,
> If death, I shall die at last
> Strong in my pride and free.

This was taken from a poem entitled "My Creed" written by Lieut. E.A. Macintosh, M.C., 51st Seaforth Highlanders, who died in 1917 in battle.

Speaking of this memorial Christopher Hussey said: "It is an achievement that demanded great sureness not only of hand but of soul. Only a courageous and essentially lofty mind could have shaped this lad's moment when the mystery of life and death was revealed to him."**

---

*Historical Catalogue of the St. Andrew's Society of Philadelphia, Vol. III, 1913-1937, p. 66.

**Hussey, *Tait McKenzie: A Sculptor of Youth*

Norval Scrymgeour in *The Scots Magazine* reported:

At the unveiling ceremony the then American Ambassador, the Hon. A.B. Houghton, said: 'Today we commemorate the Great War with the figure of a common solider—one youth separated from the thronging files of recruits pressing on from behind—one youth within sound of the pipes and drums and within sight of the Old Castle on the hill—one son of Scotland from a mansion or a manse or a mine, from a farm or a factory, from a Glasgow close or an Edinburgh lane—it mattered not. For he came from all these. He kept lonely company with his own soul in a tank or in a trench, on the sea or in the sky. And he went to his death alone.'

These words, spoken by an American, sum up the significance of the symbolic statue in Princess Street Gardens, which next to the Shrine at Edinburgh Castle, is to multitudes of men and women with memories of the loved and lost, the most sacred spot in the Scottish capital. . .

The soldier statue forming the Scoto-American Memorial encourages the personal mood. . .It is 'oor lad' who won the war.

On Dr. Tait Mackenzie's statue I have laid flowers 'of remembrance at the request of mothers and father who can never hope to see their lad in bronze. The last I laid was at the bidding of a mother, eighty years of age, an exile in South Africa. I had with me an American millionaire who had spent perhaps a thousand pounds while touring towards Edinburgh for the special purpose of keeping me company. As I laid the sprig of white heather at the feet of the bonnie Scottish laddie in bronze I bared my head. The millionaire stood, hat in hand, and when I ventured to look at him his eyes were streaming. So were mine.**

As a holiday after the demands of the Edinburgh memorial, Dr. McKenzie went on a motor trip through the Maritimes in the summer of 1928 with Dr. A. MacIntosh, Vice-President of Haverford College. At Shediac, N.B. they stayed at the home of Dr. Clarence Webster, a virtual museum of historical artifacts and art objects. MacIntosh commented later:

The conversation ranged over a variety of subjects. Dr. McKenzie could talk with authority on Canada and Canadian history, Scotland and the Scots, athletics and athletes. He had a never-ending fund of stories, amusing, touching, penetrating, which illustrated his deep understanding and love of people and his keen appreciation of their strengths and foibles.

He used both to embarrass, amuse and educate me by making me hold forth as long as I could on any piece of sculpture that we came across before he would say a word.

Despite the very considerable disparity in our ages, I have rarely felt as much at home with anyone. He was always interesting, understanding,

** Norval Scrymgeour, F.S.A. (Scot.), The Story of 'The Call' ", *The Scots Magazine*, (July 1932).

humorous, sympathetic. His keen discrimination and his quick imagination coloured every situation.

Writing to Dr. Webster later, McKenzie said:

My dear Clarence:

I am sorry to hear of your disability. I need not tell you of the importance of rest for a man with 'milk leg.' . . . We are now settled and in full stride with a lot of work ahead which keeps me busy till the last moment before going abroad. The Canadian commission still hangs fire but I am filled up with other work. Our little visit to Shediac was one of the bright spots of the summer and I am retailing many of the incidents of our conversation to sympathetic hearers at the Faculty club.

With kindest regards to you both, I am

Sincerely yours,

Dr. MacIntosh's commentary on the ability of McKenzie to tell a story was verified by Joe Brown, one-time apprentice in McKenzie's studio. Professor Brown has said Tait McKenzie was great at telling his own stories but he invariably "murdered" the retelling of another person's story, to the amusement of all present.

The same year an article which tells us something further about McKenzie the man, appeared in the Toronto *Star*. It was written by his old school chum, R.E. Knowles who had seen him when he came to Toronto to give a lecture. Knowles, a theology graduate and practising minister, paced his article with rhetoric:

'Dr. McKenzie, please tell me what is art?' McKenzie just like Peacock (they are both sons of Presbyterian ministers) has been taught to ponder before answering. And he pondered. . . . By and by he said: 'I should say that art is the graphic expression of life.'

'And which, professor, do you consider the greatest of the arts?'

'Oh, the written word. It is the most influential, most enduring. And besides,' warming up, 'the exponent gets the greatest thrill of any artist—or does the orator? And you know there is no art without thrill.'

'What is the special charm of the sculptor's work?'

'I should say it is the deliberate and progressive character of it, rounding out your creation, finding or feeling that it is ripening and glowing in your hand, touching it with life, hidden life, so to speak . . . '

'Do you believe that the body is the soul?' . . .

'It's all a mystery,' was the answer . . . 'All life and all expression of life which is art is linked together—wherever there is life there is soul—the body is the expression of the soul— . . . . It's all mystery.'

Then we both scrambled back to shore. Thereafter we kept our feet in the sand.

'Is the art ideal—devotion to it and pursuit of it, more in evidence in the U.S. than in Canada?'

'Yes, I think so—even allowing the difference in age and wealth and population. I wouldn't say that Canada's national art consciousness is high but it's growing.'

'Which work do you consider your greatest work?'

'Oh, the Edinburgh memorial by all means!'

'And what, Dr. McKenzie, do you recall with the most pleasure of all the great ceremonies of the unveiling day?'

Then the 'Bob' McKenzie as I knew him nearly half a century ago when we were at school together, paused a minute or two and the voice that answered was the voice of the lad I knew in the old St. John's Presbyterian manse at Almonte, the voice of the son of the Scotch minister, the Rev. William McKenzie. For he said: 'I believe the grandest thing about it all was when someone started and the thousands swelled the song the old 121st Psalm: *I to the hills will lift mine eyes From whence doth come mine aid.*'

A fund had been raised in Canada around 1910 for a memorial to General James Wolfe who had won Canada for the English in 1759. The project was postponed and the money lay in a Canadian bank until Canada's Diamond Jubilee of Confederation in 1927; then it was revived and McKenzie commissioned to do the statue of Wolfe for Greenwich Royal Park, London.

This was the second large memorial statue with which Boris Blai assisted. The work suffered many complications before it was finally completed and set in place.

The bronze statue took three years to complete (1927-30). McKenzie spent six preliminary months reading and studying historical material before starting work on it.

In searching for the critical moment of Wolfe's career, I came across the following sentence in Francis Parkman's *Montcalm and Wolfe.* 'Sept. 1759 . . . landing on the south side a little above Quebec and looking across the water with a telescope he described a path that ran in a long slope up the face of the woody precipice and saw at the top a cluster of tents.'

What thoughts passed through his mind as he stood there, telescope in hand? William Wood puts them in words:

'Then he looked at the Plains themselves, especially at a spot only one mile from Quebec where the flat and open ground formed a perfect field of battle for his well-drilled regulars. He knew the Foulon road must be fairly good because it was the French line of communication between the Anse au Foulon and the Beauport camp. The cove and the nearest point of the camp were only two miles and a quarter apart, as the crow flies. But between them rose the tableland of the Plains, 300 feet above the river. Thus they were screened from each other and a surprise at the cove might not be found out too soon at the camp' . . .

To paraphrase further remarks of Wood's, Wolfe knew the French expected to be attacked at one or other end of the line, Cap Rouge or Beauport, that his own army expected to attack above Cap Rouge and that nobody should expect the attack in the center between those two points. In this he was wrong for one man was thinking and never stopped thinking about it until he died and that was Montcalm.

On the 5th he had sent a whole battalion up to the Plains of Abraham. On the 7th Vaudreuil ordered them back to camp. 'The British haven't got wings; they can't fly up the Plains,' he said. On the 12th, Montcalm ordered them back, but Vaudreuil again countermanded it. 'We'll see about it in the morning,' he said. Wolfe saw through his telescope that the regiment had been taken away. He now gave up all idea of his old plans against Beauport as well as the new plans of his brigadiers and decided on his own . . .

This is the moment chosen for the statue: the moment when the great decision was made. Wolfe is represented standing quietly, his lowered telescope in his right hand, his left resting easily on his hip. He gazes straight forward, thinking it out. He wears the three-cornered hat so constantly shown in his pictures, his long full-skirted tunic, knee breeches and gaiters, with stock and ruff about the neck, and short sword or hanger in its scabbard at his belt. Over all is thrown his ample military cloak and cape, enveloping the whole figure with its long folds. The lines of the cloak carry up the outside of the pedestal of Portland stone on which he stands. The original cloak, faded and creased, still hangs in a glass case in the Tower of London.*

Much material was studied for a good replica of Wolfe's face. Of these McKenzie chose a posthumous picture from the National Portrait Gallery painted by J.S.C. Schaak, as being the most characteristic.

After the decision had been made as to the pose, the sculptor's difficulties began. The first sketch had to pass the Committee representing the donors and the Canadian High Commissioner after which it had to be submitted to the Office of Works in charge of all monuments to be erected in public places. Their attitude was one of active resistance to any encroachment on public property.

Following this, it had to be submitted to the Royal Art Commission which is composed of distinguished artists and architects, each of whom had his own opinion as to how such a work should be done.

*R. Tait McKenzie, "Major General James Wolfe." Reprinted from the *Proceedings of the Charaka Club 1935*. Pamphlet.

It had then to be shown publicly before the House of Commons and passed by them; and finally it had to have the personal approval of His Majesty, the King, as 'Chief Ranger' of all Royal Parks. It is not surprising then that this statue had a stormy period of parturition.*

McKenzie's working model of the figure was passed but controversy arose over the site, setting, and pedestal which went on for two years between the Office of Works and the Fine Arts Commission. Three plans for the statue were thrown out but a fourth was accepted and passed by all.

The 8-foot high statue stands on a pedestal cresting a grassy hill near the Greenwich Royal Observatory in Greenwich Royal Park, London. Wolfe looks toward the Thames River and the Naval College and seen from the Naval College he appears as a small, distant, lonely figure.

The pedestal bears the inscription:

> This monument
> the gift of the
> Canadian people
> was unveiled on
> the fifth of June 1930
> by Le Marquis de Montcalm.

Overburdened with work in sculpture and his many organizational commitments, coupled with a long harassing relationship between his Department and the Athletic Association, Dr. McKenzie had asked for a year's leave of absence from the university in 1929. With Ethel, he planned a holiday abroad beginning in 1930. He had already planned to resign from the university for the last time and the events leading up to this are dealt with in a later chapter.

Corresponding with his old friend, Max Ingres who was living in Paris, he wrote:

> Probably we will go to Egypt first, then Greece, then Italy, Paris, and London about May to be present for the unveiling of my statue of Wolfe on the 17th of June.

McKenzie was also waiting for the go-ahead on a Confederation Memorial for the Canadian government. This had gone through the same preposterous delays as his Baker memorial commission. To Ingres he wrote:

> About the memorial for the Parliament Buildings, they're [The Cabinet] arguing about material to be used. The Cabinet 'insists' on having it done in marble which will cost $15,000. more than doing it in bronze. The deadlock still continues and I have not been able to do any work on it.

Max, seriously ill, had written many times of his loneliness in Paris which though native to him, did not contain the friends he had in Montreal, Tait among them. His wife, too, missed Canada.

*Ibid

GENERAL JAMES WOLFE (1928–32) Bronze statue 10 feet high. Greenwich Royal Park, London, England.

McKenzie felt for his friend and from their correspondence it appears he was always trying to come up with a plan that would bring Ingres and his wife back to North America but it never worked out. McKenzie continued in his letter:

> I am sorry to hear of your feeling of loneliness and have often wished there was a possibility of having you with me especially on my travels in Europe. I wonder if it would be possible to have a trip together somewhere next spring. We must plan for it. I often dream of our bicycle tour through Picardy (1895) one of the most vivid experiences of my life . . .

> Macphail [Sir Andrew, also a friend of Max] had a serious operation this Spring. I was to meet him at Orwell but when I arrived there his brother Jim and Dorothy were both there but he did not turn up. The day I left they got word that he had been in hospital. I wrote him at once but have not heard from him at all except indirectly, word coming that he was better. I felt very anxious about him, too, because no one seemed to know what the trouble was.

Ingres was trying to sell his paintings but already the Depression which later hit North America, was being felt in Europe. McKenzie forwarded some money to Mme. Ingres on the pretence of having sold one of Max' paintings in Philadelphia. Replying in November, Mme. Ingres wrote:

> Thank you so much for sending the cash—it bucked Max up and that's what he needs. I, of course, realized it was just meant for that for with times as they are I don't really expect any sales . . . . Max says to tell you his ambition is to get well and go to live near you where he can see you and Ethel often. I wish to heaven he could.

The McKenzies visited the Ingres later in the year en route to London and the unveiling of Wolfe. It was a happy reunion for all of them. Max wrote to Tait in May:

> My dear Tait:

> . . . the few days you spent here are like a ray of sunshine in my dull life and I cannot yet realize how it came and went so quickly—like a dream—too short . . . . With our joint love to you both, I am as ever your fond old

>   Max

McKenzie never saw his friend again: later in the year Ingres succumbed to the lung and heart trouble that had plagued him for many years.

Arriving in London, in May, McKenzie found a letter from Harrison Morris of Philadelphia awaiting him, full of Philadelphia news and congratulating him on at long last seeing the Greek sculpture of which he had talked and written for so many years.

Dear Tait and Ethel:

... You were right to head for Greek and Roman antiquity. It will show you how right you are in your delineation of the human figure. The more I and others look over your book* the greater faith I have in the laws of human male beauty you have discovered for yourself. There's surely an inversion of beauty behind the surface beauty. It isn't what the churches call 'spiritual' either nor is it esoteric. But it is only visible to feeling and to eyes that go along with the laws of Nature, to get into the stream and see the Hamadryad in the tree. This at your best, you do. There! Selah!

Have been full of duty and entertainment and some of the joy I attribute to you. Also effort to my clearing up the filth of Philadelphia . . . the air is full of political noise. . .

McKenzie wrote to Morris when settled and Morris replied with a long letter reading in part:

... We're glad you've landed in London and we're admiring on the sidelines while you 'take the Salute' at Greenwich and show your best foot in London. Tait, for the life of me I can't account for the melancholy strain of your letter. Here's a young fellow at or near the top of his talent, taking fame like topping fruit from the bowl of success—My eye! What does he expect?

Yours for luck,

Harrison S. Morris.

The "melancholy" mentioned by Morris may have been due to a premonition of McKenzie's that his friend, Ingres, recently seen in Paris was going rapidly downhill. Coupled with this the frustrations involved with the Wolfe memorial and his frustrations over a number of years since the ending of the War, at the university where the Athletic Association and his department were often at loggerheads. But of this more later.

From London on the 3rd of June, McKenzie wrote to Boris Blai in Philadelphia:

Dear Blai:

The exhibition is to open the 18th June and will last until July 5th. This week the Wolfe statue is to be unveiled. I got the figure mounted and the site is very fine but the pedestal is much too high. Most people will be looking straight up his nose which was what I wanted to avoid. That is the trouble of having to deal with three different committees.

The design of the pedestal, however, is very good apart from its height.

At the unveiling, descendents of both Wolfe and Montcalm were

*Hussey: *Tait McKenzie: A Sculptor of Youth*

present, as well as the McKenzies, the long-suffering architect, A.S.C. Butler, and dignatories. The London *Times* reported:

> The Marquis de Montcalm unveiled in Greenwich Park today a statue of his great ancestor's great adversary, General Wolfe. The two commanders fell together at the Battle of Quebec and out of that mingling of British and French blood arose the united Canada which has given this monument to Britain. . .
>
> Le Marquis de Montcalm said in his address . . . . It is the fate of these two heroes who have both shed their blood in the service of their country to be forever united in the memory of men. Wolfe and Montcalm were both worthy of each other. . . . Commanders of two rival armies, hundreds of miles from their countries, both felt in the course of the campaign that death would be the price of this tragic struggle. And when Wolfe before the attack murmured thoughtfully in the dark and mystic night which surrounded his ship, the beautiful lines of Gray—'The paths of glory lead but to the grave'—there yonder in the field of Beauport wearied by so many night watches among the brave soldiers of Carillon, his Canadian volunteers whom he inspired with his iron will, Montcalm too was oppressed with melancholy and told his companions of his gloomy forebodings. Both faced death with the same disregard for life . . . their last words were for their soldiers . . . . Both leaders were mourned and respected at their tombs and citizens of two great peoples, adversaries yesterday, friends today, pay homage. Allow me to thank you for your gesture and acknowledge your great kindness, not only in the name of the descendants of the French who fought for Canada but also in the name of those who wish with pious faith to keep in their hearts, the ties which bind them to the vanished past.*

Enthusiastic comments came to McKenzie from friends and acquaintances who saw the Wolfe memorial. From Hugh Walpole, the novelist: "The Wolfe looks splendid. How much character you've got into it!" Another Londoner and novelist, Gilbert Parker wrote: "I am sure that in your Wolfe you have reached the height of your powers so far. Next to it in design, your Whitefield on the same high level. You have got Wolfe—the dreaming face in the man of action—a face that defies the usual interpretation. . . . It should captivate all who pass through that province [Quebec]. . . it ought to go to Quebec to be shown in the open air. . . . You have risen, my friend, and nought can stop it now."

McKenzie's assistant, Boris Blai, was like him interested in education and had some innovative ideas he wished to try out. Tait had advised him to buy a property, build a house and studio, and hold classes. He had taken this advice in 1927 and later conducted art classes in his home for the Oak Lane County Day School. Temple University sought him out as an art teacher and again McKenzie advised him to seize the opportunity. This led to the founding of the Tyler School of Art at Temple through Blai's efforts and he proceeded

---

*"The Wolfe Statue, A Gift of United Canada," *The Times*, London, June 6, 1930. Reproduced by permission.

to establish a first for Temple as McKenzie had for Penn—the Tyler Art School was the first university in the United States to give a degree course in fine art. Blai was the first Director.

His schedule was a busy one: teaching at the Oak Lane Day School, the Tyler School of Art and spending a day or two a week in McKenzie's studio.

A warm comradeship had developed between the two sculptors. Dr. Blai in a recent interview said he used to call McKenzie his Scottish father and McKenzie would call him his Russian son.

Blai remembers among other things, McKenzie's great sense of humour, as well as his unwillingness to hurt anyone's feelings. Once he came to McKenzie's studio and found his mentor looking depressed. McKenzie was working on a figure and didn't look up but said: "Boris, the cook's quit, the butler's left, Mrs. McKenzie is all upset and I don't know what to do." Boris thought for a few moments, then said: "Doctor, they have discovered how to put a complete meal in capsule form. You have one pill for breakfast, another for lunch, and another for dinner."

McKenzie raised his spectacles to his forehead, turned and looked up at Blai.

"When will they be on the market?" he asked.

"Oh, maybe in ten years."

"That's good," said McKenzie replacing his spectacles and going back to work. "By then, I'll be dead."

The refined, aesthetic McKenzie was not ascetic about food. He enjoyed good cooking, hearty meals and his steak—perhaps with a vintage wine—all to his mind, part of the pleasure of living.

In 1933 Boris Blai's first show in New York City took place at the Grand Central Galleries. He had left McKenzie's studio by this time, fully occupied as Dean of The Tyler School of Art. He sent McKenzie an invitation to the opening. McKenzie replied:

Dear Boris:

I am terribly sorry that I will not be able to attend your opening tomorrow. Unfortunately I have to give a lecture in Baltimore the same evening and cannot work in the two. I cannot tell you how proud I am that you are having such a good send-off and I know you will have the success you deserve.

Yours as ever,

(sgd) Tait McKenzie

Dr. Blai had the success expected and became internationally known for his portrait busts and figures in granite, wood, bronze and marble. Now in his 70's he is teaching by apprenticeship, an experience which closely parallels that of his years with McKenzie where the student learns by working with the master, a method that should never have gone out of style. To McKenzie he gives credit for his own development, claiming "RTM" taught always by example, criticizing his work but always letting the student find things out for himself. Unlike some artist-teachers, "the Doctor" was never jealous of others' successes but entered into them as if they were his own.

Blai favoured the female figure as McKenzie favoured the male physique in sculpture. Always greatly interested in the dance, Blai has modelled the four great ballerinas. His bronze of Pavlova as *The Swan* is well known. One of their last works together was the Christine Wetherill Stevenson Memorial cast in coloured cement for the Art Alliance Building in Philadelphia. This is one of the few works of McKenzie's showing the nude female figure.

University of Pennsylvania Archives

CHRISTINE WETHERILL STEVENSON MEMORIAL (1928) Coloured cement. 8 × 3 feet. Set in wall above fireplace of Art Alliance building, Philadelphia.

In the five years I had the privilege of working with him in his studio, I had ample opportunity to observe... He never hesitated to admire someone else's work or philosophy and this certainly was proof of his greatness.

The intensity of his devotion to art and his many other interests made it necessary for him to organize his life very carefully. After having spent many hours every day in the field of physical education and in research, he devoted himself to modelling in his studio. A few hours were enough for him to rest and enjoy recreation. Even Saturdays and Sundays were devoted to his art work.

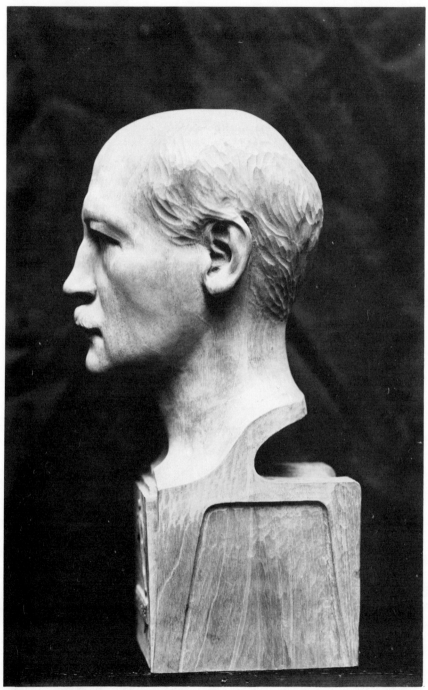

R. TAIT McKENZIE Mahogany bust carved by Boris Blai.

Once McKenzie invited Blai to come to tea with him when a Russian professor of Physical Education, also a heart specialist, was expected. Blai was to act as interpreter as it was supposed the Russian doctor spoke no English. Blai spoke Russian to the guest when he met him as they both arrived early at the studio. When McKenzie showed up, he proceeded to show the guest a number of his publications on physical education.

While I was starting to explain the contents in Russian, the Russian professor began to read the books in beautiful English.

So enchanted was Dr. McKenzie about the versatility of his guest that he gave him some movies made under his supervision and representing the work of the Department of Physical Education at the University of Pennsylvania. The professor was delighted as these movies meant a valuable contribution to his Moscow institution.*

*Journal of Health and Physical Education, V. 15, #2, Feb. 1944.

CHAPTER XI

The Constant Theme

Christopher Hussey has said: "At heart McKenzie is a thinker before he is an artist, a scientist before a sculptor, yet beauty for him is not a thing apart from life, but organically one with humanity. . . . He has a classical mind. Beauty for him is the human form in perfect health seen in graceful movement . . . the endless potentialities of life is what he most deeply feels and is the purpose that gives his sculptured forms their significance, their beauty."*

Throughout his life the interplay of McKenzie's thought and expression bore this theme for his conception of the development of the whole man.

His sculpture is not a reflection of life, but a goal for life. His physical education plans were geared to the same goal. He thought along the lines of Henry David Thoreau: "Every man is builder of a temple called his body to the god he worships, after a style purely his own nor can he get off by hammering marble instead."

Harrison Morris writing in *The International Studio* in 1920 attributed McKenzie's success to a duality of traits. He cited Coleridge as once saying that exclusive devotion to an art was not the best way to master it. "Strike and retire and you will accomplish more than if you hammer away forever." The diversity of McKenzie's interests forced him to dwell on one and then another. Lectures, writing and administrative duties at the university kept him from his studio but when he again found time for his sculpture, he viewed it with fresh eyes. He never had a chance to get stale.

He consistently shunned the ugly, the grotesque, the exaggerated—and aligned himself with the natural laws of harmony and proportion.

Occasionally he lectured on sculpture, often with slides. In one of these lectures entitled "Modern Techniques in Sculpture" he showed slides of work by Mestrovic, Eric Gill, Maillol, Carl Milles of Sweden, Bourdelle, and his own athletic work. The chiselled work showing deep African Negro and Nigerian influence he classified as belonging to a school of "distortionists." Many modern sculptors, he suggested, had turned to the archaic early forms in desperation because they could not visualize surpassing the perfection of Greek sculpture. Here he showed his own athletic works to indicate that further variation upon the themes of the Greeks could be done successfully.

*Hussey: *Tait McKenzie: A Sculptor of Youth.*

He praised the traditional work of Philippe Hébert and A.
Suzor-Coté of Quebec, and George Hill of Montreal whose panel of
Nurses graces the Ottawa Parliament Buildings. Showing a slide of
Rodin's "The Hellmaker Grown Old" he observed that it was an echo
of the traditions of workmanship left by Michelangelo. Rodin failed,
said McKenzie, when he undertook monuments which called for an
architect's ability which Rodin did not possess. Flashing the controver-
sial *Balzac* on the screen, he suggested it ressembled a monolith from
Stonehenge rather than a work of art. But for Rodin's "Eternal Spring"
he had great praise. "This shows the work of the master."

By portraying the perfect athlete, sprinter, hurdler, or whatever
athletic event in sculpture, he drew attention to the ideals embodied in
such international events as the Olympics and the spiritual idea
behind interscholastic meets.

The discus thrower had long been a subject of study for McKenzie.
One of the most famous of Greek athletic statues—Myron's
Discobolos—was generally associated with the Olympic Games and
McKenzie had tried a similar pose, but more in keeping with the
current attitude of the modern discus thrower, as he says "more
crouched."

On June 16, 1924 the McKenzies sailed on the Olympic boat, *S.S.
America,* for Paris to attend the Olympic Games. En route an
American contestant, Harry G. Frieda, posed for McKenzie for what
eventually emerged as *The Modern Discus Thrower.* Asked what he
recalled of Dr. McKenzie, Frieda recently said: "At the age of 57, Dr.
McKenzie was unusually keen, alert and sharp with an impressive
manner. Forty-six years later I haven't the slightest idea what either
of us said, but he impressed me with his keen sense of humour and
awareness of life and its meaning."

At the Paris Olympic games, McKenzie showed some of his
sculpture and again was awarded an Olympic medal.

An exhibition of 60 works of his sculpture opened July 1st at
Georges Petit Galleries, rue de Seize, Paris. The French press praised
his work for its "splendid vigor, sense of beauty and striking
exactitude."

In the summer of 1925, Hector McDonald, a member of the U.S.
Olympic swimming corps, posed for McKenzie at his summer studio in
Ipswich, Mass., for the final version of the *Modern Discus Thrower.*
Many poses were tried out, with and without the turn, resulting in the
eventual choice of the same moment of the throw as taken by Myron,
the spiral movement of the body in the pause between the backward
and forward swing.

In an article for *The International Studio,* McKenzie discussed the
technique of discus throwing and audaciously criticized Myron's
Discobolos, saying in part:

> The head in Myron's statue is turned backwards and doubtless gave rise
> to Herbert Spencer's remark that he was about to fall on his nose. In any
> movement of throwing, the head should lead and show the direction of

Frank Ross . . . University of Pennsylvania

THE MODERN DISCUS THROWER (1926) Bronze statuette. 1/2 life size.

the throw. That is why it is so hard for the golfer to keep his eye on the ball. His instinct is to raise his head in the direction he hopes the ball will go.

Every afternoon during the summer while modelling this figure, I spent one-half hour or more in this exhilarating exercise on a flat Massachusetts beach, trying it with and without the turn and found that in my case the addition of the turn added about fifteen percent to the distance of the throw. My companion, a powerful athlete, found the difference between the standing and turning throw very slightly less but it was still marked and I am concerned that the Greeks used a form very closely approximating this in the heyday of Greek athletic competition and they never bowled it under the arm.

The body should be more bent and crouched than in Myron's statue. This is necessary to give the required thrust, like the release of a compressed spring, from the loins and thighs. The left foot should be in a position to push rather than drag in the forward movement that follows. The upraised arm crosses the back to assist in the spiral or spinning movement that is essential for a good throw. The discus can be held with the face up by a twist of the arm. We have authority for both ways in modern practice as well as in records of antiquity. We also see the discus held face down although this method is not followed so often.

This figure of the modern *Discobolos* embodies these facts . . . the front view shows the spiral or circular movement about to take place . . . in an instant the coiled spring will be released . . . the discus will scale off the tips of the fingers last—and rise gracefully like a low-flying plane.*

The humanist McKenzie found further fault with Myron's *Discobolos* in "an absence in the facial expression of any hint of the severe muscular strain experienced by the athlete in the violent twisting of the torso that brings every muscle into play. This very coldness, however, is characteristic of all early Greek sculpture." McKenzie's half life-size figure was completed and cast in bronze in 1926.

Later he illustrated another technique of the throw with *The Upright Discus Thrower.*

Further athletic sculpture of this period included some of his most beautiful small works: *The Ice Bird, The Javelin Cast, The Eight, Brothers of the Wind.* A difficult work was the *Pole Vaulter.* It had long been a subject he wished to tackle but he had not found a way to show the vaulter 14 feet off the ground.

One day in San Francisco I saw a Japanese seal in jade done by a Nipponese artist in days long ago and on the four sides were landscapes showing clouds and birds. Immediately the thought came surging 'Here's the solution.'

Thereupon I set up a square shaft on which the pole and uprights were shown in relief, the surfaces decorated along the same motif of clouds and

---

*R. Tait McKenzie: "The Modern Discus Thrower", *The International Studio,* May 1926.

birds to give the impression of great height. At the top of the shaft the figure was modelled in the round and the crossbar and upper portion of uprights detached from the background.

My mind naturally turned to Nelson Sherrill as the ideal model because of his graceful lithe figure plus experience in the art of polevaulting.

Nelson fell in with the idea and posed from time to time during the winter. This was previous to his remarkable achievement of the early Spring when he astonished the athletic world by capturing the highest honours in the Indoor Collegiate Meet.*

Sherrill would walk around the studio with his feet up in the position shown in the statue and the muscles of his arms and shoulders acting almost in exactly the manner of the "push-up" in the vault. Discussing the physique of the pole vaulter later McKenzie wrote:

The pole vaulter is an all-round man. He has fine muscular development of his arms and shoulders and torso with the legs of a sprinter. Occasionally he has the advantage of great height but usually it is strength and spread of the well-balanced athlete of middle height that wins the laurels. . . . Then again it is a feat that has become greatly specialized and perfected in recent years and it is hard to realize that the light bamboo pole carefully strapped that he carries, began with one of heavy ash liable to break and impale him, an accident that did occur and that the sharp point or three spikes that were struck into the ground at the take-off are now replaced by the blunt bamboo point which finds its place securely in the sunken box in the front of the uprights as he rises to clear the bar.

The origin of the sport arose from necessity in a country intersected with small irrigation ditches which the young farmer cleared by his trusty pole and it is strange that the leap for distance has given way completely to that for height and that such extraordinary heights have been reached from 1920 steadily from Baxter at 11'-5'' (1893) to Meadows at 14.5' in the 1930's and the end is not in sight.

The inscription on McKenzie's 18-inch high statue of the *Pole Vaulter* read: "Nelson B. Sherrill of the University of Pennsylvania, vaulted over a bar 13 feet in height May 1923. The world may yet produce an athlete who will go higher by another foot."**

McKenzie's *Pole Vaulter* would have been more successful if he had used a rounded shaft and employed fantasy in the design. Christopher Hussey has suggested it could have become an attractive ornamental work. As it is, the figure and shaft are antagonistic even as the circle and the square of Nature, and this natural antagonism has not been resolved.

The McKenzies had joined the Philadelphia Skating Club in 1920 and there, Tait began to observe and make sketches of figure skaters

*R. Tait McKenzie: "The Pole Vaulter", *Pennac News*, May 1925.
**In 1976, the Olympic record for pole vaulting was 18'1/2''

THE POLE VAULTER (1923) Bronze statuette. 18 inches high.

including those training for championships. In contemplating the skater, McKenzie wrote:

> The skater comes as near the flight of a bird as possible without wings. Friction is reduced to a minimum and he swoops and soars, leaps and turns and spins toplike as if he were at last on the point of overcoming the laws of gravity.

> Watch a champion like Sonya Heine as she balances momentarily on her poised toe like a great hummingbird as shown in the medal for the New York Skating Club**, her arms and legs making a momentary cross before she swoops away—or the leap when the skater seems to float like thistledown with arms outspread. This extraordinary pose brings the artist into conflict between the truth of technique and the beauty of composition.

For his small statue, *The Ice Bird,* McKenzie found a model in Gustave Lussi, a young Swiss instructor at the Philadelphia Skating Club. He was "spare, hollowed, slim-flanked with graceful tapering limbs and slender ankles." The skater is depicted as having run forward, jumped, and turned, and is beginning an outside backward spiral. It was purchased by Lord Broughton after its appearance in a London gallery. Later copies went to several collections.

The bronze frieze, *Brothers of the Wind,* a panel of eight speed skaters, was completed in 1925. It has been eloquently described by Ethel McKenzie:

> One of the masterpieces of art, miraculously conceived in bas-relief as delicate as a vision etched in mist and snow. Epitome of speed solidified in bronze, yet evanescent as the music of Debussy . . . the reminiscence of boyish feats on frozen streams or days of student recreation on private rinks in Montreal. Yet it took the delightful Skating Club to bring it to fruition. The members followed its progress with intense interest and it was first shown in a private reception to the Club in our own home.

**In 1936, McKenzie designed this medal for the New York Skating Club.

Public Archives of Canada

BROTHERS OF THE WIND (1920–25) Bronze frieze of 8 speed skaters. Original 120 × 33 inches. Galvano 11 × 40½ inches.

Christopher Hussey said its beauty gave it "a place of its own among the masterpieces of relief."

> McKenzie's design while taking its rhythm from the movement, possesses high qualities in the abstract. The design is essentially a flowing one and is so handled that the continuity of its rising and falling lines is uninterrupted. They interweave like those bands in ancient northern ornament, the endless untiring linear rhythm which gradually developed into Gothic art. The appearance of this, possibly racial, trait in McKenzie's predominantly classic work is interesting. It is the secret of his success in both his great friezes, this and the frieze of the American-Scottish War Memorial. From forgotten depths of the subconsious, the ideas of snow and cold and his native land seem to have evoked this primative obsession with endlessly, intricately flowing line. . . .
> . . .the relief is low with well defined but softly rounded planes . . . the veiling of the lowest plane suggests vividly a misty atmosphere while the whiteness of the material implies ice and snow. These are the Brothers of the North Wind, supple, clean-limbed youths, fleeting and more deadly than the blizzard out of which they sweep in unearthly beauty.*

Brothers of the Wind was exhibited in Rome and London. A fellow American sculptor, Walter Hancock, who had seen McKenzie putting the finishing touches to it at his summer studio in Ipswich, wrote in September:

> Such a thrill as your skaters gave me yesterday is so rare I can't resist the temptation to write to you about it. To me it is one of the most beautiful friezes in existence. I am indeed happy to have seen it before going to Rome.

Later in October, Hancock wrote from the American Academy in Rome:

> The skaters have arrived and they look even better in Rome than they did in Ipswich. . . . Rome is an exciting place this year. Every Sunday is a feast day and processions of pilgrims everywhere. . . . I have a studio which is absolute perfection in every way. . . . Is there a possibility of you coming to Italy before very long?

When the frieze appeared in a London show, Forbes-Robertson, the actor, wrote to McKenzie: *"Brothers of the Wind!* Amazing! You are a genius, damn you. You are not a Scot, you are a Greek!" From Sir Campbell Stuart, Chairman of the Wolfe Memorial Committee and Director of the London *Times*, came: "What a beautiful thing *Brothers of the Wind* is!" This work McKenzie kept for his own collection, although replicas were produced and sold later.

The eminent critic, Sir Philip Gibbs, reviewed the London exhibition and wrote in the *Chronicle* in part:

---

*Hussey: *Tait McKenzie: A Sculptor of Youth.*

It seems to me and to many who have been able to see the exhibition by Dr. Tait McKenzie at the Fine Art Galleries in New Bond Street that here is something new and something good in the art of sculpture. New but not ugly, or violent, or wild, like so many modern work which desperately attempts to break with old traditions. . . . He believes in beauty . . . and achieves it though he has gone beyond the classical ideas in an adventurous purpose to express modern life with a most intimate and realistic understanding, to reveal the character of modern manhood in its ordinary workaday dress and to show the beauty of physical energy as it is seen in our playing fields and training camps. . . . Dr. Tait McKenzie is not afraid of modern clothes, of mud, of a fellow in an old leather coat, of a football crowd. He is a realist to the last button, to the attitude of the big toe, to the sinews of a horny hand, but he is a realist who does not search for ugliness, who does not get emphasis by exaggerating, and who sees the spirit that goes to youthful effort, and the supreme endurance of fatigue for the game's sake. That is how I read his purpose and how I see the work he has achieved.

Something unique in the American art world took place early the next year. An exhibition of art by physicians opened in March in New York City. Nearly 70 doctors from New York and vicinity participated and surprised the general public and the art critics with their proficiency. The show included painting, etching and sculpture. Tait McKenzie showed his small bronzes of athletes and his "Masks of Expression."

McKenzie had completed the Edinburgh Memorial and was still working on the Wolfe statue when they found a beautiful spot in Maine ideal for a summer studio. Holidaying at Asticou Inn, Northeast Harbor, in the summer of 1928, Tait wrote to Boris Blai in Philadelphia: "It's wonderful up here—mountains and sea and sand." He also expressed disgust with the Cabinet in Ottawa then haggling over the price of the Confederation Memorial.

The McKenzies discussed with Charles Savage, proprietor of Asticou, the possibility of building a studio for each of them. There was already a small building in the woods on the property and this became Ethel's piano studio where she might practice undisturbed for hours on end in a woodland setting. For McKenzie, Savage built a 20 x 40 foot studio with a north light window and a small room with a bath for his collegian male models. Both studios were on a nature trail within walking distance of the living quarters at the Inn; the McKenzies took a 5-year lease on them.

It was here that *The Eight*, his quarter life-size bronze of a crew of oarsmen bearing their shell on their shoulders, was first set up. Ethel McKenzie commented in later years how the pose, unique in athletic sculpture, was chosen by her husband:

During the early days of Spring it was our happy custom to sit on the balcony of the Sedgely Club, Philadelphia, overlooking the Schuykill River and watch the Varsity crew sweeping by in their weekly Saturday afternoon tryouts. He would invariably comment on the beauty of the rhythmic movement of the arms, moving backwards and forwards simultaneously with the oars, visioning a bas-relief he would do some day for the wall of some great indoor pool. One afternoon he noticed the crew leaving the Varsity club-house nearby bearing the shell on their shoulders as they made their way to the dock, before launching on the river.

During a happy summer at Asticou where swimming alternated with hiking over the mountain trails, McKenzie began on the work using as a model, a member of the Penn crew, their guest for the summer. Discussing the pose, McKenzie said: "All rowing men are familiar with the moment at which the crew bring the shell down to the float and at the word of command raise it above their heads ready to lay it in the water at the word of the coxswain. In this group, eight variations of the same pose are shown as the men raise the shell above their heads."

Writing to his old friend, Max Ingres in Paris in October 1929, McKenzie mentioned that during the summer he had worked on the statuette and "I sold it the day before I left Northeast Harbour although it is far from finished."

McKenzie arrived in Asticou at an opportune time when the town needed a sculptor. Northeast Harbour as a village was politically part of the town of Mount Desert which had inherited a beautiful natural parkland named *Asticou Terraces* from Joseph Henry Curtis, a landscape architect of Boston. According to Charles Savage:

> Curtis conceived the idea as early as 1909 and set up small trusts related to various land gifts, the whole being further added to and unified, together with considerable endowment as willed in 1928.

> Many years later in the 1950's, the area was much further enlarged and additional funds for certain projects provided by Mr. John D. Rockefeller, Jr. The area is really a landscape-botanical park of high order, very likely one of the finest in New England north of Boston, with an interesting botanical library, a decorative flower garden, a substantial number of wildwood and ledge paths, many of which were originally laid out by Curtis himself. It was a pleasure for me to have brought McKenzie into this project. His memorial has been a distinct addition and an important aesthetic feature.

Against a cliff of weathered granite, a flat surface was selected as a site for the memorial and was paved with granite flagstones. When McKenzie saw the site, his sculptor's imagination took hold and he was soon at work in his new studio preparing a plaster model of the project. For the medallion portrait of Curtis he used a crayon drawing done by an acquaintance since no portrait was available. Occasionally people who had known Curtis were brought in to watch the medallion portrait take shape and comment on the likeness.

The final memorial was set in place in 1932. On the broad, stone-flagged platform stands a six-foot granite slab mounted on a pedestal of rough stone. On the slab is set McKenzie's medallion portrait with the inscription: *Joseph Henry Curtis, Landscape Architect, Vigilant Protector of These Hills,* and in small letters, *The*

Asticou Terraces are his gift for the Quiet Recreation of the People of This Town and their Summer Guests. Behind the memorial stands the lichen-covered cliff bordered by spruce trees.

The same year Ethel McKenzie published a book of poetry, *Secret Snow*, which enjoyed a modest success. In his introduction to the volume, Sir Andrew Macphail stressed the evidence of her Celtic nature, "that elusive other-worldliness," while John Buchan commented that "the hard knuckle of thought behind these tunes" was never absent.

1930 was a year of changes. Following on his year's leave of absence from the university, McKenzie resigned as Director of the Department of Physical Education; he purchased a property in Canada involving much attention while it was being made suitable for occupation, and yet found time to turn out six portrait medallions of friends, as well as complete seven sports medals. The portrait studies included: Campbell Stuart, Edward Peacock, Christopher Hussey, Beatrice Harrison, Frederick Wolle, and Dr. Arthur Keith, and were presented as gifts by McKenzie.

Sir Edward Peacock wrote from London:

My dear Rob,

On my return from the country I found here *The Banker* and the inscription* upon it quite bowled me over—it went right to the spot where all the best of one is stored and remains there. Thank you again and again. I think it most successful as a portrait and as a typical bit of work, equally so, but much as I value it for both reasons, it is the inscription and what lies behind it that comes first.

Dr. Keith of the Royal College of Surgeons in London wrote a letter of thanks saying of the designation calling him "a man of science"—"I would like to be a man of science . . . I shall treasure it as your gift and when I have done with it, I hope it may get a home here as a memorial of you as much as the sitter."

Beatrice Harrison, the cellist, wrote from Surrey, England:

Dear Dr. Tait McKenzie:

At last I have received your most exquisite present. How very beautiful it is and it is being hung up here in the place of honour . . . It is so dear of you to give me such a glorious present.

Frederick Wolle, "Lover and Interpreter of Bach," wrote humbly, from Bethlehem, Pa.:

Dear Dr. McKenzie:

I do not know how to thank you for the bronze medallion which you have

*"The Banker—Edward Peacock. From his old friend, Tait McKenzie"

fashioned with rare artistry. . . . Never in my wildest dreams did I see myself sculptured and by an artist of the very first rank. I thought this honour was reserved only for the very great. . . . The great Bach whom we both admire has caught you under his spell and as he has long since gone to live beyond the stars, you have molded in lasting bronze the unworthy features of a weak interpreter. . . . What am I to do to show my genuine appreciation? Until you tell me, I can but go more deeply into my studies, leaving no stone unturned in my efforts to recreate music that has absorbed and consumed me—hoping that as it sounds out in all its glory, it may be said in coming years "And fools who came to scoff, remained to pray."

It was during the summer of 1930 after returning from London and the unveiling of the Wolfe Memorial, that McKenzie was called up to Canada to discuss a fitting memorial for his old Almonte high schoolmaster, P.C. McGregor. While in the vicinity he discovered a stone mill. Long since unused and abandoned, in picturesque surroundings, the mill kindled his imagination. Situated on a babbling stream, secluded from the passersby, it seemed an ideal location for a country home and studio.

The original owner of the Mill was John Baird who came to Canada from Scotland in 1830 and did a thriving business grinding grain into flour for the pioneer settlement of Bennies Corners.

Investigating the ownership, McKenzie found he could buy the Mill and fifty acres of land around it for $10,000.00. It must have seemed an extravagant purchase for he wrote to Ethel from Almonte, going over his financial assets in some detail, apparently in an effort to justify his intention. Former employees and assistants in his studio have remarked that he showed Scottish caution in the handling of money. Yet for all his many irons in the fire, this letter indicates that he did not accumulate wealth and as he says in it, they only managed up until World War I because of Ethel's "rigid economy and genius for making a little go a long way." His letter reads in part:

My dearest wife Ethel,

. . . I have been investing from time to time in securities and in our house and furnishings. I had hoped to have $100,000. bringing in 5% in securities by this time but I will give now an account of the income upon which we can count for the next two years. . . .

This, itemized in detail, amounted to a total of $57,000. Of the location:

The place, district and people have been associated long and lovingly with my family from my mother's and father's relation to them. They are kindly people and I like them and am happy seeing them from time to time . . . also as a straight investment it is not very bad farm land—at its lowest ebb at present. And a new highway makes this lovely river and woods available in a little over an hour from Ottawa. . . . Fitting it up as a fishing lodge will enable me to entertain bachelor friends in the Spring and Fall and to develop it according to my own taste, if you do not care to occupy it . . .

ever affectionately your
loving husband, Tait

Apparently Ethel did not object for he bought the property paying $10,000.00 cash for it, and engaged an architect to convert the building. Once made habitable, Ethel McKenzie took to it and it became a home of great charm. Her grand piano was brought from Philadelphia to fit into the spacious livingroom. Here she played sonatas to the accompaniment of the sound of the rapids in the Indian river below. A large open fireplace provided warmth and hospitable atmosphere. Huge windows with deep sills looked across the river into the woods where wildflowers, poplar, maple, and pines grew plentifully. The great mill beams were decorated with charcoal sketches of McKenzie's telling a story of an encounter between their two little dogs, Pirie and Taffy, and a neighbouring skunk.

A spacious sky-lit studio for Tait was built at the top of the building—the loft—reached by an outside staircase as well as an inside stairway from the living-room. When all was completed after some years of renovation, the McKenzies took up summer residence regularly with their cook, and chauffeur cum secretary, John Archinal.

In the Western Highlands of Scotland within sight of Skye, stand five mountain peaks known as *The Five Sisters of Kintail*. Nearby on Loch Duich is picturesque Eileen Donan Castle once the stronghold of the MacKenzie Clan, later lost to the MacRaes. The MacKenzies were pushed eastward to Brahan in Ross-shire. Once Max Ingres sent McKenzie a photo of Eileen Donan Castle suggesting "it would be nice if you fell heir to it." Perhaps his Canadian mill formed a modest substitute in his mind when he installed a drawbridge to reach the main entrance, giving it a resemblance to such a Scottish baronial keep, for he named his new summer residence, "The Mill of Kintail."

To this delightful summer home came friends from far and near. Mrs. David Gillies of Arnprior recalls driving up with Mrs. J. Macintosh Bell of Almonte when the mill was still in a stage of renovation. As they stopped the car, they saw McKenzie standing at the front door on the platform over the moat. "Let down the drawbridge," called Vera Bell. The two ladies noticed that there were no chains attached to the platform and Mrs. Gillies whose husband owned the Gillies Lumbering Company remarked "I'm sure David could find some chains for it." They told McKenzie and next day he and Gillies went off to Arnprior returning with sturdy boom chains which they attached to "the drawbridge." "Dr. McKenzie was as delighted as a child," recalled Mrs. Gillies recently. The chains are still in place today. Mrs. Gillies remembers Dr. McKenzie as being "geniune, simple in taste, with no conceit, no vanity, no pomposity."

Reginald Fairlie, the architect who had worked with McKenzie on the Edinburgh War Memorial, journeyed to the "romantic" mill and wrote from Scotland later, referring to the rapids, "I found the plodding

monotony of sound soothing." At this time McKenzie was completing
one of his few female statues, a figure depicting *Mercy*, as a tribute to
Red Cross nurses of the First World War. The original cast was at the
mill and Fairlie commented: "It is fine and dignified and expresses
something of what the spirit of nursing should be."

Male friends took pleasure in twitting McKenzie about his
farming. In October 1932, Sir Andrew Macphail wrote from Montreal
saying his main interest in life at the time was Tait's dam:

> I shall be in Ottawa soon and if the dais is finished, will go to see it and
> report to you. [McKenzie was then back in Philadelphia]. One thing is
> heavy on my mind. Upstream the planks and stone will not keep out the
> water. We must stop the flow with earth and hay, also the water will
> dribble through and then will be inclined to plow over the top.

The dam's purpose was to provide a swimming and paddling pool
above the rapids.

Macphail and McKenzie corresponded regularly and later seeing a
photo of the Red Cross memorial,* Macphail wrote:

Dear Robert,

> Your "Mercy" even in the photo is profoundly appealing. In the round it
> must be very beautiful. One day we shall see it as we saw "The
> Volunteer" at Almonte as an entirely new revelation.

McKenzie had been offered "The Freedom of Almonte" on occasion
of the town's 50th Anniversary. A ceremony and presentation of a
"gold" key to the sculptor followed by speeches and general celebration
was planned, and Edward Peacock on learning of the town's intention
wrote to McKenzie in Philadelphia:

My dear Rob,

> I have your letter and note that the medallions have been sent to Mother
> and Harry . . . . For the 'Freedom of Almonte', you ought to have it and I
> hope it will be arranged. Nothing would give me greater pleasure than to
> be there on that occasion and observe your demeanour under the ordeal.
> But I confess that the 'Freedom' which can be offered today is shorn of
> most of the prerequisites that would have appealed to you and
> me. . . . When you go to the high school, P.C. will be missing and old
> Williams, the janitor, who kicked me downstairs once, and there will be
> no John McCarter next door nor will there be any of the Knowles family
> to provide comic relief, and altogether it will be flat and savourless.
> However, in spite of that I hope you will go and if you do, you must make
> sure that at least P.J. Young, the survivor of the old lot, and Annie
> Naismith shall be there. But somehow after this recital I feel less drawn
> to the ceremony.

---

*The memorial standing outside the Red Cross Headquarters building in Washington
bears the moving inscription: "Thou shalt not be afraid of the terror by night, or the
arrow that flieth by day, or the pestilence that walketh in darkness, or the destruction
that wasteth at noonday."

I suppose it is true, as you suggest, it would give the privilege of loafing on the station platform. But what is the good of that when it is a new station and old Pat McGarry no longer carries the mail bag and Edith and Ida Thrall cannot make eyes at one from the back window of the Thrall establishment and make one's heart turn over rapidly: when Wattie Lawson's livery stable is a thing of the past and George's barber shop has disappeared along with George, the town comedian. . .

And when you come to receive your 'Freedom,' who will give it to you? Will William Thoburn be there as Mayor? Will Squire Smith pronounce the eulogy? Will the tall Youngs, and old Archie Campbell, or the McFarlands and the Sneddens be there on the platform to bless you? Not a bit of it. Some modern, smart people who have come in from God knows where will be in charge.

McKenzie did however, receive the "Freedom of Almonte" complete with the "gold" key and speeches, at the appointed time.

It was on this occasion when speaking to the students at the Almonte high school, he recalled among other things, his early schoolmaster, Mr. McCarter, who had disliked him so thoroughly, a relationship which has been mentioned before. There is no record as to whether he found the "Freedom of Almonte" rewarding or disappointing.

When resident at the Mill, McKenzie made frequent trips to Almonte where he liked to chat with shopkeepers and others; he is remembered today for his friendliness. Ethel McKenzie shared her husband's interest in the community and occasionally invited women's groups to the Mill for afternoon tea.

When the town's Handicraft Guild courageously asked McKenzie to design chair seats and rug patterns for them, he willingly did so, using native plants from the surrounding woods as models—the trilliums, cattails, wild roses. He was always interested in encouraging the artistic spirit. Once called upon to give a talk at the Ottawa Y.M.C.A. on Handicrafts he emphasized the importance of learning to use one's hands creatively—"Many college graduates are lacking in this important feature while other people have it who have had very little education."

In renovating the Mill, McKenzie came across pioneer artifacts belonging to the original owner, including some still legible but faded correspondence. Saving these for his studio, he became interested in the pioneers who had settled in the area and began to collect pioneer artifacts. Eventually he had quite a sizeable collection which is now part of the Mill of Kintail's exhibition as a historical museum.

A comfortable stone lodge for a caretaker was built near the main entrance and some years later advertising for a caretaker McKenzie described his holdings as "50 acres of which 20 are in wheat and 18 in farmland with flower gardens and borders near the Mill." An Ottawa friend and historian, Harry Walker described the Mill in 1933:

Wild life abounds and at twilight a blue heron makes the grand rounds of river and woodland. Such a sylvan Arcady must make a strong appeal to Mrs. McKenzie's love of nature. . .

Entering over the drawbridge, one is faced by the weathered portal, iron bound, that has stood sentinel throughout the years. Inside the great hand-sewn beams of white pine, stretch from end to end, imparting an atmosphere of ageless strength. Everything about the interior imparts the simplicity of the pioneer period—the wide casement windows, the hooked rugs, Mexican and Indian pottery, reposing on hexagonal pedestals cut from the shafting of the Mill. Real logs burn in the fireplace. . . Here and there splendid samples of Tait McKenzie's statuary provide an effective decorative feature.

Dominating a charming corridor vista is a reduced replica of his famous statue of Wolfe at Greenwich. . . occupying the entire upper storey is the studio where dreams are given form and substance in enduring beauty. Filtering through the urns of coloured glass, the sunlight cascades in delicate hills of amber and green. In the floodlight is the Highland lad, Tait McKenzie's *magnum opus*. The original, of course, forms the theme figure in the Scottish American War Memorial at Edinburgh . . . dining that night we glimpsed the fine attributes which have matured his genius and brought him from the obscurity of a pioneer Presbyterian manse to an assured place among those who have enhanced the values of mankind . . . the fire burned low and still we talked far into the night roaming the highways of literature and life. John Buchan and Sir Andrew Macphail and Sir Johnson Forbes-Robertson are among his personal friends. The moving majesty of Buchan's *Montrose* and the mordant wit of Macphail had captivated us both. We had also worshipped at the shrine of Rupert Brooke. . .

In spite of his sensitive reaction to the aesthetic there is something Spartan in Tait McKenzie's fibre. It is revealed in all his work. There is nothing decadent or grotesque in all his impressive cavalcade of athletic figures. Like Phidias, he has spent a large part of his time among stripped and striving youth. There he has sought and found the Greek ideal of physical perfection and has given it expression in lines flowing with light, clean rhythm. Whether it be a child's face or an athlete's figure, beauty and healthy joy of effort is vitally alive in deathless bronze. . .

Listening to the deep diapason of the river booming its symphony of Spring, one thought of John Toshack who landed near that spot in 1821 with his canoes . . . and at whose log cabin the Free Kirk minister found shelter. . .*

Boris Blai had left McKenzie's studio in 1928 to become Dean of the Tyler School of Art and although they often saw each other Blai was now fully occupied with his own work. McKenzie needed a new assistant for his studio and found one in 1931.

One day he called at the studio of Philadelphia artist friend, George Gibbs, and found him working on a painting of a prize fight.

*Ottawa Journal, May 16, 1933.

Posing for him was a young retired professional boxer, Joe Brown.

Brown had graduated from Temple University in the Spring of 1931 in the middle of the Depression, and had found little prospect of employment other than occasionally posing for sculptors or illustrators. He had done a little modelling in clay and strangely enough, on this particular day, had brought a small sculpture of a boxer to the studio to show Gibbs. McKenzie seemed impressed with the work, turned it around on the table and looked at it carefully from all angles. Finally he said: "That's very good. Is it true that you have no teacher and have taken no lessons?"*

"Yes, sir," Brown replied expecting to be complimented for his precocity.

"What a shame!" said McKenzie.

"What do you mean?" asked the student.

"It's so good, it's a shame it isn't better which it would have been if you had had training." It was a compliment with a string attached and with mixed feelings, Brown asked the Doctor for more specific criticism. "He gave it to me—right between the eyes," he recalled later. "I thanked him sullenly perhaps, but I meant it. 'I'll have to fix it,' I said."

Tait McKenzie did not let the matter end there. He recognized talent and invited the young man to come into his studio as an apprentice. Brown seized the opportunity. It was the beginning of seven and a half years of an association that was often painful but that left Brown with a great respect for his teacher, his craft, and the many tangibles and intangibles involved, he says, "in producing a work of art."

In grade school Brown had won an award for athletic achievement, a celluloid-covered button bearing a picture of a hurdler, a copy of a medallion designed by R. Tait McKenzie, and during the years that followed Brown had often gone to admire McKenzie's statues of athletes or memorial statues in the city. Having admired the sculptor from afar, it was normal that he should want his teacher to approve of his work.

> I found him to be intermittently a hard and an easy master. He had what is known in athletics as 'change of pace.' I might take a beating in the studio day after day for perhaps a week. Everything I would do would seem wrong and at times I would begin to wonder if he wasn't trying to make me quit.

> Then one afternoon when I would be near the point of discouragement he would look up from his work and innocently ask . 'Who is going to win the boxing match tonight?' I would tell him sulkily. 'All right,' he'd reply. 'We'll go and see how poorly you pick them. Would you like that?"

> A little later he would come over and give a not-too-devastating criticism of my work. . . . He was a driver but he knew when driving ceased to be a

*(Unless otherwise indicated, all quotations from Mr. Brown are taken from an interview and/or his autobiographical notes.)

constructive device, and he was plastic enough to give in when the situation warranted such a procedure.*

One of the first thing Joe Brown learned in McKenzie's studio was to sweep the floor. The Doctor advised: "We have a janitor to do this work but in doing this you will learn how to move about a sculptor's studio without knocking anything over which is very valuable knowledge."

I learned how to move a modelling stand without dumping the figure off it; how to pick little pieces of plaster out of plasticene; how to knead clay; how to build simple and complex supports for various statues; how to cast and how to colour casts; and a million and one other little technical jobs that are apparently beneath the dignity of the 'would-be genius.'

He often spoke of inanimate objects as if they had spirit. He would warn me, for instance, that if I failed to display a proper respect for the character of a staircase, I would fall down.

He impressed upon me quite forcefully at times that the first requisite of the real artist is that he is a well integrated person, interested in more than figuratively beating his chest and shouting, 'Look at me, I'm expressing myself.'

Another requisite was a healthy respect for the medium . . . To him a good statue was a successful collaboration of the clay, the model, the sculptor, and the public.*

Once Joe Brown brought a small clay figure of a boxer punching a bag to McKenzie's studio and asked the Doctor how he liked that "for two hours work." McKenzie examined it, hemmed about it, and finally said: "It's remarkable. If you don't hurry it, it will be one of your good ones."

Confident that his little statue had merit, Brown worked on it a few more hours, cast it in plaster, and shipped it off to a foundry to be cast in bronze. This cost him $34 hard-earned money. When the bronze arrived two weeks later, he hurried proudly to McKenzie's studio. The Doctor examined the little statue with concern. "You didn't fix the arm," he said. "It's withered from the elbow down." In Brown's head was revolving the sum of $34. Finally he stammered "Why didn't you tell me when I brought it for criticism?" To which the Doctor replied: "You didn't ask for criticism. You asked me how I liked it and I told you. I offered you the best advice I could—that if you didn't hurry it, it would be one of your good ones." It was a good lesson for Brown. Later McKenzie said: "You know, Joe, someday when you are dead and gone people will look at the things you have done and they'll say a thing is good—or they'll say it is bad. They won't know or care whether you spent two hours or four hours on it."

*The Journal of Health and Physical Education: R. Tait McKenzie Memorial Issue, Vol. 15, #2, Feb. 1944.

*Ibid.

He manipulated the experience so that it taught me as words never could, the value of humility. And at the same time I learned the hard way, that bronze is less plastic than clay. It was a long time before I would admit it but those thirty-four dollars were indirectly a good investment, thanks to Dr. McKenzie.*

Another painful lesson came during the first months Brown worked in McKenzie's studio. The apprentice was working on a clay head at the opposite end of the studio from the master. McKenzie noticed that he was looking into the light and walking down from his own end of the studio he explained to his apprentice that he was seeing his work in silhouette and should move so that the light was behind him. Brown thanked him and changed position. However, unconsciously, being absorbed in his work, he changed position and was again working against the light. McKenzie looked up, saw what had happened and called his attention to it. Brown repositioned himself but again returned to his original position. Very deliberately McKenzie came along, took the stand on which the clay stood and firmly moved it to the other side of the student saying: "It's hard enough to model a head in the proper light. Don't insist on being stupid about it."

His pupil was shocked and hurt. Getting his jacket from a hanger, he went down the creaky stairs thinking to himself: "That cold, old bastard wouldn't understand that maybe my problem is enthusiasm, not stupidity." Brown didn't come back to the studio for three weeks.

Then one day he returned. McKenzie, working on a medallion, scarcely looked up as his apprentice took off his coat. Casually the Doctor mentioned that he hadn't known his pupil's address and thought he might be ill. Brown went to work on the unfinished head. Later McKenzie said: "Who's going to win the fight at the Arena tonight?" Brown told him promptly and the Doctor continued: "Well, I'll take you to dinner and then to the fights just to prove you're wrong."

Mr. Brown recalls: "It was a very eloquent apology from a great man to a kid whose feelings he had hurt, and I was moved to change my mind about him being a 'cold old bastard.' "

McKenzie was thrifty and paid his apprentice very little and Brown found it hard to live on his meagre earnings but the training he received, he says, was priceless. His teacher knew and respected his materials and taught his student to do the same. "He was a tough master, but a great friend." Often he would tell his student to "visualize that figure two feet high and do it." When Brown had modelled the figure, McKenzie would say: "Now, knock it down." They were forever redoing figures, infuriating to the apprentice but invaluable for later good work. Once Brown asked McKenzie how one knew when a work was completed. McKenzie replied: "When it looks all right," showing the sculptor's instinct as his guide. Sometimes they would start a work and knock it down several times before it satisfied

*Ibid.

McKenzie. Or, if a work partly completed was not quite satisfactory to him, he would say: "Let's leave it for awhile—a week—two weeks—then go at it again, look at it, alter here or there, refine it." Thus was Joe Brown trained by perfectionist Tait McKenzie.

In the summer of 1931 while the Mill of Kintail was being renovated the McKenzies went back to Asticou where their 5-year lease was still in effect. Here McKenzie worked out the initial design of a memorial to aviation, *Triumph of Flight*, using two Penn students, Carl Periera and Nigel Altman, as models. Mrs. McKenzie likened the work to that of Renaissance artist Cellini, "whose peculiarly exquisite workmanship held an appeal" for her husband. A muscular Atlas is shown bearing on his shoulders the Globe upon which is poised a winged "Mercury." It was eventually completed in the Philadelphia studio one-quarter life size, and cast in bronze.

McKenzie followed this up with another tribute to aviation, a 6-foot statue named *The Falcon*.

Joe Brown recently recalled some of the spade work done prior to these works. For authenticity they visited the Philadelphia zoological gardens to observe a falcon. For three hours they watched the bird as it flew, ate, and struggled with the keeper. They spread its wings and counted the feathers in each wing. They noted the shapes of the individual feathers and their arrangement. They felt the wing muscles and compared the falcon's muscle structure with man's. They studied the head and facial structure.

When they returned to the studio, McKenzie ignored a falcon he had begun and went to work on the figure of the man which was part of the statue. When Brown asked him why he didn't work on the falcon wings and head which were part of the design, McKenzie replied that he wanted to see how much he had remembered when a few days had passed. He also wanted to get to know the bird, he said, "not just to meet him." Three times the men returned to the Zoo before the sculptor was satisfied that he knew all the falcon could tell him and only then did he continue with the wings and head.

Some years later McKenzie described his approach to *The Falcon* memorial which now stands outside the McLennan Library at McGill:

> The thought behind the figure is 'youth triumphant in the air'. . . . The falcon of chivalry was the companion of kings, princes, and noblemen in all lands. . . . With its pointed wings it rises in spirals to a great height dropping like a bullet on its quarry. It is the fastest and most courageous living winged thing. It is fitting, then, that these characteristics be suggested in any interpretation of the speed, daring, and indomitable courage of the modern aviator. During the war they represented the knights of old. They were in every sense 'knights of the world's last knighthood.' They brought back the spirit of chivalry that modern warfare seemed to have destroyed.
>
> I have modelled the figure to express the pure beauty of the youthful form, and have tried to follow in doing so the great tradition of sculpture. This buoyant figure is framed by four wings. They form an areola about it and give volume and background to the slenderness of the figure.

... The figure itself is visible to the spectator from the front and from either profile while from the back the spectator sees only the birdlike characteristics, the wings, the tail, and the hawk's head.

Brown recalls that it was a cumbersome thing to work on and had a "million feathers."

Brown's style did not always please McKenzie. He appreciated the vitality of his assistant's work but disliked his tendency to exaggerate. "I see you're still doing cripples" he would say noting an extra long leg or arm in the figure Brown was modelling.

McKenzie was a fan of the "fights" which Ethel McKenzie considered a vulgar pastime. Brown recalls that she had a tactic for delaying their departure when "the fights were on." She would let Pirie, the little dog, out and then tell the Doctor that Pirie had run off. He, ever the gentleman, would go down Pine Street in one direction and Joe would be directed to go in the opposite, searching for the dog. Eventually Pirie would be located and retrieved and the two men, somewhat nettled, would continue on to the Arena.

When Joe completed his prize fighter knocked down called *Dropped* in 1935, Tait was much impressed and considered it a "powerful and personal statement." He was so enthused that he asked Brown to pose for him to express his statement of the same event, and the result was *Invictus,* a half life-size study of a boxer down on one knee resting while the referee counts ten, before he will "spring back to life and to battle." The highest compliment McKenzie could pay Brown came when he completed a boxing pair called *Counter-Punch*, also in 1935. "I would be proud to sign that," McKenzie said. Shortly afterwards he recommended that it be shown at the next Olympic Games and it was accepted for the 1936 meet.

Brown worked with McKenzie on the Canadian Confederation Memorial over which there had been such discussion in Parliament for so long. It was completed in 1932. It commemorated 60 years of confederation (1867-1927) and was a project of the Canadian Clubs throughout the United States who raised the money for it from their membership of one and one-quarter million men and women. It stands in the main corridor of the Parliament Buildings in Ottawa opposite George Hill's memorial to Nursing Sisters of the Great War.

In the summer of 1935, now ensconced at the Mill of Kintail for the season, McKenzie began a long contemplated project—a memorial to his father and mother. For this he had an architect design a bench using one of the great millstones as part of the back in which he placed a bas-relief portrait of his parents, modelled and cast in bronze. "The bench to the Minister and His Wife" was placed near the Town Hall in Almonte on a grassy knoll near and facing the Mississippi River where it remains today. The portrait of Rev. William McKenzie is his likeness when possibly a young man of about 34, wearing a clerical collar. Mrs. McKenzie is dressed as she might have been at 27 when she first came to Ramsay township, with a simple lace collar and modest brooch, hair parted in the middle and brushed smoothly down and held in place by

University of Pennsylvania Archives

ROBERT TAIT McKENZIE bronze bust by Joseph Brown.

the customary net. Rough-hewn stone wings flank the circular millstone, forming back and arms of the bench. Inscribed in the stone above the medallion plaque in Roman letters is "The Bench to the Minister and His Wife." On the medallion are the dates of their life-span: William McKenzie 1824-1876, Catherine Shiells 1836-1914. On the back of the bench is carved the following lines:

> Stranger sit and rest and dream
> The noisy millstone turns no more
> Before you runs the restless stream
> That seeks the ocean evermore.

Tait McKenzie's brother, Bertram, and his family, from Ottawa visited at the Mill regularly. A niece, Dawn Knutsen, recently recalled the years when she and her brothers, John and Bob, used to come there during their summer holidays:

I remember Uncle Bob as a lovely, patient and humorous man—he always had time to listen—I can remember hiding in the balcony of his studio which he had furnished with a bed and a few other pieces so he could rest during his labours. I well remember peeking at him through the banisters while he worked on the bust of Mary Baker Eddy. He was

Lawrence Hayward

THE MINISTER AND HIS WIFE (1935) Bronze portrait plaque of McKenzie's parents, set in a millstone from the Mill of Kintail, forming the back of a bench facing the Mississippi River, Almonte, Ontario.

doing her jacket and cape and painstakingly rolling small bits of clay
into balls and pressing them flat to give a coat of mail (to my way of
thinking) effect. I was so impressed with his patience.

The summer he went to Scotland we stayed at the Mill and during our
visit my dad built me a tree house much to my delight. Of course my
brothers had to go me one better and build a higher one. We were rather
wondering what Aunt Ethel and Uncle Bob would think of our building
in their trees but when they returned Uncle Bob came in from his usual
walk through the woods the first morning and said very seriously that
there was some kind of new big crow that had invaded his wood and had
made a very strange kind of nest! I'm sure he had a lot to do with Aunt
Ethel letting us leave them there.

Uncle Bob always loved to walk in his woods and had endless paths and
charming wooden bridges built over the creek. He often found huge
puff-balls that grew as big as basketballs. . . . He adored his dogs, Taffy
and Pirie and each morning they went with him on his walks.

He took a great deal of pleasure in his Mill of Kintail—had to rebuild the
dam across the creek nearly every year as the spring thaw would bring
chunks of ice crashing against the dams and usually broke them. He had
a birch bark canoe he paddled on the lake the dam made and we all used
the waterfall as a shower. . .*

   The Mill was indeed a great source of pleasure to McKenzie. In
1936 he wrote to Sir Robert Borden at Ottawa:

Dear Sir Robert,

Can you and Lady Borden spare a day before you sail for Vimy?

I have just completed a remarkable bridge illustrating a new principle of
construction. Near the north end of it is a cold spring in which a bottle,
for dedicatory purposes, could be immersed while its beauty and utility
were being discussed. The hired man's bed is made up and an adequate
cook is now functioning in the kitchen. Ethel sends cordial greetings and
seconds the invitation warmly and 'McGregor' can call for you and return
you to your place.

Sir Robert replied:

My dear Dr. McKenzie:

Our warmest thanks to you and Ethel for your kind invitation. It would
give me the greatest pleasure to visit you but unfortunately I have to
leave tomorrow morning at 8 o'clock for Montreal where I have some
business meetings before sailing by the *Empress of Britain* on the
following day.

---

*(It is rather interesting to note that Dawn Knutsen teaches art, John McKenzie is an
art director and Bob McKenzie, Tait's namesake, is an architect.)

It is one of my chief regrets in making this journey (a highly adventurous one for a man of my years) that I must miss the 'Mill of Kintail,' the 'hired man's bed' and the communion at dawn with the spirits of those who knew and loved the Mill in its earliest days and especially shall I miss the opportunity of dedicating from a bottle duly immersed in that lovely spring, the beauty and charm of the Mill of Kintail and its gracious chatelaine.

Madge Macbeth, an Ottawa journalist and novelist, was present at the dedication ceremony and wrote many years later in her column in the Ottawa *Citizen*:

Dinner was progressing smoothly when he [Tait] cried: 'This occasion calls for a toast. Just a moment, please.' He ran to the balcony and leaning over it began to haul on a rope while singing 'Heave-ho, Heave-ho.' The guests watched curiously. Soon the neck of a bottle appeared above the rail. Tenderly Dr. McKenzie drew the bottle into the room. The old mill was not equipped with electricity. It lacked even an old-fashioned ice-box so the host had planted several bottles of his favourite wine in the stream beneath the dining room for cooling purposes.

. . . .He was an ideal host as he was an ideal guest. He never made himself conspicuous. He never sought the limelight but neither did he retire into himself, ignoring his share of the social burden. His presence was felt in a pleasant, not an exacting way and his humour was ready and kindly . . . he loved to walk about the town talking to all and sundry. He had . . . the humility of greatness.*

The Mill of Kintail is now a memorial museum and an historic site, owned and administered by the Mississippi Valley Conservation Authority. During the 1950's it was purchased by Major and Mrs. J.F. Leys and arranged as a private museum for display of their collection of Dr. McKenzie's works. Many of these remain now including original plaster models of such well-known memorials as the Scottish-American War Memorial in Edinburgh. On the hillside near by is an interesting structure reminiscent of the Greeks McKenzie so admired—Cloister-on-the-Hill, built of native sandstone. A Celtic cross of local white pine resting on stones from the Holy Isle, Scotland reminds pilgrims of McKenzie's ancestral background. A plaque in the Cloister reads:

*Madge Macbeth: "Over My Shoulder," Ottawa *Citizen*, April 23, 1955.

In Loving Memory of
The Great Surgeon-Sculptor
R. Tait McKenzie
(1867-1938)

President of the St. Andrew's
Society of Philadelphia 1924-1925

"He formed imperishable links between
the United States, Great Britian and
Canada."

This plaque inscribed by the St. Andrew's
Society of Philadelphia 1967.

In the month of May, the Mill of Kintail holds an annual Tait McKenzie Day inaugurated by Major Leys. On this day Boy Scouts, Legionnaires, Girl Guides, Medical and Physical Education Associations, Historical Societies, and others gather. The Tait McKenzie scholarship awards set up in memoriam for scholastic achievement at the Almonte High School are presented. The St. Andrew's Society of Philadelphia send representatives and noted celebrities recall Dr. McKenzie's achievements.

CHAPTER XII

McKenzie and Physical Education After the War

An eulogistic article on Tait McKenzie's success as a physical educator appeared in the sports magazine *Outing* in July 1915, entitled: "A Molder of Clay—and of Men." The author, Waldo Adler, said in part:

This native (Scotch) independence of spirit characterizes Dr. R. Tait McKenzie. Today professor in a university subject that has as yet obtained but slight recognition, he has, single-handed, put through a new departure in education and made it accepted not merely by university students [but] the public schools also with their twenty millions of coming American citizens are following his lead. With the 3,000 or more students under his charge, he has shown that an entire student body not merely a few picked natural athletes but all—the strong, average, the weak, even the sick—can be given a physical education as sound and thorough as their book education. He is the pioneer who has shown this plainly and convincingly.

Now, only one American in 1,000 goes to college but 9 out of 10 go through public school. With the public schools accepting and following his lead, McKenzie's work is beginning to affect all Americans . . . the beginner [college student] knows the first day that the grammar he must learn includes the following conjugations: to climb, to run, to jump, to swim. Once he has mastered these in their moods and tenses, he is prepared to become a student of the classics of athletics. . .

McKenzie tells the beginner why they are taught these things—because when a fire breaks out, or an auto threatens your life, or a girl is in danger of drowning, all modern inventions and machinery might as well be uninvented—the man facing an emergency has his own trained muscles *only* to depend on.

He told a little story about Dr. McKenzie.

A bunch of students were going out of the gymn one evening in winter with the Doctor in their midst. One of the men warned him that the stone steps leading to the street were very slippery to which Dr. McKenzie replied: 'Only the awkward fall!' Scarcely had the words been uttered but one foot flew out from under him and it was only by an acrobatic stunt that he saved himself from falling. The boys were laughing but Dr. McKenzie simply repeated: 'Only the awkward fall!'. . .

Partly because of his own magnetic quality Dr. McKenzie secures broader results from his system of physical education than have been achieved by anyone else. . . . The results: The number of good tennis and racquet players and teams and the popularity of fencing and boxing in and around Philadelphia certainly exceeds their popularity among older men in the other great American cities. Dr. McKenzie's influence is one of the factors that has caused this.

Although the course at Penn had itself been successful, the problems between the Athletic Association and the Department of Physical Education had never been resolved insofar as competitive sport was concerned. Developments after the War accentuated this schism. An era of inflation began around 1920 and the old frictions increased in tempo between the Council on Athletics which arranged intercollegiate sports events and the Faculty concerned with student health and welfare. The Board of Trustees adopted a resolution in 1922:

That as soon as practicable, there be established a Department of the University to be known as the Department of Physical Education and Athletics, at the head of which there shall be a Director appointed by the Trustees with general powers and duties comparable with those of a Dean of any department in the University, which Department shall be charged with the oversight of the physical life of the students of the university and shall control the teaching and management of all athletic sports, contests, exhibitions and, subject to approval of the Board of Trustees, promulgate all rules and regulations necessary for such purposes.*

"It was proposed to write this into the statutes of the University, then under revision, but action was referred to a committee and there died of anaemia so frequent after sojourn in a pigeon-hole."*

Also in 1922, the stands were enlarged on Franklin Field to accommodate 50,000 and in 1925 another deck was added to the stadium to bring it to its present capacity of 60,546. The expenditure required an annual income of nearly $250,000. Most sports events broke even or showed a deficit with the exception of football. "Obviously nothing must interfere with the extraction of the last ounce of gold from this mine. . . . The struggle between the ethics of an Amusement Enterprise and an Educational Institution which was abroad in the college world, became more and more acute."*

Speaking at the Third Triennial Conference on Education and Citizenship held in Montreal in 1926, McKenzie warned against the trends he had already seen in his own university as well as others in the U.S.:

The forcing back of contests that are suitable to young men of twenty into

---

*R. Tait McKenzie: *Physical Education at the University of Pennsylvania—from 1904 to 1931—and the Gates Plan. The Research Quarterly,* Vol. III, No. 2, May 1932.

the schools for boys of sixteen is an example. There is real danger in having boys of that age run half mile or mile races, and many a promising athlete has had his career crippled by over-enthusiastic competiton in his school life, when a little care and restraint would have prevented it.

In athletic sports, as in life, severe competition finds following it as a shadow, the danger of cheating, dishonesty and commercialism. This is especially true at the present time in American college athletics, where the tremendous interest in football has put vast sums of money into the hands of those who direct them. The answer to this is, I believe, not the abolition of these contests but rather the careful administration of the money by a responsible authority. It is a new condition and must be met in a new way.

He felt that the schools had lost sight of the true function of athletic sports in education.

At the university, McKenzie found himself out-manoeuvred and outvoted by the Athletic Council. "He was smilingly told after a galling defeat to remember that one with God was a majority."*

In 1927 he presented a report recommending abolition of dual control and reorganization of the Department. At the same time he turned in his resignation but "oil was poured on his wounds and he was urged to carry on" until a four-year teachers course in physical education produced its first graduates.

In the Spring of 1928 the first class of teachers graduated but nothing was done about McKenzie's recommendations. Again he resigned "with emphasis on the intolerable conditions resulting from conflicts inevitable when the two independent organizations, a Council and a Department, were attempting to deal with the same or interlocking problems and holding divergent views. A committee was appointed to study the question."*

McKenzie was urged to reconsider but remained firm. As an alternative, he took a year's leave of absence [1930] while the university looked for a successor. During this year he and Mrs. McKenzie went abroad and he visited physical education colleges at Geneva, Budapest, Prague, Munich and Berlin. On his return to the university in 1931, he found that the chairman of the Committee to look into his recommendations was the new university president, Thomas S. Gates. "The chairman . . . was a different kind of chairman from the others and events began to take place."*

Gates appointed a Committee of two to investigate conditions, gather information and report to him and asked McKenzie to continue in office as an advisor to the Committee. They visited colleges in the U.S. from coast to coast, collected data from alumni, faculty, students, and in February 1931, presented a complete and exhaustive report on the structure and working of physical education in colleges in the

*Ibid.

United States. Upon this study, President Gates set up what was called *The Gates Plan*.

One of McKenzie's recommendations had been a separate division within the Department for Hygiene or Student Health and Gates adopted this. His plan included a Dean for the Department of Physical Education, responsible to the President of the University alone, with three divisions under him, each headed by a Director. One division looked after Student Health including examination of incoming students, care of sick, isolation of infectious cases, personal hygiene and sanitation with an advisory board from the Medical School. There was another division for Physical Instruction which included class work, intra-mural sports, teacher training, and coaching. Finally, the most important change—a division of Intercollegiate Athletics to manage competitive sports on which the old Council would serve only in an advisory capacity. An umbrella budget covered all three divisions so that the interscholastic events and their gate receipts assumed no more importance than non-commercial events. "In other words, sports were given back to the students, teaching to the Faculty, and the deficit to the Treasurer."*

Other changes included curtailment of football training and the choosing and appointing of coaches of faculty calibre and placing them on the Faculty.

Dr. E. Leroy Mercer of Swarthmore became the first Dean of the revised Department and McKenzie stayed on for two months in the Spring of 1931, going over budgets, records, appointments and assisting him generally in assuming his new responsibilities. Penn was reluctant to lose McKenzie's fund of knowledge and experience and conferred a Research Professorship of Physical Education upon him and he was asked to continue for a year or two more in an advisory way while *The Gates Plan* was being implemented and tested.

In May, comment on this Plan came from Dr. James Naismith his old colleague of McGill days, then at the University of Kansas teaching physical education. He wrote in part:

My dear Rob:

. . . I think the whole scheme will ultimately be the one used in the majority of the institutions like Pennsylvania. I notice they give you credit for helping them in their survey of the work.

. . . I have a photograph of you in your track suit taken while you were still at McGill. I would like to have a picture of you that I could hang up in the office, as I believe it is a good thing to direct the attention of our majors in physical education to the men who have been prominent in this work. We use your book as a text and also as a reference in a number of our courses.

. . . We would like to go home to Almonte but may have to put it off for another year. I hear frequently from Uncle Pete Young. I wish that sometime, Will, you and myself could be in Almonte together so that we could enjoy an outing on the river and visit some of the old scenes.

*Ibid.

Sir Edward Peacock wrote from London about the same time:

> You have certainly been industrious as well as inspired. R.O. Sweezey of Montreal, a very prosperous grad of Queen's University, was here the other day and he and Campbell Stuart and I had a good deal of discussion about a new Principal for Queen's. Campbell was looking over your work and suddenly had an inspiration and said: 'There is the man.' As a result Sweezey was instructed to get in touch with you as soon as he gets to the other side and find out: (1)whether you are the man, (2)whether it would interest you, (3)whether it could be brought about. . . . You may feel that you are not prepared to put on new fetters and are going to enjoy the liberty to carry on your work in sculpture for which you have been longing for many years. . . . I am looking forward to seeing you in the Spring.

There is no evidence that the position of Principal for Queen's University at Kingston, Ontario, was ever offered to McKenzie. The subject does not appear again in correspondence or among his papers at the University of Pennsylvania Archives.

McKenzie's physical education involvements after the War included the preparation of several textbooks on physical education and physical therapy. In the early 1920's he was helping Dr. James H. McCurdy, M.D., Secretary-Treasurer of the American Physical Education Association, prepare a textbook on *Physiology of Exercise*. Dr. McCurdy was a distinguished lecturer, but had difficulty turning out an easy-to-read textbook for the layman. McKenzie read various chapters and suggested changes. Lengthy correspondence ensued. McKenzie pulled no punches in criticism and suggestions. At the same time, his remarks show his kindly nature and unwillingness to upset McCurdy. In March 1922 he wrote:

> Oh, my dear McCurdy. Why did you not work up your manuscript so that it would be in shape for publication? It is as if you invited us for dinner and showed us a pile of potatoes and cabbages and a fine fat steer and said, 'There is your dinner.'
>
> The material is of the best but I am afraid it will take a good deal of work before it is in shape for publication. . .
>
> It seems to me in general that you have not kept clearly in mind the fact that it is to be a definite, carefully arranged and logical treatment of the subject of physiology in its relation to exercise, that anything not directly bearing on this should be left out and that everything bearing on it should be explained with the utmost clearness and simplicity and reinforced by the account of experiments. . .
>
> What I find is that you do not seem to have been working to a definite and clear-cut plan. Much of the material is evidently in the form of a lecture, some of it is technical and some popular in character.
>
> On the other hand I don't want you to feel that I am doing nothing but finding fault. It is only because the stuff is so valuable and much of it is

*Ibid.

original that I feel it should be presented in the best possible form, and I believe that as it is now it will not make the impression or have the wide circulation that it should have.

In September the next year they were still working on the text and he is writing to McCurdy:

> I want to say how much I appreciate the way in which you take the very unpleasant criticisms that I have had to make on the manuscript. I want you to feel now and always that the purpose is to get a book which will do you credit, because, after all, you are the man who signs it.

> It is perfectly clear to me as well as to yourself that you can put across the material in a lecture course and I would say that perhaps it is because of the ability in a lecture course to answer questions that you are inclined to take too much for granted in writing the text. If you could put yourself in the attitude of someone who does not know anything about the subject, and who must have it explained without having to ask questions and receive answers, I believe it would help you to visualize what I believe is the weak point of your manuscript as a text book.

Eventually in 1924, the book was ready for the publishers. McKenzie also helped with criticism and editing of Dr. Fred E. Leonard's (Oberlin College, Oberlin, Ohio) *Guide to the History of Physical Education,* and wrote the preface.

About this time a physical education series was prepared in which McKenzie was much involved. He also acted as editor and consultant on a book which E. Norman Gardiner of Cambridge was writing, contrasting the ancient and modern athlete. In a letter to Gardiner dated March 23, 1923, Tait apologized for his tardiness in sending material to England due to his many other commitments and advised:

> I would suggest that in writing the historical part that the story of the Greek and Roman periods be curtailed as far as may be possible and that you include the revival of the Olympic Games with some account of each of the festivals up to the games at Antwerp. . . . I would also suggest that you give a paragraph to the Relay Games at Pennsylvania which are the largest track games after the Olympics, and are now international in character as teams from Oxford, Cambridge and France take part in them yearly.

> You will notice among the pictures, a number showing technique, especially the high jump. There is not much about the high jump in Greek literature, but there has been great experimentation done by high jumpers in America who have developed three distinct styles, as shown in the pictures. The roll-over of the Californians, the reverse turn as shown by Oler of Yale, and the still classic form as shown by Langdon of Yale which is the one usually taught and I think the best. . . . It might also be well to go into the technique of the hurdles, the hammer, shot and pole vault.

> I am enclosing three good pictures of typical modern stadii, the Yale Bowl which is a coliseum, the Ohio stadium which is a horseshoe, and the

Franklin Field stadium in which the stands and the gymnasium are combined in one architectural scheme giving greater versatility to the plant than any of the others. You doubtless got a picture of the great stadium about to be erected at Wembley which should make a very interesting chapter on 'Stadiums: Ancient and Modern.'

If you can get at your manuscript this Spring and have it out by June it would be possible to have the book issued next October and thus secure the sale at the opening of the college year. I would advise you not to hurry it, however, if you want to devote more time to it.

In his years of studying athletes and their techniques, Dr. McKenzie had kept a diary of his observations and conclusions. He had also amassed a large collection of photographs of athletes and athletic events, supplementing these with his own sketches. Of the high jump he remarked:

It is a pleasure to walk over to the corner of Franklin Field, sit down on a bench and watch the high jumpers go through their religious rites before competition. Carefully measuring their distances, marking them with offerings—sweater and cap, or shoe, or a handkerchief, placed on an exact spot to guide them to their approach. Each with his own personal idiosyncrasy and superstition—changing them by a few inches as the bar rises and the tension increases.

No event on the athletic program requires more delicate adjustment of coordination or more perfect timing as this explosive display of agility and the high jumper is silent and thoughtful during a contest—weighing and considering, concentrating his attention on the small details of technique that go to make perfection.

Tall and slender as a rule the high jumper stands, awaiting the effort. With care he cleans any possible dirt from the spikes of his shoe, on which he depends for a firm take-off. . .

It was Page's story of his method in *Outing* that started me studying the technique of it in 1887 and by following the directions of this wonderful athlete who cleared 9'' above the ordinary, I improved my own performance from 5'-4'' to 5'-9''—a height that was quite sufficient for the few competitions that were then open . . . then came Sweeney who showed in his variation of it at the Harvard Summer School, pushing the record up to 6'-5 5/8''* and finally the extraordinary discovery of the Western Robert Van Horne of California in which he took off with the foot nearest the bar contrary to all tradition and rolled over the bar landing on hands and the same foot from which he took off. . .

The center of gravity never reaches the level of the bar but the legs, hips, shoulders and arms each in turn thrown over it while the rest of the body is at a lower level. It is a thrilling demonstration of perfect timing of effort and doing what seems to be impossible.

The collaboration with Gardiner continued by correspondence

*In 1976 Olympics, the gold medallist Jacek Wszola of Poland, cleared 7'4-1/2''

until McKenzie had time to meet him in England. On the 24th of May 1923, he wrote in part:

My dear Gardiner,

This year we do not get overseas, but will spend the summer in California where I am giving a couple of courses at the summer school at Berkley.

... In the chapter fourteen it seems to me important that the high jump be described and also that the pole vault and hurdles which are very distinct modern contributions to the athletic program be described. The discus emphasizing the throw with the single or double turn taken from the hammer throw would seem to me an interesting addition.

In Chapter Sixteen you already show the style of the javelin and an illustration of the javelin throw would be interesting and instructive. I may say that at our Relay Games and at the Olympics, the javelin is becoming a very popular event and we have enormous entries as we have for the discus. ... I cannot help thinking it might be well to introduce some modern examples in contrast to ancient methods such as invention of the boxing gloves by Sargent Broughton, the change brought about in the protection of the hands, the swinging blow using the hand like a club instead of like a foil, the division of fighting into rounds, and such other changes as would show its development.

It might also be interesting to have some of the different forms of wrestling. ... I would be very glad to have the revival of athletic art as a concluding chapter but it would have to be very carefully worded so as not to appear like an advertisement for the editor!

... I think somewhere in the book you might emphasize the movement that is at present very strong in America toward the combining of physical training in its most rudimentary forms with competitive athletics under one department in colleges as well as in the schools. They have hitherto been separate and frequently antagonistic.

The two men discussed the text more satisfactorily when the McKenzies went over for the Olympic Games held in Paris in 1924. Gardiner's book entitled *Athletes of the Ancient World* was published in 1930. In it Gardiner included McKenzie's bronzes, *The College Athlete, The Modern Discus Thrower,* and *The Sprinter,* calling them in his preface, "the nearest modern parallel to the athletic art of Greece."

Tait McKenzie attached great importance to his connection with the American Physical Education Association (now called the American Association for Health, Physical Education and Recreation)*. Many of his fellow founders of the Society for Directors of Physical Education in Colleges, had been early members and leaders in physical education.

The history of the Association went back to 1885 when Dr.

* Its Canadian counterpart is The Canadian Association for Health, Physical Education and Recreation.

William Anderson, later physical director at Yale, called together about sixty teachers, to organize a society of physical education. The result was the "American Association for the Advancement of Physical Education" with Dr. Ed. Hitchcock of Amherst College as first president. Tait McKenzie joined in the early 1900s and played a prominent part in formulating ideals and policies. In his autobiographical notes, he outlines the value of this association and his role together with interesting by-products of his involvement:

> Starting as a small society it enlarged under the able secretaryship of J.H. McCurdy until it numbered over 1,000. . . . During my first [1912] presidency, we met at Newark and the second year at St. Louis. This convention was marked with bitter controversy over the Constitution and time and energy wasted. I was elected to a third term and served part of it but by the Spring of 1915 I was in England on active war service and far from San Francisco and the scene of the Convention.

> The great values of these conventions were and are meeting and talking with leaders in the work. One can soon decide after talking with a man whether his written statements are trustworthy or not, and the demonstrations of gymnastics, athletics, by school children and students in the great armories of cities like Newark, St. Louis, Cincinnati, were full of suggestion to those who went with eager and open mind. . .

> In 1907 I went to the International Congress of School Hygiene in London at the Imperial Institute at Kensington. Before the meeting the president, Sir Lauder Brunton, invited me to dine at his house in Portland Square. It was an old-fashioned stone house. The waiting room with its magazine-strewn table became the dining room by night with its glass and silver. He had invited a picked company of about a dozen. When the table was cleared, pencils and notepaper were passed and to my astonishment he said: 'Now, Dr. Tait McKenzie will tell us about the experiment he is carrying on at the University of Pennsylvania and will, I am sure, be willing to answer any questions you ask.'. . .

> So I told of the work and we discussed the school and college in relation to physical education until a late hour. I gave a paper on the subject at the Congress, illustrated with pictures of the class and other work at the University of Pennsylvania and so started a friendship with Sir Lauder that ended only with his death. He was keenly interested and anxious to have a system somewhat similar to ours introduced into the colleges and universities of England and Scotland and it was at this request that I wrote and read a paper before the Royal Sanitary Institute of London on *Our National Scheme of Physical Education*. More than one meeting was held in his house, even in 1916, but he was a broken man. His favourite son had been killed in battle and he said to me: 'I always cut out and sent him medical items of interest when I wrote to him and I would like to send them now to you.'

> Alas, it was not for long. He wrote me in 1917, 'The lamp continues to flicker.' But the flame was soon extinguished and a great physician and a great and lovable man passed to his reward. It was with a shock of surprise that in the summer of 1925 while living at Darnick Tower we

paid a visit to Bowden Church and saw the inscription on a tablet in his memory. . .

At the 1908 Congress on Physical Education held in Brussels McKenzie had met Monsieur Demeny "who with his paper gave a demonstration of the rhythmic curvilinear movements in contrast to the static or angular movements of the Swedes which bid fair to make a real contribution to the physical education of France and the world."

These international conventions have continued and the revival of the Olympic Games gave occasion to tie up these conventions with the Games themselves. . .

In Amsterdam in 1928, Professor Baylendick of Gronigen was the head of this Convention and of the laboratory that was exhibited at the stadium for the study of physiological problems and at the Congress held in the old University of Amsterdam, I read a paper on the relation of art and athletics, illustrated by works of my own and showed many pictures of the work at Penn.

. . . We bring away from conventions such as these much more than we bring. One may be so wrapped up in one's own little world that these outside influences may make but little impression. I have met men at them who were like the man who traded a horse for a mule and who was so busy talking about the horse that there was no time to learn the habits of the mule he was getting. . . . But it is a dull mind that fails to carry away something of value from contact with the best minds in his own field and this informal education can be of greater value and more service than the formal lecture and the reading of a textbook by yourself.

These gatherings were always a stimulus to McKenzie and he rarely missed an occasion to meet with the medical and/or physical education fraternity. On the medical side, McKenzie was a Fellow of the College of Physicians of Philadelphia, a member of the County Medical Society, and a member of the Charaka Club of New York, an exclusive group of men outstanding in the medical profession who met once a month for dinner and "congenial conversation."

"All his life he had warm friendships with such giants in the profession as Doctor Weir Mitchell, W.W. Keen, Harvey Cushing, J.W. White, Charles Frazier, Edward Martin, and when in England he never failed to visit his old friends, Sir William Osler, Regis Professor of Medicine in Oxford, and Sir Clifford Albutt, occupying the same position in Cambridge."*

Dr. McKenzie was one of the founders of the American Academy of Physical Education. In 1926 Dr. Clark W. Hetherington of the School of Hygiene and Physical Education at Stanford University in California, had called together William Burdick, Thomas Storey, Jay B. Nash and Tait McKenzie, doctors of like mind engaged in the physical education at universities. This group formed the nucleus.

*Journal of Health and Physical Education: R. Tait McKenzie Memorial Issue, Vol. 15, #2, page 52.

The original five elected five more by ballot, and these again elected five more until by 1930, 29 members had been elected to the fellowship and a constitution was drafted. Fellowship in the Academy indicated leadership in the field.**

The only Canadian besides McKenzie included was Dr. A.S. Lamb, Director of Physical Education at McGill University.

Dr. McKenzie acted as chairman and later became the first president. At the first annual meeting held December 31, 1930, he addressed the gathering of distinguished doctors and physical educationalists, outlining the Academy's aspirations and achievements:

> Twenty years ago a great philosopher and thinker in our ranks, Luther Halsey Gulick, thought there should be such an Academy to encourage research and original creative work in physical education, and many hours were spent in reading manuscripts, discussing them and judging their merits with intention of making awards, but the child of his imagination was born before its time. It dwindled in the atmosphere of struggle and strain. Every member of the group was fighting for bare recognition of his subject in a hostile educational work, and so it died and is almost forgotten. Today we enter on the same experiment. What are our chances?

> Physical education is now firmly entrenched in the statute books governing education of nearly all the states. . . . If one picks up the catalogues of such publishers as Macmillan; Barnes, Lea and Febiger; and Saunders to mention a few, one finds textbooks on our subject (most of them by our own Fellows), occupying prominent places on their educational lists. In Budapest, I saw rows of them on the book shelves of the Royal Hungarian College of Physical Education. They have even penetrated to Berlin, Zurich and Dresden. American methods and ideas are being spread abroad more and more throughout Europe and South America, as well as among our own people. Such an organization as ours is in the air, so to speak. Already in Europe a Scientific Society* has been formed, limited to forty members, to take leadership in all investigations on subjects connected with physical education.

He discussed the systems of physical education he had seen operating in Europe during his tour of universities. He was most impressed with the Berlin Stadium under Directorship of Carl Diem:

> We enter the Stadium which seats about 40,000. Inside is a cycle track, then a running track and field. Opposite is the swimming pool, 100 meters long, divided into three sections for teaching. In the rear are the barracks for athletes, dining room, laboratories and classrooms. In one laboratory are x-ray pictures of athletic injuries; spicules of bone showing in tendons at the site of old sprains; injuries to joints; fractures and dislocations; hearts; big and small, before and after exercise and prolonged training; all taken with German thoroughness and precision.

**See Appendix for Founding Fathers of the American Academy of Physical Education.

*Scientific Society of Physical Educations with headquarters in Berlin.

And now we go through a long tunnel which burrows below the race track of the Berlin Jockey Club and come up on a plain divided into fields with ranges of tennis courts along the edge; light and airy dormitories for women; near them an out-of-door circle surrounded by shrubs and trees for dancing; an amphitheatre for lectures and demonstrations; and on to the running track and athletic fields. . .

Here is a great institution drawing its students from all over the world, America included, and aiming to lead the world in physical education. Eventually it will be the center for post-graduate work in physical education just as the clinics of Vienna attract physicians who wish to specialize in their subject and get the most advanced work in it.

In 1932* America will be invaded by students and professors of such institutions as these and they will be eager to see for themselves what we are doing.

He enumerated an eight-point plan for the Academy which included recognition and encouragement for those who were making a contribution to physical education, directing the attention of promising students to the field, and awarding scholarships, medals, and diplomas for essays or research.

The Academy accepted his plan in principle and a program was drawn up for participation in the 10th Modern Olympiad to be held in Los Angeles in 1932. In conjunction with the Los Angeles Institute for Foreign Relations and the University of Southern California, the Academy arranged a course of lectures with Professor William LaPorte of the University of California (a member of the Academy) as chairman. This series included reports from representative authorities of the work being done in France, Poland, Germany, Finland, Japan, and England. McKenzie gave an illustrated talk on "The Athlete in Sculpture" and took a class around the gallery describing and commenting upon the Olympic Exhibition of Painting, Sculpture and Architecture relating to sport, from all parts of the world.

In his talk, McKenzie pointed out that modern athletics offered the sculptor poses not known in the days of the Greek Olympics when athletic sculpture was the order of the day:

The modern high jumper has exercised an ingenuity of style in the 'Reverse', the 'Roll-over' and the 'Scissors' that give it a thrill the Greeks never had. The modern athletic program has other events peculiar to itself. Heaving the 56-pound weight for height by a handle is an Irish contribution. Throwing the hammer, first practiced on the village green in Scotland, and the putting of the 'shoulder stone' is now standardized into the 16-pound shot-put from a seven-foot circle. . .

Perhaps the most interesting race in the modern program is one the Greeks never saw—the flight of the hurdlers. . . . Swimming and diving were part of the daily life of the Greeks but we have no records of

*1932 Olympics held in Los Angeles.

competition in them as part of their athletic program. In the modern Olympic Games, water sports have a section to themselves and bring competitors from all over the world. The flight of the diver and the flat plunge of the racer each lends itself to the sculptor's interest. . . . The rhythmic sweep of the oars in a college eight was a sight the men of Attica never saw although the Athenians had their own regattas and torch or relay races on foot and on horesback. . .

He also spoke of winter sports that should inspire the sculptor and wound up his talk with:

Wherever untrammeled youth is found—in camp, field, beach, or gymnasium; on land or in the river, lake, sea or swimming pool, there should be the sculptor with his appraising eye, his cunning hand, and his will to record his impressions, if an adequate interpretation is to be made of this great renaissance of athletic competition in which we are living, for the most part unconsciously and all to often with an unseeing eye.*

With a few other lecturers and officials, McKenzie met daily for breakfast in the apartment of J.G. Merrick of Toronto where the informal group prepared a breakfast from purchases made at the nearby market the previous day. Merrick recalled later: "It was delightfully intimate and the most pleasant human element of the Games that year."

Los Angeles had gone all out in providing for the Games. Called by one reporter as "unique in the history of international gatherings" was the Olympic Village—"a veritable city of champions, designed especially for their particular needs and comforts with its 550 rose-coloured stucco, two-room cottages . . . covering a tract of 331 acres, the site being selected for it spectacular view and ideal climatic conditions." There were miles of roads graded especially for the event, green grassy plots, shrubs and palm trees to give a homey appearance to the village. "Miles of water mains, every known kind of bath for the athletes, a shower in each house and wash bowl in each room . . . for the first time since the men of ancient Greece pitched their tents on the plains of Elis, participants in the games were housed and fed in a complete community designed for the purpose. The success of Olympic Village was an outstanding feature. . . . German authorities are planning to make every effort to continue this successful experiment for the Eleventh Olympiad in Berlin."**

Attachés of various countries had offices in the Village and were supplied with interpreters to handle language problems.

On Saturday, July 30, 1932, the opening day, the sun shone brilliantly in a cloudless blue sky where blimps and airplanes droned overhead while flags of all nations fluttered from the ramparts of the

---

*R. Tait McKenzie: "The Athlete in Sculpture." *Journal of Health and Physical Education,* November 1932.

**Hartley d'Oyley Price: "The Tenth Olympic Games", *The Journal of Health and Physical Education,* November 1932.

immense stadium and a vast, expectant throng of 105,000 awaited the opening. After the playing of the "Star-Spangled Banner" came the Parade of the Nations with Greece, the Mother of the Olympics, leading the procession and the others following in alphabetical order. It was a thrilling spectacle with the uniforms of every nation displaying national colours. The Olympic Torch lighting the way for international goodwill, flamed high above the peristyle of the stadium as the athletes took their oath before a hushed assembly.

The Olympic flag with its five interwoven circles of blue, black, red, green, yellow (representing five continents) on a background of white waved from the flagstaff as representatives from 39 countries marched from the field—the women to Chapman Park Hotel (their residence for the Games) and the men to Olympic Village.

If the Academy of Physical Education had had any qualms about impressing the European schools with America's ability to carry off an international event, their minds must have been at ease as the days of competiton progressed. The Olympic Committee and the Los Angeles authorities seem to have spared nothing to ensure its success.

"Rowing drew thousands to the Long Beach Marine Stadium where the course is considered one of the most ideal of its kind in the world," reported Hartley Price. "Owing to its advantageous position, it is not affected by wind or tide. This course represents the untiring efforts of the city of Los Angeles to provide the best possible equipment yet devised for such an event. It is the result of considerable excavation and the diverting of water from the Pacific Ocean into it. It is the only rowing course in the world that is lined throughout its length with bleachers on both sides."*

There was something for everyone, no matter what one's taste as a spectator. At the track were hurdles, broad and high jumps, shot put, races, steeplechase, pole vault, discus and javelin throw. There was a fencing stadium for those who enjoyed watching this graceful art. At the Rose Bowl in the evenings one could watch cyclers jockeying for position on the track or go elsewhere to observe weight lifting, boxing and various kinds of wrestling. Water sports ranged from swimming to water polo in addition to rowing and yacht races.

At Elysian Park Range was pistol and rifle shooting. Hockey type games drew large numbers of spectators. "Lacrosse, a fast sensational game new to Californians, found a popular response. This contest was between the Canadian Nationals and John Hopkins University. Much to the delight of the audience, Will Rogers announced a part of the final contest. He humorously enlarged upon the apparently murderous intent of participants as they wielded their clubs during the play."*

There were gymnastics, football, and lastly the decathlon and pentathlon—a series of events calling for the utmost in strength, stamina and skill without which no Olympiad was complete.

Price reported:

No competiton of early Greece can quite compare with our modern

*Ibid.

decathlon event. The greatest pride of early Olympiads was the all-round athlete, but he was never called upon to perform in any series of events that demanded the endurance called for today. For two consecutive days, contestants are required to engage in ten different sports: 100-meters, broad and high jump, shot put, 400-500 meter run, 110-meter hurdles, discus, pole vault, and javelin throw. This is particularly exhausting to even the most rugged.

The track and field events showed Finland outstanding in the javelin, Poland in the 10,000-meter run, Argentina in the marathon, Italy in the 1500-meters, Japan in the hop-skip-and-jump, Great Britain in the 800-meters, Ireland in the 400-meter hurdles, and the United States in the sprints, broad jump, pole vault, shot put, and the relay races. In the women's events, the United States reigned supreme.*

The pentathlon of the early Greeks had consisted of running, leaping, wrestling, throwing the *diskos,* and the javelin or spear. The modern pentathlon "is perhaps the best all-round test of ability in the athletic world."*

Included in the five events are revolver shooting (rapid fire at a disappearing target), fencing, swimming, cross-country running, and cross-country horseback riding. In the equestrian phase of the proceedings consisting of a series of jumps as well as cross-country riding, the men are not permitted to inspect the course until the day before the ride, and then may only walk over it. They may not try out their mounts until fifteen minutes previous to the ride*

The climax of the five-day contest is a run over more than two miles of difficult territory. The contestants . . . claimed that the steeplechase course and the 5000-meter cross-country were the stiffest that had ever been faced by modern Olympic contestants.*

Sweden was again champion of the pentathlon "an unblemished record held since its introduction into the Games in 1912."*

An equestrian event on the course considered the most difficult in the history of the Games brought the Olympiad to a close on August 14th. Commandant LeSage and his "magnificent horse *Taine*" brought hearty cheers from the assembly before the hush fell over the Stadium for the closing ceremony.

Marching slowly from the west end of the Stadium came the standard bearers of the flags of all nations. Colourful, richly silken, the flags waved and fluttered in the late afternoon sun . . . the band played softly; a fanfare of trumpets sounded from the peristyle; the boom of an artillery salute announced that the Olympic flag was about to be furled for another four years; the flaming torch grew dimmer—and faded entirely. Tinged with the sadness of farewell, officials made their closing speeches; the standard bearers took their exit amid the glorious crescendo of the chorus of 2500 voices singing 'Aloha, Farewell to thee.' Then taps, eerily solemn, climaxed this impressive, almost mystical ceremony.*

*Ibid.

Public Archives of Canada

OLYMPIC SHIELD (1928–32) Bronze medallion. 5 foot diameter. First shown at the 1932 Olympiad in Los Angeles. 18 inch galvano shown here.

Tait McKenzie's *Shield of Athletes* exhibited at the games won the Olympic Art Award for the year. The symbolic work depicts the Spirit of Olympia (a female form) helmeted and garbed in archaic drapery. "Her outstretched hands are bringing together two athletes representative of the modern Olympic revival who shake hands in token of the friendly spirit in which athletic competition should be conducted."**

These figures are in high relief and are surrounded by a laurel wreath and border. Immediately circling this are panels depicting field events: throwing the hammer, casting the javelin, the pole vault, the high jump, putting the shot and scaling the discus, while below are a group of hurdlers in full flight.**

** Hussey: *Tait McKenzie: A Sculptor of Youth.*

(In 1937-38, a replica of the *Shield of Athletes* was given to Tokyo for their new Olympic building and it was adopted at the Olympic Games held in Tokyo in 1964 as the official *Olympic Shield*. Many athletic groups use the Shield for award purposes.)

Four small octagonal panels show individual athletes in the high jump, broad jump, an athlete tying his shoe, and one preparing to lift a weight. Words in the border below the figures of *Flight* read: *Mens Fervida In Corpore Lacertoso* (an eager mind in a lithe body), the aim of the Olympic Games. Above are three words: *Fortius* (stronger), *Altius* (higher), *Citius* (swifter).

Above and below these octagonal panels are the qualities cultivated by athletic competition: *Celeritas* (speed), *Agilitas* (agility), *Fortitudo* (courage), *Aequitas* (fair play). In lower relief are other useful qualities: *Accuratio* (accuracy) and *Elegentia* (grace).

Above the central medallion is a winged figure. Surrounding the lettered and enriched border is a frieze displaying a foot race from start to finish showing every part of the stride. There are 60 figures in the frieze alone and 90 male figures and one female in the entire Shield, the largest number of human forms ever represented on a medal. This was a remarkable piece of work.

At the tenth Modern Olympiad, William A. Carr, a graduate of Penn, ran the 400-meter in 46.2 seconds. McKenzie asked Carr to pose for him for it seemed to him that his small-boned slight figure with its well-balanced, muscular development should be preserved in sculpture. McKenzie portrayed him first in an easy, relaxed standing position characteristic of the athlete at rest. A 12-inch high sketch study was also made of him showing the runner in full stride with his peculiarities of style—a long forward reach of the leg and a somewhat restricted movement of the arms from side to side, rather than backward and forward as in the average runner. The standing pose was later reworked for the William Irvine Memorial Group commissioned for Mercersburg Academy, Mercersburg, Pa.*

Tait McKenzie was overjoyed with the American presentation of the Olympic Games which he called "incomparably the greatest and most beautiful festival, ancient or modern, up to the present time."

Later he designed a seal for the Academy of Physical Education showing a torch being passed from one runner to the next as in the Olympic ceremony. This typified the American Academy and its ideal of "increasing knowledge, raising standards, and raising the profession to the level of the other learned professions."

From the time of the revival of the Olympic Games, McKenzie had rarely missed a meet. His experience and knowledge in the field of physical education continued to involve him in a consulting capacity, not only in the United States but in European countries where universities were reluctant to include the subject as part of the curriculum. Writing to McKenzie from Minto House, Chambers Street, Edinburgh in 1934, Ronald Campbell discussed the problems of setting up such a department at the University of Edinburgh:

---

*Robert Michelet, Swimming Champion, statue, and a portrait medallion of Wm. Mann Irvine, "Dreamer and Scholar, Builder and Worker", set in a memorial slab, completed this memorial group.

Physical education as it is conducted in this country is lacking in purpose and healthy emotion. By the widest stretch of the imagination, it cannot be defined as 'education'. . . . For example, the Swedish system I consider is an apotheosis of posture, the very negation of creative impulse. Even as a system it was shaken from its foundations by the War; in France it was discarded as static and lifeless. The national reaction to it has been the popular adoption of Niels Bukh's system with his vigorous disjointed movements which from an ethical point of view have as much purpose as some glorified form of St. Vitus' dance!. . . . Every attempt to start an institution for teaching of physical training instructors in England has failed. On the other hand we have our games, voluntary institutions where the pulse beats naturally and in tune with our national temperament. Our British games give us an opportunity to carry out the highest ideals of life. . . . Physical education must not be isolated to the gymn; it should pulsate between classroom and gymn, playgrounds and countryside. For every physical expression, there is a physical equivalent. What a dynamic inspiration this reaction of mind on body and body on mind. Properly directed it should be the greatest, most dynamic and fruitful force in education.

The same year his old friend, Lord Aberdeen died at the age of sixty-four. A telegram arrived from Lady Aberdeen on the 4th of March reading: "Aberdeen passed home peacefully today." Writing to her, McKenzie said:

I have just been reading 'We Twa'* again and it has brought back such a flood of memories that I am putting down some notes with the idea of publishing my 'Reminiscences' later on (I have already had an offer from an English firm for such a book but have been too busy with other things to consider it seriously). I do not know if you realize how much my association with you both had broadened and enriched my life. . .

As for your own enquiry about myself, I find a curious indifference as to what the future may hold. One plans as if one were to be immortal, at the same time realizing that each day may be the last and that one has to stand very much on one's record as it has already been written. My heart goes out to you in your loneliness.

Affectionately, as ever

RTM

Only close friends knew that McKenzie's heart had been a source of trouble to him for some time though perhaps it was guessed when the Olympics were held in Berlin in 1936, and he passed it up.

Prior to the annual meeting of the American Academy of Physical Education, he wrote to Agnes Wayman arranging lectures for the occasion that he would be unable to speak to them.

I am under strict medical orders about undertaking anything which involves excitement or strain of any kind on account of a coronary

*Lord and Lady Aberdeen, *We Twa*, Vols. I & II, 1925, W. Collins, Sons & Co. Ltd., London, England.

University of Pennsylvania Archives

Dr. Tait McKenzie as the guest of the Marquis and Marchioness of Aberdeen, House of Cromar, Deeside, Scotland in 1933, with Her Majesty Queen Mary.

condition of the heart which has been bothering me. Sometimes I am all right but at others it would not be wise for me to do certain things such as making a public address before a large crowd such as would be there. I am hoping to be able to be there and will be glad to be there if all goes well. . .

I am anxious to get the Academy in some kind of shape so that it can be handed over to a successor in good working order. For that reason I am working on the St. Louis program.

The American Academy of Physical Education had suffered a somewhat tempestuous career during McKenzie's tenure as president. Some members elected to the Fellowship disputed the value of the Academy in achieving anything practical in the field. Much of McKenzie's time was spent in lengthy correspondence persuading or pacifying or explaining the whole purpose of the Fellowship and he was frequently exasperated by complaints of members who required the achievements of the Academy to be visible in black and white although much of the influence of the Academy was intangible.

The group met in St. Louis in April 1936. Dr. A.S. Lamb was still the only Canadian admitted to the organization. Five women were included in the Fellowship by this time: Miss Jessie Bancroft, Lake Placid Club. N.Y.; Dr. J. Anna Norris of the University of Minnesota; Miss Agnes Wayman of Barnard College, New York City; Elizabeth Burchenal of the American Folk Dance Society, New York City; and Miss Mabel Lee of the University of Nebraska.

At the annual meeting Dr. John Brown, Jr. stated his views of what the Academy should be and his remarks were recorded by McKenzie later as being in agreement with his own.

The Academy should be a fellowship, not just a research organization and should have some spiritual values which could not be obtained in a meeting necessarily hurried. . . . There should be no sense of pressure in meeting . . . time enough should be given to indulge in the various phases of discussion . . . there should be time to pay homage to members who had passed on, properly induct new members into the Academy, the opportunity for the sharing of concern and ideas with debate around any topic or project. This should not be primarily a meeting of old people, but a meeting of kindred spirits who have matured in the fire of experience and leadership. This should be an opportunity for them to warm their hearts and renew their spirits and go away refreshed and inspired. It should be a time to thank God that we are still here and can rededicate ourselves to this movement.

Dr. McKenzie sent a telegram asking that plans be made for completion of a biography of Dr. Clark Hetherington "whose long and active life has been devoted to the establishment of physical education in states and institutions from coast to coast." McKenzie felt Hetherington's writing should be in print and available for consultation of students in the field. Dr. Frank S. Lloyd of New York University and N.P. Neilson of Leland Stanford University agreed to collaborate on this valuable work. Again the assembly of Fellows nominated Tait McKenzie as their president. Dr. Arthur H. Steinhaus of George Williams College, Chicago, became secretary, an appointment which pleased McKenzie—he expected Steinhaus "to breathe new life into" the Academy. Steinhaus had done some clay modelling and criticising his work later, Tait wrote:

> There is no doubt that if you become active in sculpture it will interfere with your practice. I would strongly advise you to keep your sculpture as a hobby for the present for two reasons: (1) it is an exceedingly uncertain and capricious profession, and (2) the professional associations which you make among the medical men are likely to be much more agreeable and lasting than those you would make among artists. The artist plays a lone hand whereas the medical man is part of a great fraternity speaking a common language.
>
> . . . In my own case, my interests were primarily medical . . . it was only on my return from active service that I had to make the decision as to whether or not I would continue my private practice. I decided against it, but kept on with my college professorship until three years ago.

McKenzie was pleased that Steinhaus and Brown would represent the Academy at the Eleventh Olympiad in Berlin that July. The American group sailed on the *S.S. Manhattan,* July 15, 1936. Another event McKenzie would not have missed but for his heart condition, was the International Congress of Physical Medicine held in London. Dr. William McFee, friend and associate of the Academy of Physical Medicine, wrote to him later (July 9, 1936):

Dr. and Mrs. Tait McKenzie (about 1932)

Dear Dr. McKenzie:

Having returned from the London session of the International Congress of Physical Medicine, I am reminded of your courtesy in giving me letters of endorsement and introduction to some of your good medical friends in London . . . the men concerned were very glad to have a message of regard from you and wished me to convey theirs in return, as they hold Dr. McKenzie in very high regard.

The presentation of the subject of Physical Education under leadership of Lord Dawson was one of the highlights of the Congress. . . . It is my particular pleasure to inform you that you were elected to Honorary Membership in the New England Physical Therapy Society at its annual meeting. . .

During the latter part of the year McKenzie began to put in order articles published and material collected over the years on the modern athlete in sculpture. This would be an elaboration and extension of lectures and articles possibly illustrated with his own work, re-emphasizing his life-long theme and its relationship to physical perfection. It was his intention to produce a book-length manuscript, and it would include scientific data from his observations and records during his tenure at the University of Pennsylvania. It would be of value to the physical educationalist as well as a contribution to the world of art. The manuscript was not completed but portions have been already quoted herein relating to the characteristics of the perfect pole vaulter, discus thrower, et cetera, scientific data upon which McKenzie based his sculptural versions.

CHAPTER XIII

A Birthday Party at Seventy

On May 26, 1937, Tait McKenzie celebrated his seventieth birthday and in honour of the occasion, the Franklin Inn Club hosted a birthday party at Valley Forge Golf Club to which many of his friends and associates were invited. Each was asked to contribute a poem or limerick to McKenzie.

One may imagine the scene:

A small, spare man, meticulously dressed in a black suit, his pince-nez slightly tilted as he scans some of the tributes, turning to a friend beside him to make a few dry remarks or smile humorously. Occasionally his high infectious laugh is heard for some of the guests, mostly members of the Franklin Inn Club, are called upon to read aloud their poetic efforts. Often enough tears are mixed with laughter in McKenzie's eyes. Obviously he is enjoying the whole affair. Someone recalls McKenzie's early days in Philadelphia as a member of the Club where he often met male friends for lunch. There was the occasion of their burlesque show in 1909 when Tait appeared as a dancer and was billed as:

Tait Isadora McKinzy
The Scotch Highball—
Scotch Songs and Sword Dances
Real sword—real kilties—real legs

Twenty-eight years later the many friends he had made in Philadelphia and beyond have come together to pay tribute to one they consider "a great man."

Dr. David Riesman of Philadelphia pointed to McKenzie's distinction as a sculptor in his poem.

To R. Tait McKenzie
On His Seventieth Birthday
May 26, 1937

The blood of Bruce and Wallace
Flows in his sturdy veins
And from the skies of Inverness
His eye its colour gains.

The silent grandeur of the glen
The dancing moon on Monan's rill
Have gone into his flesh and bone
And do pervade it still.

The love of freedom and of space
These two I would suppose
His mother gave to him
The Lady of the Snows.

He does not paint in poignant lines
Pangs of a homeless mouse
Nor does address his burning words
To a lady's bonnet's louse.

Of marble and of lustrous bronze
His poetry is made
Not through the ear but through the eye
Our souls it does invade.

And we're the better if we find
The poet's soul in stone
And make him feel we share his dreams
And that he's not alone.

And all our hearts go out to him
On this fair day in May
May he through many years to come
Work on in stone and clay.

Richard Warren wrote:

To R. Tait McKenzie

You model Youth, creating from the clay
The very spirit of the athlete's soul
When he, triumphant, winning, crowned with bay
At last achieves the ever sought for goal.
What tribute can I pay to you whose art
Has greatly thrilled since first I saw it stand
As masterful, yet simple, far apart
From those who merely fashion with the hand?
You love your work, to splendidly portray
The clean limbed athlete in his youthful pride,
Your heart and hand together have held sway,
The statue *lives* and youth is deified!

Limericks included one from Austin K. Gray, Librarian in Philadelphia:

'Please come to my attic next Wenzie
To see what I've done,' said McKenzie:
'I've made such a statue,
It's modern, and dratue!
It's just the last word in stark frenzie!'

Dr. Rebecca Wright of the Massachusetts Institute of Technology wrote:

> Many friends has a sculptor named Tait
> Who count him as one of the great
> At three score and ten
> He ranks with young men
> Though his posture is rather more straight.

Following a sumptuous dinner, E.W. Mumford, Secretary of the University of Pennsylvania, delivered a witty eulogy, including a run-down of the McKenzie clan history. It is quoted here in part:

The man we delight to honor tonight has an old distinguished ancestry. The first of his line of whom we have any record is now commonly known as 'the Neanderthal Man,' but the later 'Piltdown Man' and the justly famed 'Cardiff Giant' are also of his family. It was always a good fighting and yet artistic stock. Originating in Central Europe it struggled north with a war-club in one hand and a carving tool in the other, pausing now and then in a limestone cave to scratch a picture of a bear or an aurochs for the sheer joy of self-expression. When it reached the sea the tribe crowded its last remaining opponents into the channel and, annoyed that they preferred drowning to further good honest fighting, pushed on past them, swam to the cliffs of Albion, gave a shout of satisfaction and started working north through the Cymric. It was a sad day when they reached the Shetland Isles and discovered the deep sea beyond and no one left to quarrel with. One of these islands is still named 'Yell.' It perpetuates their heartfelt outburst of rage and disappointment.

There was only one course left to them. They divided into two bands, calling themselves the Picts and the Scots, and started to fight each other. It kept them busy and happy until the Sassenach pushed up from the South. Then they joined forces once more and have been fighting the Sassenach ever since. . .

I have always thought R. Tait McKenzie came from the Pict side of the clan. Of the two divisions the Picts were always a shade handier with the carving tool. . .

Mumford went on to point out that the Scots, as they became known, after a few centuries "dropped the war club" and contented themselves with "quietly slipping in among other people, out-smarting them and leading them around by the nose." Eventually some migrated to Canada, among whom were McKenzie's parents, and settled down to raise families and educate America. Tait McKenzie was born there and at an early age indicated his potential genius.

On the morning of his first anniversary, his parents decided it was time to find out what Rab was good for. They set him in the middle of the floor, and put near him a Bible, a bottle of pills, and a lump of clay. He swallowed the pills, seized and squeezed the clay, set the Bible on edge and jumped over it. They couldn't make up their minds what this portended. But Rab knew. He had already decided that for a man of his parts, at least three professions were indicated. He was on his way to becoming a physician, a sculptor, and a professor of physical education.

Passing over the unimportant details of his education at McGill, his athletic triumphs and his early professional development, we find him at length in Philadelphia where his genius came to full flower as Director of Phys Ed at the University of Pennsylvania, an orthopaedic surgeon with the British Army during the Great War, and finally, as a sculptor.

I need not name for you his brilliant successes in the latter field. Every freshman at the University still breathes his name with reverence as he kisses the toe of McKenzie's *Youthful Franklin**. . . his bronze figures in athletic poses have inspired thousands of young sculptors. . .

Commenting on McKenzie's personality, Mumford said "you find him a modest, unobtrusive chap, always ready to listen to another's story and laugh at another's joke. He is the best of company in the world because he has a geniune interest in all humanity, a keen curiosity as to human progress, a love of books, and a veritable passion for ideas. His generosity is as unfailing as his understanding. So, gentlemen, a skirl o' the pipes and a good deep toast to Robert Tait McKenzie, a braw Scot, gallant gentleman, and a true friend."

With visible difficulty, Dr. McKenzie regained his composure. When the sound of bagpipes and the cheers had died down, he rose—a small, erect figure, and began to speak in a voice still tinged with emotion. Looking back into childhood, he saw himself as a small, shy boy who had perhaps a low level of vitality, in any case one who had a very "moderate physical equipment." Will power and ambition changed this slowly. "The actual achievement of these youthful athletic exploits were for the most part, rather mediocre in reality. They might be compared to the crude bronze of a statue as it leaves the mold—unimpressive in color to the eye, full of roughness and imperfections."

He went on to speak of his gradual development through gymnastics at McGill and his gradual involvement in physical education. It was of physical education for everyone that he spoke mostly and its value to the ordinary fellow—not the competitive athlete. McKenzie's lifetime message to his fellow man (and woman) was capsuled in his comments:

The man who is well educated physically is not the football hero or the tennis star. He is the one who has practiced many forms of sport and who retains the memory of many of its great sensations. One who can recall the explosive effort of the sprint or the leap . . . the calculated timing of the pole vault or the shot put . . . one who has disciplined himself to physical pain to hang on in the mile race when his leaden feet seem impossible to lift, who has felt the ecstacy of placing a right-hand cross-counter to the chin without a return, or the scoring a clean hit on the mark with the foil. One who has faced and conquered the fear of the giant circle on the bar or a back somersault from the shoulders of an acrobatic partner, one who has felt the sweet sensation in the hands of a

*One of the duties set down for freshmen by their monitors at the U. of Penn.

low straight drive of the golf ball . . . for the memory of them remains and when he sees them done by his successors, he relives these experiences with an intelligence, knowledge and intensity of emotion that is quite unknown to the physical ignoramus. . .

It is memories such as these that go far to compensate for the very real loss of vigor that age must submit to and when joined with the increasing ability to boast unchallenged when one can find listeners, of what one once could do and did do when young, they almost tip the balance in favour of age. . .

Now in his sunset years, he found great satisfaction in recalling his own experiences in sport and athletics as he watched the feats of others. Physical education had also taught him how to conserve energy.

All the accumulated experience of an active life, all the ruses learned, all the hidden ways of saving energy and unnecessary movement, the acquired skills of years, come to his aid and there is a peculiar satisfaction in accomplishing skillfully and without undue effort what the young and unskilled have to struggle for without avail.

One is like the veteran pugilist who bears down on his young and eager opponent in the clinches, blocking his leads with ease, making him swing and miss, keeping him off balance, and using the ring as Tommy Loughran did so that when the bell closed the round, he was always at his corner while the antagonist had to walk across to *his* corner.

He found pleasure in re-reading classical literature not touched since college days.

Re-reading the story of Caesar's Gallic campaigns have stirred me as few things have in recent years. . . . I read these stories at college, but then they were a sort of mental gymnastic exercise, a maze of uncouth words to be parsed and analyzed. The vivid story of the exploit, the uncertain outcome, the fearful odds faced were all to me a new discovery. Caesar did the things one feels oneself doing in the same grand manner. . .

It is only with the increase of years that we get a true appreciation of style, and as we browse among familiar books, new beauties peep out like the hepaticas and violets when we take our familiar daily walk in the spring woods. Old books reveal new qualities, and we realize how much we missed along what seemed familiar and well trodden paths. George Borrow stands a new reading to me every year. . .

Gardening, strolling, swimming, even the hot room has its place in the program. It keeps the skin active at least. The old man can make his skin act even without muscular effort by high temperature in the hot room and if he follows it with 'ersatz' or substitute exercise of a general massage, he can approximate the effect of a good workout. . .

He advised his hearers that one must strive for poise, mental as well as physical at age 70, and "accept the arm of youth with grace, if not with gratitude."

Seventy years of health and strength, mental and physical is a pretty good run; at that age one can call it a day; and if we sign on for a short extension of the contract, it should be only on the condition that the care of the old machine be not too burdensome. As soon as it begins to creak too loudly and when it takes all our time and attention, let us hope it may be promptly scrapped, painlessly, if possible. If not, let us retain at least our fortitude.

He expressed regrets for not having done certain things he had chances to do and for not recording interesting adventures and occasions in his life which gradually faded as time passed so that he could not now recall the complete details. One also regretted little kindnesses that one should have done and didn't and the wrong let go unrighted .

Outlining his work of a lifetime in medicine, sculpture and physical education, he saw little hope of immortality for himself unless it were to be in his sculpture. He could see little reason for personal survival of the soul after death. "Imagine coming into a group of bores one has suffered from during life, reinforced by those who have preceded and followed us! Intolerable! Would it not take the edge off the joy of meeting one's few friends across the Styx?" Viewing the cheapness of life as shown in Nature, McKenzie could see no reason to believe man's soul more favoured than those of the lower forms of life.

During the Great War, I once saw battalion after battalion entrain for the front. Every half hour a train left for 24 hours a day and for six days. Everyone knew that few would return. They went like cattle to the abbatoir, most of them scarcely thinking of it, more probably thinking of their next meal or the immediate comfort of their bodies. What was the lasting impression left with me? It was of the cheapness of human life. The giving of it was the cheapest contribution man could make to a great cause . . . the chances of survival are with the artist whatever his medium, and if his work is in touch with universal emotion it will be constantly reincarnated even if his name is lost in the shuffle.

One conjectures that in the minds of his hearers arose pictures of some of his major works of sculpture—the vibrant, striding boy figure of the Cambridge memorial set in the busy thoroughfare of the English college town; the imposing statue of James Wolfe perched on the hill overlooking the Naval College and the Thames of London in Greenwich Royal Park; the youthful, visionary figure looking to the Castle in Edinburgh's Princess Gardens—McKenzie's favourite—"The Call;" or his small athletic bronzes—*The Athlete, The Modern Discus Thrower, Brothers of the Wind,* or the medallions *The Joy of Effort, The Punters.* Perhaps McKenzie himself recalled the words of his earlier biographer, Christopher Hussey who wrote of the sculpture: "The entire work may be looked upon as a kind of reference dictionary for future generations who may come to study the technique of the 20th Century athlete in action."

Yet despite his somewhat dubious regard for the durability of his work, his athletic medallions and his Olympic Shield have continued in use among athletic groups as awards for over forty years and "the end is not yet in sight."

CHAPTER XIV

Last Works

In 1934 McKenzie had submitted designs for a medal for the International Congress of Mathematics, held every four years. His designs were chosen and he completed the medal in time for the Congress meeting in 1936 in Oslo. On one side, the sculptor showed the head of Archimedes in profile. The surrounding inscription translated reads: *To transcend one's human limitations and master the universe*, a translation from the Roman poet Manilius. On the reverse side was an inscription which translated reads: *Mathematicians gathered together from the whole world honour noteworthy contributions to knowledge.* Behind the inscription is a laurel-branch and in the background can be seen the diagram of a sphere contained in a cylinder. The determination of the relation of these two forms was one of the outstanding achievements of Archimedes and this diagram was engraved on his tomb. The medal was produced in gold and is awarded to mathematicians selected for their outstanding contributions to mathematics.

McKenzie had been commissioned by the Georgia Society of Colonial Dames of America to create a memorial to the Scottish Highlanders who fought against the Spanish and established "New Inverness" in 1736. McKenzie reworked the pipe band portion of his Edinburgh memorial frieze and called it "The Pipes of War." It was cast in bronze and set into a Georgia pink marble monument. The memorial surrounded by flowers and shrubs is located on an island at the intersection of highways US17 and GA99 in Darien, Georgia (former site of "New Inverness"). McKenzie attended and spoke briefly at the dedication ceremony held in May 1936.

Commemorating the 40th Anniversary (in 1934) of the famed Penn Relay Carnivals, he modelled a frieze of relay runners in low relay and titled it *Passing the Baton*.

The same year he was approached by the American Association of Anatomists to produce a memorial medal to their first president, Joseph Leidy who had once been a professor at the University of Pennsylvania. Replying to a letter from member Dr. W.F. Addison at Woods Hole, Mass., McKenzie wrote:

> I would be much interested in doing your Anatomical Medal. I recently did one for the International Congress of Mathematicians which was similar in character but had a portrait of Archimedes. Leidy would make a fine subject with his noble head.
>
> If you can get 200 subscribers at $10.00 each, you could give them each a

medal to pay for the models, dies and medals and still come out even. It would leave something under $1,000 as the sculptor's fee. This plan has been carried with success several times and I could go further into particulars if you think the plan feasible. I hope you can carry it out as it is a fine idea.

Also completed in 1936 was a medal for the Skating Club of New York featuring Sonja Heine. In 1937, McKenzie completed a portrait of neurologist, Dr. Henry Donaldson, the Harold Pratt Pool medal, and began work on another athletic statue. He also completed a portrait medallion of Tom Daly, "Laureate of the Lowly", and a portrait medallion of his close friend and Philadelphian John R. Sinnock, engraver with the U.S. Mint. The same year, Sinnock modelled a portrait medallion of McKenzie.*

As far back as 1931 he had promised to design a seal for the American Association of Physical Education but because of the world-wide Depression, nothing further was done about it until 1935-36 when under Agnes Wayman's term as president the suggestion was revived. Funds were secured and in 1937 McKenzie proceeded to complete the work begun some years earlier.

The seal showed profiles of a typical American college boy and college girl. For the boy he had plenty of examples from his study of athletes and students at the University of Pennsylvania. In order to select the correct features of an average American college girl, he painstakingly wrote to the deans of the women's colleges asking for photos of girls whom the physical directors considered as typical. These he studied carefully along with a number of models who posed for him.

He found the predominant American boy was tall, broad-shouldered, thin-hipped with a low square forehead, blunt nose, very straight eyebrows with high cheekbones, square jaw, and prominent chin.

He asked for frank criticism of students, teachers and other visitors to his studio while working on the girl's head. A favourite question was "If you saw that face at The Salon in Paris, where would you say she had been born?" The answer was usually: "In America."

In his autobiographical notes, McKenzie complained: "Why do girls pluck their eyebrows and paint in arched eyebrows high up on their forehead? It gives the permanently surprised look of a startled fawn."

He found that the typical American girl was inclined to have a short, slightly-upturned nose; full lips but not heavy, the chin broad rather than pointed. "The face is broad rather than thin; and the head round rather than long."

"We are fortunate at this time" wrote McKenzie in 1937, "in the

*In 1967, the centennial of Tait McKenzie's birth date, a commemorative medal was struck by the Medallic Art Company of Danbury, Conn., showing Sinnock's portrait of McKenzie on one side, and on the reverse McKenzie's Olympic Shield. It was made available to numismatists, collectors, museums in a choice of silver or bronze and is still available.

fashion of wearing the hair. We have passed through the nightmare of the close boy-like bob, and now the hair comes down to the level of the chin and covers the ears giving a beautiful line and mass."

Each member of the Seal Committee came to the studio and all approved of the final design. McKenzie had already conceived a development of the seal—his last large sculpture in the round, a herm.

Discussing his approach to creating this unique memorial to American youth, McKenzie wrote a paper and presented it before the American Academy of Physical Education in New York City:

> The custom of marking the boundary of one's property by a stone dates from the beginning of time; and to an artistic and imaginative people like the Greeks, it was only natural that the creation of such a pillar or column should offer a chance for decoration.
>
> *Hermes,* among his many duties, presided over the division of land and it was natural that his head should adorn the top of many of the posts. So often was it used that they became known as 'herms', a name which persisted when the idea spread to their use as garden decorations marking the end or division of a walk.
>
> . . . It is with this in mind that I have taken the form of the colum or herm on which to combine the masks of two students to represent the best types found in our American colleges, the finished product of this great movement for physical education, sports and outdoor life that is the outstanding feature of the last forty years. They are not all averages determined by compass and tapeline; they are not averages at all. They are ideal if you will; but ideals on a solid basis of fact and a consensus of opinion and judgment. . .
>
> The heads are just above life size and the column is six feet six inches in height, and could be used as a memorial award. It is designed to be cut in marble.
>
> What does the American college girl look like? What kind of boy would we consider as representative of our American college and university? These are the questions that the *Column of Youth* is designed to answer.*

The herm was completed and cast in Georgia marble in 1938.

In October 1937 while still at the Mill of Kintail, after summer residence, McKenzie received what one might consider as one of life's little compensations for one's efforts. A letter arrived from a stranger, James F. McCurdy, a Canadian then in London, England.

Dear Sir:

I have had the pleasure of writing to Lady Aberdeen and in the letter I said something of admiration for the Scottish-American War Memorial.

---

*R. Tait McKenzie: "The Column of Youth", read before the American Academy of Physical Education, New York, N.Y., April 22, 1937. Later printed in *The General Magazine and Historical Chronicle*.

In a return letter, Lady Aberdeen says: 'Do tell Dr. McKenzie some day how you feel about it.' But, sir, I have nothing to say of value. I can only admire the work as any thoughtful observer might, with all my heart. I saw it only twice—in September. It was my first visit to Edinburgh. Nevertheless, I felt fairly thrilled, almost to tears. 'The Call' is so completely simple and reverent and humble and modest. The whole conception, the seated figure, the pose that of Archie Gordon. I knew him in Canada forty years ago, when they used to come to New Richmond, P.Q. where I was a minister. It is the face of a young man aware of his trust, of his duty, and resolved to do it in the name of God. It is the 'face of an Angel'. And the upward look not at the Castle but to God Himself. It moved one mightily. It inspired one to go and try to do his best himself . . . as I stood there a gentleman and his wife from abroad I judged were just moving away. We nodded to each other. They seemed as moved as I.

I personally beg to thank you for that great work.

Yours sincerely,

(sgd) James F. McCurdy

In November 1937 McKenzie wrote to his friend, Dr. William McFee in Boston:

Dear McFee:

I should think that the autumn would be the best time for the meeting of the Academy. . . . I am fairly busy with my art work. Formerly I used to do three days' work in a day but now the proportion is reversed and I do one day's work in three.

He had promised to complete a fresh bas-relief of his portrait of Lord Aberdeen for the Scottish National Portrait Gallery in Edinburgh. He was also making arrangements for a marble bust of Archie Gordon to be made from the original bust. On December 13, 1937, he wrote to Lady Aberdeen:

Dear Lady Aberdeen:

I have been putting off writing to you from week to week pending further news on the bust of Archie which is now in the hands of the March brothers.

I have just heard from Sydney who is in Canada right now and reports everything going alright. The plan is to have it cut in the rough during the winter, sent out to Canada, and then have the two of us complete it at my studio next Spring. . . . I trust you will accept this marble when it is finished as a slight token of my appreciation of the many kindnesses I have received at your hands, and Dr. Henry wishes to be associated with this as well.

. . . On the night before we sailed I had a talk with Sir John Stirling

Maxwell about His Ex and suggested that a replica of the plaque I did for Haddo House would be appropriate for the National Portrait Gallery of Scotland. In this he cordially agreed, brought it up before the Board, and the Curator has written me saying that they would gladly accept a replica in bronze. I am now working over the wax preparatory to casting it and I hope to have it ready in the New Year. Would you like me to send it to the Gallery? I cannot tell you what a great pleasure it was for me to do this in his memory and in small recognition of the great part he played in the affairs of the Empire.

I have been reading with great interest the life of the Premier Earl and can readily see how 'His Ex' wanted to have it published in order to put in permanent form the real story of his career. I know it threw new light on it to me as I had always considered him as partly responsible for the Crimean War and did not know he had fought against it so consistently until his hand was forced. It is strange how often these misconceptions about one's work persist as you yourself know from experience. The main thing, however, is to do one's work and let them talk. It is what one actually accomplishes that really matters, not what other people say about it. . .

Since I came back I have been fairly busy doing a medal for Amherst* and the Bicentennary Medal for the University of Pennsylvania and a sketch for a statue to go to Honolulu as a tribute to a great swimmer who was an Olympic champion. His name is Duke Kahanamoku and his name 'Duke' was given him because he was born on the day the Duke of Cornwall (afterwards George V) visited the island.

Otherwise life has been going quietly and I have been reading on going to sleep your *Musings*** which brings back memories and deeds of other days. Perhaps the greatest consolation we have as we get older is our ability to live in the past.

Ethel joins me in Christmas greeting and I am, as ever,

Yours affectionately,

(sgd) R. Tait McKenzie

The bicentennial Medal mentioned in this letter was issued to commemorate the 200 Anniversary of the University of Pennsylvania and was the last medal completed by Tait McKenzie. On one side is shown a *Herm* crowned by two heads facing back to back. One head is that of Benjamin Franklin, founder of the University, as an old man crowned with bays to represent the past, the other head is of a youth looking to the light for guidance in the future. The inscription *Temporis Lux Acti Illustret Posteritatis Viam* (Let the light of the past illumine the pathway of the future) with a lighted lamp of learning on

---

*Amherst College Pratt Pool Medal

**Ishbel, Marchioness of Aberdeen and Temair, *Musings of a Scottish Granny,* Heath Cranton Limited, London, 1936.

one side of the *herm* and a light bulb symbolic of Franklin's interest in electricity and Provost Edgar F. Smith's pioneer work in the purification of tungsten on the other side of the background. The reverse side of the medal reads: "University of Pennsylvania 1740-1940" with its motto *Leges Sine Moribus Vanae*. The shield of the University is centered showing two open books and a dolphin, chevron and plates. For the 1940 celebration, the University planned to show their collection of Tait McKenzie's sculpture.

In January of 1938, E.D. Mitchell, Secretary of the American Physical Education Association, wrote from Michigan University:

My dear Dr. McKenzie:

A letter from Prentice-Hall publishers reports an interview that their representative, Mr. Bloss, had with you recently regarding the book covering the relation between physical education and art. I am encouraged to know that you are interested in this project. I realize that you are already working on the book on 'The Modern Athlete in Sculpture' and that it would be impossible for you to give much time to a second book.

Mitchell suggested that a younger man undertake the research and McKenzie act in an advisory capacity suggesting contents, source of material, and possibly editing the work. Since Tait had already written relative articles through the years, these could be woven into the text.

One such article I remember was included in the Olympic Games issue of *The Journal of Health and Physical Education* of November 1932. [quoted previously in Chapter XIII] I shall look forward to seeing you sometime this Spring and then we can discuss the matter more fully. In the meanwhile I shall be giving some thought to possible collaboration and will have some names for you to consider when we have a meeting.

Also in January came a letter from a committee of the House of Commons in Ottawa asking him if he would undertake a memorial to Sir Arthur Doughty, Dominion Archivist. In February McKenzie wrote to a young Ottawa sculptor, Roland Beauchamp, who had occasionally worked with him in his studio at the Mill of Kintail.

My dear Roland,

I am arranging to come up to Ottawa some time in the next couple of weeks to look over the material and make a start on the preliminary sketches. According to my present plan I will do the small sketches here, submit them in May and do the working model about three or four feet during the summer in Almonte and point it up and do the large figure in Philadelphia next winter.

I want to thank you very much for your offer to work for me and if there is any chance of work for you, you may be sure I will not forget. . . . I

think your bust of the Master Barber is very life-like. . . . I will look
forward to seeing you when I come up.

Dr. Webster wrote to McKenzie from Shediac, N.B. in March:

My dear Tait,

I have rejoiced to read that you were commissioned to make the Doughty
memorial. It would be a shame to let anybody else have it. . . . I hope you
will remember my Museum Collection when the work is well advanced. I
should like to preserve a sketch of the figure, perhaps one of your
working drawings. . .*

In the midst of writing and sculpture commitments, McKenzie was
also trying to arrange annual meetings in his official capacity as
president of both the American Academy of Physical Education and
the American Academy of Physical Medicine.

The Annual Scientific Session of the Academy of Physical
Medicine was planned to be held in Washington in October. He went
over to Washington to arrange space at the Willard Hotel and sent out
a letter to the Fellowship showing his vision for the Academy in the
following paragraph:

Every profession must have an organization such as ours composed of its
leaders who have the best interests of their chosen work at heart, capable
of taking and maintaining this lead in the cultivation of their own
special field and of conducting and preserving its ethics and traditions
among their confreres, maintaining a dignified and friendly relationship
with other departments of medicine and with the whole scientific world.
It is especially necessary in work such as ours which has so recently
attained official recognition. Such a body as ours can prove its worth and
fulfill its destiny only by constant alertness in keeping its Fellows
informed, and making them familiar with new discoveries in physical
medicine made by individuals here and abroad.

May I urge upon you then to help by calling the attention of the Program
Committee to promising research that might be considered for the
Program of the Washington meeting next October, by planning to attend
the meeting yourself, and taking part in its discussion, and by
recommending to the Membership Committee candidates whom you
consider worthy of election to Fellowship. . .

The Committees set up for the Annual Meeting included two
non-Americans, Dr. Isi Gunzburg of Antwerp, Belgium, and Dr.
William F. Roberts of Saint John, N.B., Canada.

In March, McKenzie took a much-needed rest. Along with two
medical friends, Dr. Norman Henry and Dr. Edward Hodge, he took a
cruise to the Bahamas and while there, happily filled a portfolio with

---

*The Doughty memorial was later completed by Emmanuel Hahn, Canadian sculptor. It
stands in Ottawa on the grounds of the Public Archives of Canada.

watercolour sketches. During his absence, Joe Brown, his assistant in Philadelphia, heard of an opening at Princeton University to teach boxing. Brown had a theory about boxing, went to see them and talked it over with the "brass" securing their consent to demonstrate his ideas to a group of students. On the strength of his demonstration, he was hired. When McKenzie returned from his holiday, he was "pleased as punch" about the appointment and as proud, says Brown, as if it had been his own. Later Mr. Brown became professor of both sculpture and boxing at Princeton.

In April McKenzie wrote to Lady Aberdeen at Gordon House in Scotland:

I have just had word that the bust is as near completion as they can bring it in the London studio, and I have written today asking them to send it to the Mill of Kintail so that I may complete it myself in my own studio. It should be there early in May and there is a possibility that I will be able to bring it over myself about the end of June. . .

The University of St. Andrews [Scotland] proposes to give me a degree of Doctor of Laws at the congregation in June. As this is the first recognition of any kind that I have had from a Scottish university or civic body, I am naturally pleased and would like to be there to receive it in person; so I am going to use every endeavour to come over on that occasion although it will have to be a flying trip as usual.

I have started work on the statue of Sir Arthur Doughty, the Canadian archivist, to go in front of the Archives Building in Ottawa and this will keep me pretty busy together with another commission that I have to do, a statue for Honolulu. It is extraordinary how my work is scattered abroad. The Honolulu commission will involve a trip to the Islands and we are planning to make it next Fall direct from the Mill so that we would not open the house until near Christmas. These plans are, of course, tentative and may be changed.

I have just got back from two weeks in the Bahamas, a much-needed holiday which has done much to renew my youth.

I sincerely trust that you are in your ususal vigorous health, and I have the hope that we may yet have one more evening together.

About this time the McKenzies made a journey to Ottawa in regard to the Doughty memorial, briefly visiting the Mill of Kintail and on to Montreal. Arthur S. Lamb, Director of the Physical Education Department at McGill University, later recalled:

On his last visit to Montreal, I was privileged to have Dr. McKenzie as a luncheon guest with some of his old Montreal friends. After lunch we visited the Montreal Art Gallery where his *Onslaught* holds a place of honour. We then adjourned to the home of Sir Andrew Macphail for afternoon tea.

They had been intimate friends from their undergraduate days and as they chatted about their experiences as room-mates—the hard-boiled landladies, the odd jobs they performed to supplement their incomes, the critical but kindly assessment of their teachers, and the practical jokes of the students of that era—I could only conclude that these two famous men were reliving the joyful and fascinating experiences of normal, mischievous boyhood.*

McKenzie had been trying to interest renowned orchestra leader Leopold Stokowski, then in Philadelphia and living in Rittenhouse Place, in pibroch music and had obtained lore from Scotland on the pibroch and sent it to him. Stokowski was trying to find a "good pair of Scottish bagpipes." In a letter accompanying the material McKenzie wrote: "I hope next summer you will have a chance to seriously look into what I think is a genuine and interesting type of folk music."

Tait McKenzie had long been interested in the folk arts and as far back as 1916 had been a member of the American Folk Dance Society, quite capable himself of turning in a good performance of such Scottish specialties as the Sword Dance. From the time the Folk Arts Center was established in New York City, he was on the governing board and also served as Vice-President. He was as well one of the first American artists to participate in the Center's activities. Despite the other pressures of the year of 1938, when the Canadian Folk Arts through cooperation of the Canadian government held an exhibition at the Folk Arts Center in New York in April, McKenzie attended pleased that Dr. Marius Barbeau, renowned authority on Indian and French-Canadian Folklore, was to lecture. Dr. Barbeau had collected folk songs of early French Canada for many years and for the occasion, brought along with him the best folk singer he knew, an old "habitant" farmer from Quebec. The unsophisticated farmer was dressed in rough clothing in contrast to the intellectuals who attended. He spoke only *patois* French but had an unlimited store of folk songs to more than illustrate Dr. Barbeau's talk. He also had a merry twinkle in his eye characteristic of the French-Canadian.

Following the lecture there was a reception attended by critics, the press and folk-lorists. A guest at the function later reported:

In the midst of the noise and chatter, I heard singing and there off by themselves in a corner were Dr. McKenzie and the farmer, each with their arms around each other's shoulders, their heads together, singing *En roulant my boule roulant* in complete understanding and companionship.*

Those who knew of Tait's heart condition must have been very alarmed but it was the sort of thing they might expect of him.

The annual meeting of the American Academy of Physical Education was held in Atlanta, Georgia on April 22nd. Again Dr. McKenzie was elected president and said on the occasion: "Well, this once more, but this is the last time." He was in excellent spirits after

*The Journal of Health and Physical Education: R. Tait McKenzie Memorial Issue, Vol. 15, #2, February 1944.
*Ibid.

DUKE KAHANAMOKU (unfinished) (1938) Last sculpture of Tait McKenzie. 12 inches high. Working model of Hawaiian Olympic swimming champion.

his Bahamas trip. His presidential statement reiterated his hopes and aspirations for the organization:

> The Academy should be something a little different from any other organization in physical education. Too many people are oppressed with the machinery of their work and miss the beauty of the finished product. The worker at the loom sees only the mechanics and never realizes the beauty of the completed pattern. We need a body that concerns itself with the ultimate pattern of what comes from the factory, letting others do some of the mechanical work if necessary. We need people not just to gather data and publish it, but to think through the results and their implications. We need a group that will make authoritative statements and be didactic about it. . .
>
> If we can bring about the discovery of one truth about physical education . . . the Academy will not have been found in vain. We may not be able to give material assistance to those working toward this end, but we can pay with the more valuable coin of appreciation and understanding to the workers in the field.*

The members presented him with an embossed Scroll in appreciation of his leadership and the seal designed for them. Dr. John Brown, Jr. in presenting the Scroll spoke of the high esteem in which they held McKenzie and their deep appreciation of his contributions and leadership in their field.

Following the convention, the McKenzies returned to Philadelphia. The following Thursday, April 28, 1938, the day was busy as usual. McKenzie worked in his studio all morning on the model for Kahanamoku, attended a board meeting, lunched at the Franklin Inn Club with friends, then later climbed four flights of stairs to an attic studio of a young sculptor who had asked for his criticism. He went home, phoned Ethel who was arranging a charity musicale for her club, and asked her if he could come over to meet her with the car at a downtown restaurant. He crossed the hall to call his chauffeur and "the summons came swift and sudden."

The following Saturday the annual Penn Relay Carnival was held at the hour of his funeral service. The flag waved at half mast on Franklin Field as an announcement was made to the contestants and spectators assembled:

> If you will look at the southwest corner of this field, by the building in front of which stands Tait McKenzie's statue of Benjamin Franklin, you will note that the colours are at half mast. They are thusly flown out of respect to a great man. It is fitting that on this, the day of Tait McKenzie's funeral, we should rise and by a moment's silence show our regard and affection for this renowned representative of the University of Pennsylvania who as sculptor, physician, educator and administrator knew, depicted and furthered, as few others, *the joy of effort* as exemplified by these Relay Games which he knew and loved so well.

Many thousands present rose and stood in silence with bowed heads. Then the carnival continued. "The last race was run. The final trophy won."

*Ibid.

Postscript

So wide was Dr. R. Tait McKenzie's influence in physical education, medicine, the arts, that hundreds of people felt a personal loss in his passing. The great and the humble alike mourned. Tributes poured into the McKenzie home on Pine Street by the hundreds. A few have been selected for publication here to show the esteem in which he was held. Over and over the same phrases were used to describe him both from friends and those who had met him casually: "His endearing qualities of humour, friendliness, and fairness."

It is unique that a man who achieved so much should incur more love than jealousy, and engender devotion in both friends and associates. He lived in a day when men were not ashamed to express their feelings. One such wrote to Mrs. McKenzie: "My heart cried when I got the news of Dr. McKenzie's death. I felt I had lost one of my wisest and truest friends." The same feeling was multiplied many times among others who knew him well. There were also those who knew him only by his works and from Scotland came a message to his brother, William at Cambridge, who passed it along to Ethel McKenzie, writing to her:

From Yetholm, a village near Kelso of which Mother talked to us when children, comes this tribute: 'The example of his mind, soul and life will never die as long as his memorial in the Gardens [Princess Street] lasts and who can judge the good it has done already in the minds of people. The loss is great to a country that needs such minds, but he has got a Higher Call and his work awaits him.'

Another telling tribute came from a newspaperman who reported:

I was reading the news story of the death of Dr. McKenzie when a stereotyper stopped beside me and said he had known Dr. McKenzie. He said that when he came to this country a green Swede boy, his first contact was with Dr. McKenzie who it seemed, took a great liking to him. He was taught a lot by the doctor and at times posed while the Doctor and a Mr. Mason sketched him and others for a type they desired for their work. . . . He said no matter when or where he met the Doctor he was always treated like a gentleman. He related several instances when he thought he did not amount to much and thought he had no friends, Dr. McKenzie had something worthwhile to tell him. . . . The man filled up when talking to me and his last remark was: "Mr. Kennedy, the only thing I can think of is 'May God bless him!'

From the State Capital at Harrisburg, Pennsylvania, came a

tribute that perhaps bears quotation in full. It is on the letterhead of the State Art Commission and dated April 29, 1938.

Dear Mrs. McKenzie:

When the news of your husband's sudden death came this morning, I frankly felt that the dart of the Dark Angel had hit the wrong man, for I might well have taken his place in that respect, being older and much more physically burdened than your great and very distinguished husband.

But I want to remember him because of his impregnable honesty and equally well-based kindliness. Great artist that he was, he was never severe with those whose poor work he was endeavouring to better. His promptness to render service, even at considerable sacrifice, was no small part of his very great value to the State in which he attained eminence not only as sculptor but as physician and as physical instructor.

In my hand as I write is his letter to his friend Dr. Laird, which it was my honor to hand to Governor Pinchot at the time of his [McKenzie's appointment to the State Art Commission] appointment. In that letter he expresses his feeling of gratitude to the United States, and particularly to Philadelphia, for the opportunities he so nobly developed, and expresses great pleasure that he has been able to do the things asked of him in the way of 'paying my debt to public service.'

But most of all I shall think of him as the kindly friend with the smile that always preceded a word of help.

While I could not but sympathize with you very deeply, I do feel like congratulating you on the way in which this great and useful life ended, without a long siege of pain and in the full fruition of noble work nobly done.

Yours very truly,

(sgd) J. Homer McFarland

Some wrote to Mrs. McKenzie citing works of sculpture yet to be done and regret that the master's hand would never manifest these works. Julian S. Myrick wrote from New York: "I am only one of the many that had the pleasure of meeting and knowing him in his various activities but I had a real affection for him and what he stood for and am only sorry he was not spared for many more years to complete the ever unfinished work which he had in mind. Dr. McKenzie was to have designed the Altar in the Sports Bay of the Cathedral of St. John the Divine but we never completed the funds so that he could do it and I had always wanted this Altar to be his work."

Archibald Campbell, his old Canadian friend and historian, wrote from Perth, Ontario, reiterating his 28-year friendship with McKenzie from the time he had met him at the Royal Academy exhibition in

London where McKenzie's *The Onslaught* was displayed, later meeting him in Ottawa, Montreal, and at the Mill of Kintail. He spoke of plans for further works of sculpture made by McKenzie:

> In Dr. McKenzie's letter to me, dated 13th October 1937, expressing regret at his inability to be present at the opening. . . of my museum [Historical Museum, Perth, Ontario] he remarked: 'We will have to take up the Mair memorial next year, if we have not acquired wings before that. I make short plans myself.' In replying I think that I said that I hoped that it would be a long time before either of us 'acquired wings'. Then in his letter of the 11th November last, Dr. McKenzie wound up saying: 'Next summer, if we are all in the land of the living, perhaps we can take up the question of the monument to Charles Mair [Canadian poet born at Lanark, Ontario not far from Almonte and the Mill of Kintail]. At that time I never dreamt that there was a likelihood of early passing but I fear that he even then had a premonition of what was to happen. . .

Sir Edward Peacock wrote from England:

> I loved him as almost my oldest and dearest friend. . . . Long separation seemed to make no difference. We always picked up the threads naturally when we met, just as if there had been no separation. Of course it is the man I think of—the best of him—a most lovable creature. To the world, of course, he will be the creative artist and unlike most of us, he has left much for the world to remember and admire. . .

Dr. Charles Wilson wrote from Bremner, Alta., expressing his sympathy to Mrs. McKenzie and naming another commitment of sculpture planned for McKenzie:

> It is only a week or two ago since I saw my sister-in-law, the woman senator of Canada [Senator Cairine Wilson] passing through here and fulfilled a request of Tait's to have her sit for him when he visited Ottawa this summer for a bust of her as the first woman senator of Canada, which she assented to. . . . I am more than grieved to learn of his death for we were old house-mates in Montreal.

Dr. McKenzie had long since instructed his lawyer, Sam Scoville of Philadelphia, whom he called his "oldest and dearest friend," as to his funeral arrangements. He had requested that upon his death, his heart was to be removed from his body under direction of his family doctor, Dr. William D. Stroud, and "delivered to him so that he may confirm or otherwise his diagnosis of my case and complete his record." It was such a request as a medical man might be expected to make. He further requested that his heart be delivered to the Scottish-American Memorial Association, taken to Scotland and buried near his favourite work, *The Call*, in Princess Street Gardens, Edinburgh. This was not as orthodox. His body, he further requested, was to be cremated and if possible interred in the British Officers Plot of Northwood Cemetery in Philadelphia.

Investigation of his wish for burial in Princess Gardens revealed that regulations prohibited such an act, but permission was eventually granted by St. Cuthbert's Parish Church nearby for burial in their churchyard.

His close friend, Dr. Norman Henry, then President of the St. Andrews Society of Philadelphia Memorial Association, travelled to Scotland to fulfill McKenzie's wish. On September 7th, the annual memorial services were held at the Scottish-American War Memorial and on the same day the heart of R. Tait McKenzie was buried in the south-east corner of the St. Cuthbert's churchyard within sight of his favourite work, *The Call.* His monogram *RTM* inscribed on a stone of the church is all that marks his burial.

The Scotsman magazine reported:

> The burial service was simple and brief. Lord Provost Sir Louis S. Gumley, His Grace the Duke of Atholl, K.T., Dr. J. Norman Henry, President of the Scottish-American Association of the United States of America, and Mr. E.M. Campbell, W.S. acted as pallbearers. The casket of dark polished oak with silver mountings for the white cords was reverently lowered into the grave which was lined with ivy and privet leaves.

> . . . Four wreaths were placed on the grave. They were from Mrs. Tait McKenzie. . . . The Franklin Inn Club of Philadelphia, Dr. and Mrs. Norman Henry, and Lochiel and Hermione Cameron of Lochiel, 'in remembrance of a very happy friendship.'

> Among those present were Lady Gumley, the Lady Provost, the Marchioness of Aberdeen, the Marquess of Ailsa, Mrs. Norman Henry, Mr. C.R. Nasmith, the American Consul, and the Rev. Dr. Alexander MacMillan, Toronto, a friend of Dr. Tait McKenzie for forty years.*

The British Officers Club with whom he had associated, requested permission to engrave his name on their "Cross of Sacrifice" in Northwood Cemetery "because he identified himself so closely with ex-servicemen and with their joys and sorrows," but his ashes were not buried there, but later shipped to Scotland. Memorial services were held both at St. Peter's Episcopal Church in Philadelphia and at Almonte, Ontario, the home of his childhood.

At the 16th Annual Meeting and Scientific Session of the Academy of Physical Medicine held October 24-26, 1938, a special exhibition of his bronzes—*The Flying Sphere, The Sprinter, The Athlete, The Ice Bird, The Modern Discus Thrower,* and *Unvanquished*-was included in the program. Mrs. McKenzie carried on as Honorary Chairman for the Social Program for the visiting ladies.

In a broadcast on the Academy meeting over the Radio Station WOL in October, "The Chesapeake Bay Philosopher" said, after discussing inventions in medicine and other matters related to the work of the Academy:

The Scotsman, September 8, 1938.

There is a very human and admirable touch to this year's Academy meeting. One of their late presidents was a physician named Dr. Tait McKenzie. He was a medical man. He was always eager to examine new developments. He never got his feet stuck fast in yesterday as one of our modern poets puts it. But he never got his mind stuck between the pages of textbooks and the trade journals of medicine either. Sometimes I wish every doctor in the country could be made to see that some self-expression outside his professional interests—writing about old china—studying architecture—or playing some instrument in concerts—would do as much for him as some of things he does for us. . .

Dr. McKenzie expressed himself as a sculptor and as a very fine artist in that medium. . .

Dr. McKenzie's death, a few days after the close of the Atlanta Convention of the American Physical Education Association, in which he had taken an active part, was a great shock to thousands involved with physical education. The Association soon formed a committee to arrange a suitable memorial to the man who had once been their president and who had worked so long for the elevation of physical education "to the place of dignity which it held in the Golden era of Athens."

World War II intervened but contributions poured in from personal friends, medical associates, fellow artists, students in the United States and in other countries. The committee purchased *The Column of Youth* from the McKenzie estate, had it reproduced in creme Alabama statuary marble and arranged to present it to the National Education Association to be placed in the headquarters building in Washington. Subscribers were presented with bronze copies of McKenzie's medallion *The Joy of Effort.*

The Column of Youth was unveiled on Saturday, December 13, 1947. McKenzie's life-long friend and associate, Dr. Jay B. Nash, reviewed McKenzie's life and career and said in part:

This column is tangible evidence of the high esteem accorded Dr. McKenzie in physical education. Those of us who were privileged to sit with him at tea or stand in his studio on Pine Street in Philadelphia felt deeply his warm spirit of friendship. In committee meetings, his scientific thinking was always helpful. However, it was at the banquet table, at forum discussions, watching a track meet or a sunset, with small groups of his intimate friends, that his words and sparkling personality gave 'wings and fire' to creative aspirations*

A plaque hung on the wall to the right of the statue reads:

A memorial to R. Tait McKenzie—artist, physician, teacher—was conceived by the American Association for Health, Physical Education and Recreation to perpetuate the memory of their former president, who as a physical educator brought great honour to the profession, and as a

*Journal of Health and Physical Education, Vol. 19, #2, February 1948.

sculptor won international acclaim. 'The Column of Youth' a study of the typical college youth was selected for the Memorial because it symbolizes much of his work. The original column was produced in marble by Louis Milione.

Dedicated December 13, 1947.*

As a man, R. Tait McKenzie had a wide influence. Joe Brown who worked in his studio at the time of his death, recalls that he was as proficient at handling people as in handling clay, and he had a knack for bringing out the best in a student.

A New York city sculptor said of McKenzie: "He was very helpful to me in regard to my work and he was an inspiration to every young artist, as the very embodiment of what a sculptor and a great gentleman should be."

Hector MacQuarrie wrote from England: "I recall all he did for me, how he pointed to the artist and said: 'Be one!' and I have never written a sentence without thinking of him and trying very hard."

A Philadelphian Harold D. Eberlein said once. "I have never known Tait to say an unkind or uncharitable word about anyone—even when there was ample provocation—and I have known him to do many kind things quietly and unobtrusively."*

Elizabeth Pitt, a cousin, recalls how he set her on a course for a career in physical education when few women were in the field. Following courses in Swedish and Danish gymnastics, she secured a position as a physical education instructor at the fashionable ladies college, Bryn Mawr. The McKenzies provided her with a key to their house in Philadelphia where the attic bedroom was hers whenever she chose to come over from the college for a weekend. She later taught phys ed for the Y.W.C.A. in Toronto.

Once Tait McKenzie wrote: 'Fifty percent of the value of being right is to be right at the right time." He was a man of his time and in the right place at the right time. With the revival of the Olympic Games in the late 19th Century, the Western world was ripe for structured physical education and for sculpture idolizing the perfect athlete, *after his kind* or according to the sport portrayed.

Francis Fisher Dubuc once wrote an article on McKenzie entitled: "A Sculptor of Soldiers and Athletes" which points out rather well the reason for McKenzie's success:

> His soldiers and athletes are never alien or impersonal. One senses the joy of accomplishment, the consciousness of duty well performed, of victories won, by the silent eloquence of their plastic energy expressing the spirit of the man, his deep convictions and intense emotionalism beneath the mask of his Scotch reserve. His work embodies the spirit of our times; the sentiment expressed is always tempered and strengthened by realism, a realism that never impinges upon that underlying and unmistakable principle of true beauty which is inherent and endures

*Ibid.

regardless of popular belief or criticism. His technique is subordinated to sentiment, but these qualities are quite distinct and sentiment after all, is the most important consideration in a work of art. 'It is life and soul,' says Sir Joshua Reynolds 'and without it, a work of art is a dead letter—technique is secondary.'

It is an artist's duty and privilege to give permanency to things that others feel but cannot express,' said Dr. McKenzie to the writer. 'Before anything I want to give something people can understand and sympathize with, not merely clever studies of anatomy or classic compositions of a person buried beneath the dust of centuries. . . . There is as much sentiment in a Kakhi uniform as in a Roman toga or suit of armor—more in fact, for this day and generation and for those who will come after us.'. . .

While his work has often been compared to the athletic art of the Greeks, it is in none of its manifold forms pseudo classic, but rather a genuine expression of our present day civilization. Tait McKenzie's art will live.*

Of his sculpture, Alfred Petrie, former curator of the National Medal Collection, Public Archives of Canada, considers that McKenzie's was unique and cannot be compared with other sculptors, contemporary or earlier ones. In modelling Olympic athletes, the classical Greek sculptors portrayed the fashionable proportions of the day while McKenzie in a later era portrayed the actual according to the sport depicted. Because he ignored the fashion in sculpture of his day, Mr. Petrie thinks any comparison with McKenzie's contemporaries odious. In examining McKenzie's work from another angle, one must consider that he had an abundance of fine physical specimens to choose from as models, whereas the average sculptor, outside the field of physical education, does not have this choice of selection.

Of his medals, Mr. Petrie remarked that again, in designing athletic medals or medallions, McKenzie stuck to actual proportions or the ideal according to physical education statistics in contrast to athletic medal design of today where the trend is toward big-muscle athletes. Mr. Petrie observed some change in McKenzie's work from *The Joy of Effort* period to later work such as *The Punters,* modelled in the late 1930s, the latter being more stylized and higher in relief. He considers McKenzie's war memorial statue of Capt. Guy Drummond in the Public Archives of Canada Collection, as being one of the finest memorial work.

R. Tait McKenzie's art lives on, such medallions as *The Joy of Effort,* and the Olympic Shield continuing as awards to the present time. Two of McKenzie's athletic bronzes, *The Plunger* and *The Sprinter*, were chosen by the Canada Post Office for commemorative stamps marking Canada's hosting the Olympic Games in 1976. That year The Olympic Travelling Sports Art Exhibition included representative works of his athletic sculpture.

---

*F.F. Dubuc: "A Sculptor of Soldiers and Athletes," *Arts and Decoration*. Date unknown.

He himself said he could see no hope of immortality for man except through art, but Rosalind Cassidy of the American Academy of Physical Education, thought of yet another way for him when she said of him: "in his great genius and art in human relationships he is one of the Immortals."

APPENDIX

Major Collections of Sculpture by Robert Tait McKenzie

Lloyd P. Jones Gallery, Gimbell Gymnasium, University of Pennsylvania, Walnut Street at 37th Street, Philadelphia 19104

1. *Modern Discus Thrower,* bronze statue
2. *The Eight,* bronze statue
3. *The Plunger,* bronze statue
4. *Brothers of the Wind,* plaster frieze
5. *Masks of Expression,* 4 heads, bronze
    Effort
    Fatigue
    Exhaustion
    Breathlessness
6. *Football Kickoff,* plaster
7. *The Joy of Effort,* bronze
8. *Crawford C. Madeira,* bronze portrait plaque, from Mrs. Crawford C. Madeira.
9. *Lord Burghley (Olympic Hurdler),* plaster plaque
10. *Olympic Shield,* plaster. 60'' diameter
11. *The Punters,* bronze medallion
12. *Radiance,* bronze medallion. On loan from Mr. and Mrs. Robert Glascott.
13. *Relay,* plaster medallion
14. *Relay Carnival,* bronze medallion
15. *Scottish American Memorial "The Recruiting Party",* plaster and wood frieze
16-17 *Society of Medalists Medal,* Bronze. Obverse side "Strength", and reverse side "Speed."
18. *J. William White,* portrait in the round, bronze and wood.
19. *Athlete* statue. Bronze
20. *Aviator,* plaster statue
21. *Boxer,* bronze statue
22. *Competitor,* bronze statue
23. *Capt. Guy Drummond,* plaster statue
24. *Flying Sphere,* bronze statue
25. *Ice Bird,* bronze statue
26. *Invictus,* bronze statue

27. *Robert H. Michelet,* plaster statue
28. *The Onslaught,* bronze group statue
29. *Pole Vaulter,* bronze statue
30. *Relay,* bronze statue
31. *Standing Athlete,* bronze statue
32. *Supple Juggler,* bronze statue
33. *Triumph of Wings,* bronze statue
34. *Youthful Franklin,* bronze statue
35. American Physical Education Association medal, copper 10″ diameter.
36. Athletic awards won by Lloyd P. Jones.
37. *William Carr No 1,* bronze statue
38. *William Carr No 2,* bronze statue
39. *Champion* (D.G. Lowe) bronze statue
40. *Cleaning Shoe,* bronze statue
41. *Diver,* bronze statue
42. *Grotesque #2,* bronze
43. *Handball Player,* bronze statue
44. *Poet Roy Helton,* bronze portrait medallion
45. *High Jumper Cleaning Shoe,* bronze statue
46. *The Loop,* bronze
47. Medals: gold-plated bronze for:
    Swimming
    Golf
    Tennis
    Track and Field
    Wrestling
    Fencing
    Gulick Award
    A.L.M.B.
    A.L.M.G.
    Oxford
    Cambridge
    Brothers of the Wind
    Joy of Effort
48. *Modern Discus,* statue
49. *Relay Runner #1,* bronze statue
50. *Safe at First,* plaster
51. *Shot Put Grotesque,* bronze statue
52. *Shot Put Hop,* bronze statue
53. *Shot Put Preparing,* bronze statue
54. *Shot Put Ready,* bronze statue
55. *Shot Put Resting,* bronze statue
56. *Sprinter,* bronze statue
57. *Sullivan Award,* gold-plated bronze medallion
58. *Taking Count,* plaster
59. *Head-on Tackle,* bronze
60. *Tackle,* bronze
61. *Upright Discus Thrower,* bronze statue

62. *Watching Pole Vault,* bronze statue
63. *Winded,* bronze statue
64. *Wounded,* bronze statue
65. *Winner,* bronze statue
66. *Wrestlers,* bronze
67. *Head of R. Tait McKenzie,* bronze bust, life size, by Joe Brown (on loan from Joe Brown)
68. Oil Portrait of R. Tait McKenzie by Maurice Molarsky.
69. *Line Play,* plaster relief (from Percy D. Haughton Memorial)
70. *Punt,* plaster relief, (from Percy D. Haughton Memorial)
71. *Candlesticks,* 12'' bronze
72. *Clarence S. Bayne, Class of 1895,* plaster relief
73. *Ellwood Charles Rutschman* (Father of Penn Basketball). bronze medallion. Gift from John Munzi and Jack Shapiro.
74. *American Academy of Physical Education medal.* Bronze seal
75. *Sesquincentennial medallion,* bronze sports medal. Gift from R. Mifflin Hood.
76. *Relay Runners,* bronze medal. Gift from R. Mifflin Hood.
77. *William Patrick McKenzie,* plaster bust
78. *Wisconsin Palman Qui Mervit Ferat,* bronze plaque
79. *Fencing Club of Philadelphia medal*
80. *Winter Sports,* White metal frieze
81. *Blighty,* bronze statue, on loan from Professor and Mrs. Philip Ruff.
82. *John McClure Hamilton,* bronze portrait medallion
83. *Hector MacQuarrie,* bronze portrait medallion
84. *Miss Katherine Clark.* Bronze medallion
85. *Frederic Wolle,* bronze medallion
86. *Arthur E. Shipley,* plaster medallion painted bronze colour
87. *Ethel O'Neil,* stone plaque
88. *Lenape Club medal.* Bronze
89. *Jacobs Bond.* Bronze-coloured plaster portrait medallion
90. *The Boy Scout,* Bronze statue, On loan from the Philadelphia Council, Boy Scouts of America.

"The Mill of Kintail" Collection of R. Tait McKenzie Sculpture, The Mill of Kintail, R.R. 3, Almonte, Ontario.

1. *The Sprinter,* — plaster figure in the round
2. *The Athlete,* — white plaster statuette
3. *The Skater* — plaster relief plaque
4. *Brothers of the Wind* — original working model, white plaster, relief plaque.
5. *Brothers of the Wind* — bronze relief plaque replica
6. *The Joy of Effort* — small bronze medallion
7. *Laughing Athlete* — bronze statuette
8. *Tumbler* — bronze nude youth with outstretched legs
9. *Tumbler* — bronze nude youth with bent knees and arms

10. *Shield of Athletes* — full-size original plaster medallion
11. *The Call* — full-size main figure for Scottish-American War Memorial. Bronzed plaster
12. *The Marching Scots* — Original full-size background frieze for Scottish-American War Memorial. Bronzed plaster.
13. *General Wolfe* — original working model, polychrome plaster statue
14. *The Boy Scout* — 3-inch copper and plastic trophy
15. *The Home-Coming* — bronzed plaster original sketch for monument statue in Cambridge, England
16. *Dorothy B. at Sixteen* — plaster, polychrome relief portrait
17. *Doctor S. Weir Mitchell* — bronzed plaster plaque
18. *Hector MacQuarrie* — bronze plaque
19. *Sir Edward Wentworth Beatty, K.C.* — bronzed plaster bust
20. *Christopher Hussey* — bronze plaque
21. *Edward and John* (Fernberger children) — bronze circular plaque
22. *Walt Whitman* — bronze medallion
23. *George Frederick Scott* — plaster negative mould of portrait plaque
24. *Ethel O'Neil McKenzie* — concrete relief portrait plaque
25. *Sir Edward Peacock* — bronze relief plaque
26. *Kathleen Parlow* — polychrome plaster plaque
27. *W.P. McKenzie* — life-size bust, bronze
28. *Mother and Father* (McKenzie) — original small plaster relief sketch for medallion for memorial bench
29. *Pelham Edgar* — plaster relief plaque
30. *Canadian Confederation Jubilee Memorial* — plaster original working model of memorial in Parliament Buildings, Ottawa
31. *Canadian Confederation Jubilee Memorial,* Alternative — plaster sketch design
32. *University of Pennsylvania Bi-Centenary Medal* — bronze relief medallion
33. *Grotesque Candle Stick* — statuette
34. *Sun Dial* — South Face
35. *Sun Dial* — West Face
36. *Award for Distinguished Service to Canadian Mineral Industry* — lead medallion, obverse side
37. *Award for Distinguished Service to Canadian Mineral Industry* — lead medallion, reverse side
38. *American Academy of Physical Education Award* — plaster plaque
39. *Award for Distinguished Service to Canadian Mineral Industry* — negative mould of reverse side
40. *Society of Mathematicians Medal* — bronze-coated medallion. reverse side
41. *Society of Mathematicians Medal* — bronze medallion, obverse side
42. *University of Pennsylvania Bi-Centenary Medal* — bronze medallion

43. *R. Tait McKenzie, Surgeon* — white plaster bust by Joe Brown
44. *R. Tait McKenzie, Physical Educator* — bronzed plaster bust by Joe Brown
45. *R. Tait McKenzie, Sculptor* — white plaster bust by Joe Brown
46. *Trial Design for Canada 50¢ Piece* — pencil on plaster
47. *Trial Mould for Canadian Coin* — plaster
48. *Negative Mould for Canada 50¢ Piece*
49. *Positive Mould for Canada 50¢ Piece*

The College of Physicians of Philadelphia Collection of R. Tait McKenzie Sculpture, Medals and Badges.

1. *Bust of R. Tait McKenzie,* plaster, by Joe Brown.
2. Four studies in bronze of the progress of fatigue in athletes, showing "Effort," "Dyspnoea", "Fatigue", Exhaustion.
3. *The Athlete,* bronze statue.
4. *Head of Aesculapius,* Mary Ellis Bell Prize Medal for Undergraduate Medical Research, bronze.
5. *Dr. William Wood Gerhard* medal, bronze. The Gerhard medal of the Pathological Society of Philadelphia.
6. *Dr. Dudley Allen Sargent,* bronze medal.
7. *Florence Nightingale-Saunders* bronze medal.
8. *American Association of Anatomists 50-Year Medal* portrait medallion of Professor Joseph Leidy.
9. *Dr. Crawford Williamson Long,* Portrait medallion showing Dr. Long administering ether to a patient.
10. *Dr. Francis Kinloch Huger.* Reduced replica of bronze portrait medallion in Medical Hall of the University of Pennsylvania
11. *College of Physicians of Philadelphia Medal.* Bronze.
12. *University of Pennsylvania Bicentennial Medal.* Bronze
13. *Henry H. Donaldson, Ph.D., M.D..* Bronze portrait plaque.
14. *Dr. William Henry Drummond,* bronze portrait medallion.
15. *Dr. Sir Wilfred T. Grenfell.* Portrait medallion.
16. *Dr. Chevalier Jackson.* Bronze medallion.
17. *Sir Robert Jones,* bronze portrait medallion.
18. *Dr. William Keen.* Reduction from original portrait plaque modelled from life on half-size scale. Life-sized bronze in the Library of Brown University.
19. *Sir Arthur Keith.* Bronze medallion.
20. *Dr. Silas Weir Mitchell.* Portrait medallion sketch in plaster.
21. *Dr. Horatio Robinson Storer.* Bronze portrait medallion.
22. *Relay Carnival of the University of Pennsylvania.* Large plaque showing Benjamin Franklin in a chair shaking hands with first of four members of a relay team.
23. *Rejoice: O Young Man in Thy Youth.* Medal of male figure throwing ball. Bronze.
24. *Joy of Effort* medallion.
25. *University of Pennsylvania badge:* reduction of Bicentennial medal.

Public Archives of Canada, National Medal Collection

1. *J.R. Sinnock's 1967 Struck Medal* commemorating the Centenary of Dr. Robert Tait McKenzie's birth. Features McKenzie's profile head.
2. Series of seven Medallic Awards given by the Intercollegiate Conference of Athletic Associations (I.C.A.A.) to athletes of mid-western U.S. universities:
    ICAA Award for Fencing
    ICAA Award for Golf
    ICAA Award for Gymnastics
    ICAA Award for Swimming
    ICAA Award for Tennis
    ICAA Award for Track (Running)
    ICAA Award for Wrestling
3. *The Punters.* 3 inch diameter medallion
4. Galvano of above. 18 inch diameter
5. *The Joy of Effort.* 3 inch diameter medallion
6. Galvano of above. 18 inch diameter
7. *Brothers of the Wind.* 5 inch medallic plaque
8. Galvano of above. 40-½ inches long
9. *The Society of Medalists* medal. Shot-putter on obverse and runners on reverse. 2-⅞ inch diameter
10. International Nickel Company (INCO) *Nickel Award Medal* for distinguished service to the Canadian Mineral Industry. Obverse design features "Vulcan" and a miner; reverse is of a beaver. 3 inch diameter.
11. *Archibald Lampman,* portrait medallion. 11-¾ inch diameter
12. *Robert Barr,* portrait medallion. 8-⅞ x 10-⅞ inches diameter
13. *Shield of Athletes* (or Olympic Shield). Galvano. 18 inches diameter
14. *Wilfred Campbell,* portrait plaque. 11 inch diameter. From Mackenzie King Collection
15. Montreal Intercollegiate Winter Sports Union Awards to William Ball. Design features speed skater. 2-⅛ inch diameter medallion.
    Awarded to Dr. Ball for:Cross-Country Skiing-1928,1931,1933;
    Ski Jump — 1929, 1932;
    Combined Event 1933;
    Downhill Ski Racing 1934.
    From Dr. William Ball Collection.
16. *Capt. Guy Drummond.* Memorial Statue. Bronze. 42 inches high. Acquired for the Public Archives by Dr. Arthur Doughty, Dominion Archivist.

The Joseph B. Wolffe Collection of R. Tait McKenzie Sculpture, The University of Tennessee, Knoxville 37916, Tennessee.

1. *Column of Youth*

2. *The Sprinter*
3. *The Supple Juggler*
4. R. Tait McKenzie Portrait by Sidney March
5. *Tait McKenzie* Portrait by Boris Blai
6. *Tait McKenzie* Portrait by Joe Brown
7. *The Pole Vaulter*
8. *Wounded*
9. *Winded*
10. *William Carr,* Portrait Sketch
11. *Grotesque,* Why Not #1, Shot Putter
12. *Grotesque,* Why Not #2, Boxer
13. *Upright Discus Thrower*
14. *Relay Runner #1*
15. *William Carr,* Full Stride Sketch
16. *High Jumper Cleaning Shoes*
17. *Sprinter,* Small, Copy of No. 2.
18. *Shot Putter, Resting*
19. *Shot Putter, Preparing*
20. *Shot Putter, Hop*
21. *The Lenape Club Medal*
22. *Walt Whitman* (Franklin Inn Club) medal
23. *The Aesculapius Medal*
24. *The National Junior Forum Award medal*
25. Souvenir, R. Tait McKenzie medal
26. *The Punters,* medallion
27. *Buzzie,* medallion
28. *Mazzie,* medallion
29. *Sesquicentennial Sports Medal* (Philadelphia)
30. *Playground Association Medal* (Ariston)
31. *Playground Association Medal* (Level One)
32. *Public School Athletic League* (New York) medal
33. *ICAA Track and Field medal*
34. *Amherst Pratt Pool medal*
35. *Society of Medalists medal*
36. *Skating Club of New York medal*
37. *Bicentennial medal of University of Pennsylvania*
38. *Joseph Leidy (Anatomists) medal*
39. *Forbes-Robertson as Julius Caesar* portrait medallion
40. *Buzzie* (Charles Harrison Frazier) portrait medallion
41. *Mazie,* (Frazier) portrait medallion
42. *William Cornelius Covenhoven Van Horne,* child portrait medallion
43. *Viscountess Folkstone,* portrait medallion
44. *Horatio R. Storer,* Medical Numismatist, portrait plaque
45. *Grant Mitchell,* actor, portrait medallion
46. *The Joy of Effort,* medallion
47. *Pennsylvania Relays medallion*
48. *Brothers of the Wind,* plaque
49. *Paul Dougherty,* painter, medallion

50. *ICAA Swimming medal*
51. *ICAA Wrestling medal*
52. *ICAA Tennis medal*
53. *ICAA Golf, medal*
54. *ICAA, Fencing medal*
55. *ICAA Gymnastics, medal*
56. *Passing the Baton* medallion
57. *Eugene Paul Ullman* medallion
58. *Discobolus,* Plaque #1
59. *Discobolus,* Plaque #2
60. *International Nickel Company medal*
61. *Mathematics Award*
62. *John R. Sinnock* (portrait by R. Tait McKenzie) medallion
63. *R. Tait McKenzie* (portrait by John R. Sinnock) medallion
64. *The Joy of Effort,* Springfield College award
65. *American Legion Award,* Girls medal
66. *American Legion Award,* Boys medal
67. *ICAA Scholarships medal*
68. *U.G.I. 50th Anniversary medal* (Philadelphia)
69. *Walter Burns Saunders* (Florence Nightingale) medal
70. *Edward Longstreth* (The Franklin Institute of Invention) medal
71. *William James Young* portrait medallion
72. *The Chancellor's medal* (University of Buffalo)
73. *William Wood Gerhard* (The Philadelphia Pathological Society) medal
74. *The Winner*

Yale University Art Gallery, 111 Chapel Street, New Haven, Conn.

1. *The Onslaught*
2. *The Pole Vaulter*
3. *The Icebird*
4. *The Joy of Effort*
5. *The Javelin Cast*
6. *The Upright Discus Thrower*
7. *The Modern Discus Thrower*
8. *Shot Putter*
9. *The Flying Sphere*
10. *The Competitor*
11. *The Plunger*
12. *The Relay*
13. *The Sprinter*
14. *The Athlete*

Affiliations:

Fellow, Royal Canadian Institute

Fellow, American Medical Association
Fellow, College of Physicians of Philadelphia
Fellow and President (at time of death), American Academy of Physical Education
President (at time of death), Academy of Physical Medicine
President, American Physical Education Association, 1913-14-15
President, Society of Directors of Physical Education in Colleges, 1912
Vice-President, Collegiate Society of Gymnasium Directors
Vice-President, American Folk Dance Society, New York City

Member of:

State Art Commission of Pennsylvania (at time of death)
The Art Alliance of Philadelphia (at time of death)
English-Speaking Union, Philadelphia (at time of death)
St. Andrew's Society of Philadelphia (at time of death)
National Sculpture Society (at time of death)
Franklin Inn Club, Philadelphia (at time of death)
Athenaeum Club (London, England) (at time of death)
Author's Club (London, England) (at time of death)
Society of Medalists (at time of death)
Philadelphia Academy of Fine Arts
Royal Academy, London, England
Royal Canadian Academy
Rittenhouse Club, Philadelphia
Charaka Club, New York City
Century Club, New York City
University of Pennsylvania Club

Also a member of standing committees in physical education, sculpture, in Philadelphia and elsewhere.

Editor of a series of textbooks on physical education.

Honorary Degrees:

McGill University, LL.D., 1921
University of Pennsylvania, A.E.D., 1928
St. Andrews University, St. Andrews, Scotland, LL.D., 1938.

Founders of the Society of College Gymnasium Directors

Charles Stroud, Tufts; F.H. Cann, New York University; Dr. James A. Babbitt, Haverford; Dr Caspar Miller, University of Pennsylvania; Mr. George Velta, Trinity; Dr. W.G. Anderson, Yale; Dr. Watson L. Savage, Columbia University; Dr. R. Tait McKenzie, McGill University, Montreal; Mr. George Goldie, Princeton University; Dr. Dudley A. Sargent, Harvard University; Dr. Edward Hitchcock, Amherst College; Dr. J.W. Seaver, Yale University; Dr. Cummings, Swarthmore; Dr. W.A. Bowler, Bates; Dr. Paul C. Phillips, Amherst College; Dr. G.W. Banning, Colgate.

Founding Fathers of The American Academy of Physical Education (1930) 29 members.

Clark W. Hetherington, R. Tait McKenzie, M.D., William Burdick, M.D.; Thomas Storey, M.D; Jay B. Nash, Ph.D., Carl Schrader; J.H. McCurdy, M. Howard Braucher; Amy Homans; William Stecher, M.D.; E.H. Arnold; George Meylan, M.D.; Jesse F. Williams, M.D.; William LaPorte; C.W. Savage; John F. Bovard, Ph.D; Paul C. Phillips, M.D.; A.S. Lamb, M.D.; F.R. Rogers, Ph.D.; John Brown, M.D.; J. Anna Norris, M.D.; E.C. Schneider, Ph.D.; Elmer D. Mitchell; C.H. McCloy, Ph.D.; Elizabeth Burchinal; Arthur H. Steinhaus, Ph.D.

*Short Biographical Sketch of Mrs. R. Tait McKenzie**

Nee: Ethel O'Neil. Poet, pianist, lecturer. B. Hamilton, d. John Hamilton and Hannah (MacGowan) O'Neil; educated, Hamilton Collegiate Institute, Hamilton Conservatory of Music, studied piano with private teachers in New York and Berlin; married Dr. R. Tait McKenzie at Chapel Royal, Dublin, Ireland, August 18, 1907 (Died April 28,1938). Followed profession as concert pianist in America and abroad; teacher and head of department of music in Science Hill School, Shelbyville, Kentucky; appointed advisor to Tait KcKenzie collection of bronzes, University of Pennsylvania 1939; lecturer on ancient musical instruments. Member: Daughters of the British Empire (recently William Blake Chapter), Society of Ancient Musical Instruments, Animal Rescue League, Art Alliance, Poetry Society of America. Honorary member: Art, Contemporary Faculty Clubs. Presented to Court of St. James, 1927; King George and Queen Elizabeth, 1937; 1939; Episcopalian. Clubs: Acorn, Sedgley (Philadelphia); Garden, Sesame (London). Author: *Secret Snow* (book of verse) 1932; *Angel Musicians* 1928. Contributed biography of Jessie Wilcox Smith to *Philadelphia Golden Book 1937;* Catalogue Tait McKenzie Collection, University of Pennsylvania, 1939. D. 1952. Buried in St. Peters Episcopal Church Cemetery, Philadelphia.

*Most of this information from: *Who's Who in Pennsylvania,* edited and compiled under direction of Albert Nelson Marquis, Vol 1. (1939), the A.N. Marquis Company, Chigago.

CHRONOLOGICAL LIST OF WORKS IN SCULPTURE BY R. TAIT MCKENZIE

Before
1902:   Tentative works in low relief
Two plaques of Speed Skaters, about 8 × 12 inches. (One currently in Mill of Kintail Collection)
Medallion portrait, *The Mother*, 12 inch. Plaster patinate. *Four Masks*, life size, illustrating violent effort and the progress of fatigue. First described before the International Congress on Physical Education, Paris, 1900: published with description in *Journal of Anatomy*, England, October 1905. Since then greatly revised and described in *Exercise in Education and Medicine* (W.B. Saunders). Set of the masks in the Museum of Royal College of Surgeons, London, England; Anatomical Department, Cambridge University; and Medical Museum, McGill University, Montreal, Canada.

1902:   *The Sprinter,* bronze statuette, 1/4 life size. Completed after three years work. Modelled from average measurements of one hundred sprinters, showing typical sprinter in typical crouching start, then recently introduced. Shown at Society of American Artists, 1902; Royal Academy, London, 1903; Salon, Paris, 1904. Copies in Fitzwilliam Museum, Cambridge, England, and many private collections. Used as Intercollegiate Trophy (Track and Field) in Canada, and elsewhere.

1903:   *The Athlete,* bronze statuette, 1/4 life size. Modelled from the average of four hundred Harvard students, the fifty strongest taken over a period of eight years. First shown at Paris Salon, 1903; Royal Academy, London, 1904; Roman Art Exposition, Rome, 1911. Copies in the Ashmolean Museum, Oxford, England; Museum of Natural History, New York; Toronto Art Gallery and Osler Library, McGill University, Canada; and in many private collections. First copy owned by Society of Directors of Physical Education in Colleges.
Archibald Lampman, bronze bas-relief portrait. 12-inch; galvano reduction 2 inch. Trinity College, Toronto, Canada.

1904:   *Jeffrey Macphail,* bronze bas-relief, 12 × 16 inches. Galvano reduction 2 inches high.
Dorothy B (Browne), bronze bas-relief portrait, 12-inch diameter. Shown in Paris Salon, 1904. Galvano reduction 2 inch.

1905:   *Robert Barr* (Novelist), bronze, bas-relief portrait, 8 × 12 inches. Galvano reduction 2 inches.
Wistfulness, bronze medallion of Stuart Guilford McKenzie (nephew). 2-inches Galvano reduction 1 inch. Originally owned by William P. McKenzie, Cambridge, Mass.
Discobolus No. 1. and No. 2, 4 × 7 inches.
The Boxer, bronze statuette, 1/4 life size. Shown at the Society of American Artists Show in 1906. In private collections.

1906:   *The Supple Juggler,* bronze statuette, 1/4 life size. Shown at the Royal Academy, London, England, 1908; Paris Salon, 1909; Roman

Art Exposition, 1911. Acquired by Metropolitan Museum, New York, and private collections.

The Competitor, bronze statuette, 1/2 life size. Shown at Paris Salon, 1907. Acquired by Metropolitan Museum of Art, New York; National Gallery, Canada; Springfield College, Mass.; and in private collections.

Wilfred Campbell (poet), bas-relief portrait, 12-inch diameter. Galvano reduction 2 inches. Set in a memorial bench of granite in Beechwood Cemetery, Ottawa, Canada. Original owned by Mrs. Campbell

Maizie and Buzzie, two portrait medallions of children, 8-inch diameter. Galvano reduction 2 inches and 1-inch. Originally owned by Dr. C.H. Frazier, Philadelphia, Pa.

Public School Athletic League Medal, 1-1/4 inches. For New York City. Reproductions in bronze, silver, or gold.

1907:   *Dr. William Henry Drummond* (poet). Bas-relief portrait, 12 inch dia. Galvano reduction 2 inches. Original in Western Hospital, Montreal. Reductions — Harvard University and other collections.

Forbes-Robertson as Caesar, bas-relief portrait. 9-inch diameter. Galvano reduction 2 inches.

Gertrude Elliott as Cleopatra, bas-relief portrait. 9-inch diameter. Galvano reduction 2 inches.

Charles Wharton Stork (poet) bas-relief portrait, 9-inch diameter. Galvano reduction 2 inches. Originally owned by Dr. Stork.

Dudley Allen Sargent, bas-relief portrait, 12-inch diameter. Medal reduction 2 inches. Owned by the Alumni Association of The Sargent School of Physical Education. Medal struck to commemorate 25 years of service.

1908:   *Amie Hampton Clark,* bas-relief portrait, 10-inch diameter. Owned by Mrs. C. Howard Clark. Galvano reduction 2 inches.

Clarence Howard Clark III, bas-relief portrait, 12 × 16 inches.

William Cornelius Covenhoven Van Horne, bas-relief portrait of child. 6-inch diameter.

Charles Brockden Brown (novelist). Bronze portrait plaque. 14 × 16 inches. Galvano reduction 2 inches. Franklin Inn Club.

James Fletcher, F.R.S.C., F.L.S. (Entomologist, Botanist, Naturalist) High-relief bronze portrait medallion, 14-inch diameter. Set in memorial stele of granite with fountain on grounds of Central Experimental Farm, Ottawa, Canada. A tribute of the Ottawa Naturalists Club.

George Newhall Clark, bronze portrait medallion, 9-inch diameter. Set in tablet, Ponfret School Chapel.

Bertram Stuart McKenzie, bas-relief portrait, 9-inch diameter.

William Patrick McKenzie, bas-relief portrait, 12 × 18 inches.

Eugene Paul Ullman (artist). Bas-relief portrait, 12-inch diameter.

Carrie Jacobs-Bond ("At the Piano") bas-relief portrait, 13-inch diameter.

1909:   *The Relay,* bronze statuette, 1/2 life size. Shown at Roman Art Exposition, 1911. In Montreal Art Gallery, Springfield College, Mass., and collection of Viscount Ridley.

Lisl Medallion, bas-relief portrait, 9-inch diameter; galvano reduction 2-inch. Originally owned by Dr. Charles Stork.

Guglielmo Ferrero (historian of Rome) Bas-relief portrait, 9-inch diameter.

Paul Dougherty (artist) Bas-relief portrait, 9-inch diameter.

Dr. S. Weir Mitchell, bas-relief portrait, 16 × 28 inches. Re-study for Franklin Inn Club, Philadelphia, 1915. Re-study with changed inscription for Library of University of Pennsylvania, 1917. Reduction 4 × 7 inches. 100 copies issued by Franklin Inn Club. In Harvard University, Pennsylvania Museum, and other collections.

Dr. W. W. Keen, life-size bas-relief portrait, 26 × 45 inches. Library of Brown University, Providence, R.I. Four reductions, 16 x 28 inches for family. Reduction 4 × 7 inches for Harvard University, Pennsylvania Museum, and private collections.

Dr. Nathaniel Chapman and *Dr. Samuel Jackson,* bronze plaques 38 × 54 inches for medical school, University of Pennsylvania, Philadelphia.

Francis Kinloch Huger, bas-relief portrait, 18-inch diameter. For Medical School, University of Pennsylvania. Reduction 3-inches for Harvard University, New York Numismatic Society and Medical Hall, University of Pennsylvania.

College of Physicians Medal, Bronze, 2-3/4 inches. To commemorate opening of new building of College.

Mrs. Bradbury Bedell, bas-relief portrait, 12 × 16 inches. Originally owned by Margaret Bedell, Catskill, N.Y.

1910:   *Dr. Arthur Adderley Browne.* Bas-relief portrait 26-inch diameter. Medical Library, McGill University, Montreal.

Baron Tweedmouth, Baroness Tweedmouth, two bronze portrait panels with life-size heads, 14 × 8 inches mezzo relief, for fountain at Tomich, Ross-shire, Scotland.

Edward Walter Madeira. Bas-relief portrait, 12 × 16 inches. Originally owned by Louis C. Madeira.

1911:   *The Onslaught (1904-1911)* Football group in bronze, 40 inches long. Figures 1/4 life size. Shown at Royal Academy, London, England, 1912. Acquired by Montreal Art Gallery and University of Pennsylvania. Copies in private collections.

Series of small sketches of athletes in action (at about this time): *The Plunger, Man Watching Pole Vault, Discobolus* (forward swing), *Shot Putter Preparing, Shot Putter Resting, Shot Putter Ready, High Jumper Cleaning his Shoe, Wounded, The Tackle, Relay No. 1, Relay No. 2,* University of Pennsylvania collection.

Dr. William Gardner (gynocologist). Bas-relief bronze portrait, 18 × 27 inches. McGill Medical Library, Montreal, Canada.

Dr. Crawford W. Long. Bas-relief portrait, 18 inches diameter. Medical School, University of Pennsylvania. Replica with changed lettering for University of Georgia, Athens, Ga. 1921. Reduction 3 inches.

Sign Board for Franklin Inn Club, Philadelphia. 14 × 18 inches. Bronze.

Captain William Foster Biddle. Bas-relief portrait, 12-inch diameter. Episcopal Academy, Philadelphia.

Honourable Archie Gordon. Plaster bust, life size. Haddo House, Chapel, Aberdeenshire, Scotland.

Working model of *Benjamin Franklin,* 1/2 life size. Copies: Newark Museum, N.J.; Philadelphia Public Library, and private collections.

1912:   *Mrs. Tait McKenzie.* Bas-relief portrait, 12 × 17 inches. Bronze.

Kathleen Parlow. (violinist). Bronzed plaster portrait plaque, 15 × 30 inches. Now in Mill of Kintail collection. Almonte, Ont.

The Joy of Effort. Bronze medallion, 46 inch diameter. Set in wall of stadium, Stockholm, Sweden. Reduction 20 inch. Used by Philadelphia Board of Education as William A. Stecher Award for contribution to field of health and physical education. 3-inch reduction for use as medal, available to various groups.

American Playground Association Medal–"Ariston" Bronze medallion, 10-inch diameter. One inch reduction. Award for athletic tests.

Re-Study of Public School Athletic League Medal for New York City — "They are swifter than eagles."

Katherine Clark. Bas-relief portrait, 10-inch diameter.

Honourable Sir George A. Drummond, K.C.M.G.. Bas-relief portrait, 36 × 52 inches. St. Margaret's House, Montreal.

General Henry Morris Naglee, memorial high-relief portrait medallion 30 × 50 inches. Set in marble column, St. James Park, San Jose, California. Architect: Paul P. Cret.

1913:   *Dr. John Herr Musser.* Low-relief portrait plaque set in tablet 32 × 26 inches. University Hospital, Philadelphia.

Wisconsin University plaque, 5 × 9 inches. 1 × 2-inch reduction medal awarded to athletes at University of Wisconsin.

Dr. Horatio R. Storer, Medical Numismatist, Bronze bas-relief portrait, 12 × 27 inches. Reduction 3 inches. New York Numismatic Society, Harvard University, and private collections.

Clarence S. Bayne (Baseball team captain) Bronze plaque, 20 × 40 inches. Set in wall of the gymnasium facing Franklin Field, University of Pennsylvania.

1914:   *Fencers Club of Philadelphia* medallion, 7-inch diameter. Bronze medal—4-inch reduction.

Dr. John Herr Musser, bas-relief portrait medallion, 12-inch diameter. Outdoor Department, University of Pennsylvania Hospital, Philadelphia.

Franklin Institute Medal of Honour, 3 inches diameter. Awarded for distinguished service to science.

Dr. John Bonsall Porter. Bas-relief portrait plaque, 12 × 18 inches. Original owned by John Bonsall Porter.

The Youthful Franklin (1910-1914). 8-foot high bronze statue. Stands outside Weightman Hall and Franklin Field, University of Pennsylvania, Philadelphia. Pedestal by Paul P. Cret. Replica in 3-foot bronze, Brookgreen Gardens, S.C.; Chapel Hill, University of North Carolina; The Newark Museum, N.J.

The Boy Scout, bronze statuette, 1/4 life size. Ten copies issued. Owned by Sir Robert Baden Powell, and members of the Philadelphia Scout Council to whom the copyright was presented by the sculptor.

1915:   *Honourable Thomas Ryburn Buchanan,* portrait plaque, 18 × 32 inches. Low relief. Originally owned by Mrs. Thomas Ryburn Buchanan.

Crawford C. Madeira, bas-relief portrait plaque, 12 × 16 inches. Owned by Louis Madeira.

1916:   *Intercollegiate Athletic Association Scholarship Medal.* Bronze, 3-inch diameter.

1917:   *Intercollegiate Athletic Association Track and Field Medallion.* Bronze, 8-inch diameter. 3-inch and 1-1/2-inch medals.

Lieutenant Hector MacQuarrie, R.F.A., Sketch portrait, 12 × 17 ins.

Sir Robert Jones, K.B.E., bronze portrait in relief, 12 × 16 inches.

Reduction 5 × 7 inches. Original owned by Sir Robert Jones.

Sir Wilfred Grenfell, K.C.M.G. Bas-relief portrait, 8-inch diameter. Originally owned by Sir Wilfred Grenfell.

Philip S. Collins, Sketch bust, under-life-size. Done for Red Cross. Originally owned by Philip S. Collins.

1918: *Luther Halsey Gulick,* memorial medallion. 22-inch diameter. For Gulick Camp, Sebago, Maine.

Over the Top, sketch for proposed war memorial.

Mrs. Nicholas Biddle, bronze portrait bust, life-size. Owned by Mrs. J. Bertram Lippincott.

1919: *The Fountain of the Laughing Children.* Erected in memory of Rosamond Junken Mallery in Athletic Playground, Philadelphia.

Joseph Pennell, sketch plaque, 12 × 16 inches. Owned by Mrs. Joseph Pennell.

John McLure Hamilton, portrait in relief, 12-inch diameter.

Fred G. Morris, sketch medallion, 10-inch diameter.

Walt Whitman, bronze cast medal, 5-inch diameter. Issued by Franklin Inn Club, Philadelphia.

Boy Scouts Memorial plaque. 18 × 36 inches. For Scout Council, Philadelphia.

Altar of Dedication, 30 × 72 inches. Memorial to Captain Howard C. McCall, Church of the Saviour, 39th Street, Philadelphia.

Captain Guy Drummond, bronze statuette, 1/2 life size. National Medal Collection, Public Archives of Canada.

Blighty, bronze statuette, 1/2 life size. Shows a Seaforth Highlander. H.M. the Queen's Collection, Balmoral Castle, Scotland.

Rev. George Whitefield (1913-1919). 8-foot bronze statue. Dormitory Triangle, University of Pennsylvania. Pedestal by John Harbeson.

Grotesques. Door knocker and candlesticks.

Edward Longstreth Medal of Merit, 2-inch and 1-½ inch diameter, bronze and silver. Franklin Institute of Philadelphia Award for Invention.

1920: *Elizabeth Butler Kirkbride* "Philanthropist". Bas-relief portrait medallion, Kirkbride School, Philadelphia.

Sir Arthur Shipley, G.C.B.E., bas-relief portrait medallion, 12-inch diameter. Christ College, Cambridge, England.

Honourable Christopher G. Benson, bas-relief medallion, 10-inch diameter.

The Aviator, statuette, 1/2 life size, of Lieutenant Norton Downes, St. Paul's School, Concord, Vermont.

Intercollegiate Winter Sports Union Plaque. Bronze. 8 × 9 inches.

Flying Sphere, bronze statuette, 18 inches high. White collection, University of Pennsylvania.

1921: *Sara Yorke Stevenson,* "Archaeologist, journalist and civic worker." Bas-relief portrait plaque, 12 × 16 inches. Art Museum, Philadelphia.

Lenape Club medal, 6-inch diameter. Lenape Club, University of Pennsylvania, Philadelphia.

Philadelphia Sketch Club medal, 4-inch diameter. Cast medal. Philadelphia Sketch Club.

William James Young, bronze portrait in relief, 12-inch diameter. Reduction 3-inch. For General Palmer E. Pierce, New York.

John Kendrick Bangs, 8-inch sketch medallion.

Pelham Edgar, "literary critic." Bas-relief 8-inch sketch medallion.

Francis Pizzi, 8-inch diameter sketch medallion.

Achilles Club of London Medal, 12-inch. Reduced 1-½ inches.

Lord Seaforth, inscribed "James Alexander Francis Henderson Stewart McKenzie, from his clansman, R. Tait McKenzie, Brahan, August 1921". portrait plaque, 12 × 16 inches.

The Marquis of Aberdeen and Temair, portrait plaque, 12 × 16 inches. Haddo House, Aberdeenshire, Scotland.

Pan, fountain head with spouting mouth. Dr. John L. Todd, Montreal and Dr. Charles Wharton Stork, Philadelphia.

1922:   *Dr. J. Wm. White,* portrait medallion, 12 inches. Set in fountain wall, Rittenhouse Square, Philadelphia.

Grotesque Knife Rests, two.

Paperknife.

Why Not? One. Shot-putter statuette, 10″ high. Bronze.

Why Not? Two. Boxer statuette, 10″ high. Bronze.

American Legion Award (for boys). 3-inch and 2-½-inch medals. Bronze.

The Home-coming (1920-1922) Monument to the men of Cambridge, England, who fought in World War I. Bronze. Unveiled by Duke of York, 3rd July, 1922.

Radnor Memorial – "Over the Top", bronze panel 44 × 65 inches, in mezzo relief. Memorial to soldiers of World War I, for St. David's, Pennsylvania. Architect, Adams.

Viscountess Folkestone, bronze portrait medallion, 10 inches. Owned by Viscountess Folkestone.

1923:   *Joseph Trimble Rothrock,* portrait medallion, 12 inches. For memorial in State House, Harrisburg, Pennsylvania.

Grant Mitchell, actor. Bronze portrait medallion. 12 inches.

Alexander Wilson, naturalist, portrait medallion, 12 inches. For Memorial Museum of Natural History, Philadelphia.

William Cooper Proctor, portrait plaque. 24 × 40 inches. Proctor Hall, Graduate School, Princeton, N.J.

Aesculapius, bronze cast medal, 5-inch and 3-inch. Award founded by Dr. Edward Krumbahr for research, University of Pennsylvania. Known as the Mary Ellis Bell Prize for undergraduate medical research.

Luther Halsey Gulick Memorial Medal. 2-1/2 inches. Originally owned by New York Physical Education Society. Now awarded annually by American Alliance for Health, Physical Education and Recreation.

Memorial Table to Samuel Chew, 18 × 48 inches. Marble. Old St. Peter's Church, Philadelphia.

Sir William Osler, portrait medallion, 36 inches. John Hopkins Hospital. Re-study for medical library of McGill University, Montreal, Canada. Bronze.

The Javelin Cast, bronze statuette, 18 inches high. White Collection, University of Pennsylvania, Philadelphia.

The Volunteer, bronze statue, 8 feet high. Rosamond War Memorial, Almonte, Canada. Architect: John Harbeson.

Henry Labarre Jayne, tablet, bronze, 24 × 36 inches. American Philosophical Society, Philadelphia.

Lieut.-Col. George Harold Baker Memorial, Bronze, 7-foot high. Lobby of House of Commons, Parliament Buildings, Ottawa, Ontario. John Pearson, architect.

Pole Vaulter, bronze statuette, 18-inches high. Wolffe Collection, University of Tennessee.

1925: *John Cadwalader,* portrait plaque, 12 × 16 inches. Institute for the Blind, Overbrook, Pennsylvania.

Relay Carnival Medal, University of Pennsylvania. Three sizes: 18 inches, 8 inches, and 2 inches in diameter. Owned by the University of Pennsylvania.

American Legion Medal, school award for girls. 2-1/2 inches in diameter. Bronze.

Dr. Chevalier Jackson, bronze portrait medallion, 12 inches.

Radiance, medallion, 18 inches in diameter. Health award for Philadelphia Schools, presented by Dr. James Anders. Original owned by Mr. and Mrs. Robert Glascott. Now part of Lloyd P. Jones Gallery collection, University of Pennsylvania.

The Ice Bird, bronze statuette, 1/2 life size. Collection of Lord Broughton.

Wm. Wood Gerhard, 2-inch bronze medal. Gift of Dr. Arthur Gerhard to the Philadelphia Pathological Society.

Brothers of the Wind (1920-1925) Bronze frieze of eight skaters. 120 × 33 inches. Galvano 11 × 40½ inches. Also 5-1/2 × 1-3/4 inch reduction.

The Chancellor's Medal of Honour, bronze, 3-inches in diameter. For Buffalo University, Buffalo, N.Y.

The Plunger, bronze statuette, 30 inches high. Presented by William P. McKenzie to the University Club. Boston, Mass.

The Victor, bronze, 8-foot statue. Memorial to soldiers of Woodbury, N.J. Pedestal by John Harbeson, architect.

Violet Oakley, bronze portrait plaque. Estate of Violet Oakley, Philadelphia.

1926: *Sesquincentennial Sports Medal,* Plaster medallion, 14-inch diameter. Galvano reduction 2-inches, bronze.

Three Hours for Lunch Club, New York City, cast medal.

The Champion, sketch of Douglas Lowe, 12 inches high.

Dr. Edgar Fahs Smith, bronze 8-foot memorial statue. Campus of University of Pennsylvania, Philadelphia. Horace Trumbahr, architect of pedestal.

The Modern Discus Thrower, bronze statuette, 28 inches high. White Collection, University of Pennsylvania, Philadelphia.

1927: *Percy D. Haughton Memorial,* portrait plaque of Percy Haughton, 32 × 20 inches. Two panels showing football plays, 28 × 58 inches. H.A. Walker, architect. Soldiers Field, Cambridge, Mass.

Memorial Table, County Medical Society, Philadelphia. Carved in wood by Boris Blai from design by R. Tait McKenzie.

Scottish-American War Memorial "The Call" (1923-27). Figure 8-foot high, bronze. Recruiting party frieze, 25 feet long, bronze. Princess Street Gardens, Edinburgh, Scotland. Reginald Fairlie, architect.

1928: *Christine Wetherill Stevenson Memorial,* for Art Alliance in Philadelphia. Portrait plaque with two supporting figures in lunette, 8 × 3 feet. Cast in coloured cement. Above fireplace in Art Alliance building.

Ellwood Charles Rutschman, bronze portrait medallion, 34 inches in diameter. Fraternity House, Philadelphia.

Dean Andrew Fleming West (1925-1928). 8-foot high bronze

memorial. Placed in quadrangle of Graduate School, Princeton University, Princeton, N.J. Pedestal by Cram and Ferguson.

General James Wolfe (1928-1932). 10-foot high bronze statue for Greenwich Royal Park, London, England. A.S.G. Butler, architect.

Shotputter (The Hop), bronze statuette, 10 inches high. Collection of Clifford M. Swan.

The Winner, bronze sketch of sprinter, 12 inches high.

The Upright Discus Thrower, bronze, 12-inch high statuette.

Dudley Allen Sargent, bronze plaque and flagpole frieze, 6-inch diameter. For Sargent Camp, Peterboro, New Haven, Conn.

Walter Hampden, actor. Bronze portrait medallion, 11-inch diameter. The Players' Club, New York City.

Roy Helton, poet. Bronze portrait medallion, 11 inches in diameter. Lloyd P. Jones Gallery, University of Pennsylvania.

Lord Burghley, Olympic Champion for 400-meter hurdles, 1928 Olympics. Plaque 32 × 40 inches. The Marquess of Exeter, Burghley House, Stamford, Lincolnshire, England.

1929:　　*Florence Nightingale-Saunders Medal,* bronze, 2-1/2 inches in diameter. American Nurses Association.

Billie Brengle, child's portrait medallion.

Andrew G. Curtin, Governor of Pennsylvania (1861-1867), and *John G. Parks,* Major-General, 9th Army Corps of Pennsylvania: Bronze busts 2-1/2 feet high, mounted on 7-foot high gray granite pedestals in Vicksburg National Military Park, Vicksburg, Mississippi. Erected by the State of Pennsylvania in 1930.

1930:　　*Olympic Shield,* 5-foot high medallion. Contains 91 figures. Won art award at 1932 Olympiad. Original plaster model at "Mill of Kintail", Almonte, Canada. 18-inch bronze galvanos used as awards by athletic and other associations. Also 2 and 3-inch medal reductions.

Series of medals awarded by Inter-collegiate Conference of Athletic Associations (ICAA) to athletes of mid-western universities in the United States :

ICAA—Swimming—10-3/4-inch bronze medallion, 1-7/16-inch medal.

ICAA—Tennis—10-3/4-inch bronze medallion, 1-7/16-inch medal.

ICAA—Fencing—11-1/2-inch bronze medallion, 1-7/16-inch medal.

ICAA—Wrestling—11″ diameter medallion, 1-7/16-inch medal.

ICAA—Golf—11-1/4-inch medallion, 1-7/16-inch medal.

ICAA—Gymnastics—12-inch medallion, 1-7/16-inch medal.

J. Frederick Wolle, "Lover and Interpreter of Bach", bronze medallion, 11-1/2-inch diameter. Lloyd P. Jones Gallery, University of Pennsylvania.

Campbell Stuart, portrait medallion. Bronze.

Edward Peacock, "Banker". Bronze portrait plaque.

American Academy of Physical Education Award. Bronze medallion.

Christopher Hussey, "Man of Letters". Bronze portrait plaque.

Sir Arthur Keith, "Man of Science". Bronze portrait medallion. 10-inch diameter.

Beatrice Harrison, "Cellist". Bronze portrait plaque.

1931:　　*James Sullivan Memorial,* bronze cast medal, 5-inch diameter. National Junior Forum.

Sir Edward Wentworth Beatty, K.C. Bronze bust. Plaster model at "Mill of Kintail", Almonte, Canada.

Ellis Paxon Oberholtzer, American historian. Portrait medallion.

Triumph of Wings, Bronze statue, 46 inches high. Memorial to aviation.

The Falcon, re-study of "Triumph of Wings". Bronze, 6-foot high statue. At McLennan Library, McGill University, Montreal, Canada. Gift of G. Gordan Lewis in memory of Eva Maud Lewis, 1953.

1932:   *Joseph Henry Curtis memorial.* Bronze medallion portrait set in memorial granite slab, Asticou Terrace, Mount Desert, Maine.

United Gas Improvement Company Medal. (Philadelphia). 2-inch and 3-1/2-inch bronze.

The Eight. 1/4 life size. Bronze group of oarsmen. Library of Fine Arts, University of Pennsylvania; Lloyd P. Jones Gallery, University of Pennsylvania.

Canadian Confederation Memorial (60 years). 14-foot high, marble. Parliament Buildings, Ottawa, Canada.

Dominion Memorial Medal (1867-1927). 5-inch diameter, bronze.

Alma Mater, Girard College Memorial (Philadelphia) Frieze. 72 × 96 inches. Granite.

Edward and John (Fernberger children) Bronze circular plaque.

1932-33: *Three Punters.* 46-inch bronze medallion. Galvano reduction 18 inch diameter. 3-inch and 1-inch bronze medals.

1933:   *Franklin Inn Club Medal,* 3-1/4 inches.

Jane A. Delano Memorial. Marble statue depicting "Mercy", dedicated to nurses of World War I. Stands in Garden Court, Red Cross Headquarters Building, Washington, D.C.

Robert and Ethel McKenzie. Profile bas-relief, portrait plaque of Dr. and Mrs. Tait McKenzie.

The Laughing Athlete. Statuette. Mill of Kintail, Almonte, Canada.

International Nickel Company of Canada Medal. 3-inch platinum award for distinguished service to the Canadian Mineral industry through the Canadian Institute of Mining and Metallurgy. Nickel replicas also given to recipients. Also available in bronze.

1933-34: *William A. Carr* (1932 Olympic Champion of the 400-meter race) 12-inch sketch showing Carr in full stride. Bronze. J. White Collection, University of Pennsylvania.

William A. Carr in standing pose. 10-inch high bronze sketch statuette.

William A. Carr One-half life size (36-inch high) bronze statuette in standing pose. Part of Mercerburg Academy Memorial group, Mercerburg, Pa.

1934:   *William Mann Irvine* (Ph.D., LL.D. "Dreamer and Scholar, Worker and Builder") 32 × 23-inch high relief bronze portrait plaque set in 9-foot 7-inch × 4-foot 3-inch stele for Irvine Memorial at Mercersburg Academy, Mercersburg, Pa. Limited bronze copies of plaque 12-inch high × 4-inch wide.

Back Outside Loop. 10-inch high, bronze skating statuette.

Invictus, 20-inch high bronze statuette.

Robert Henry Michelet ("Brilliant student, a fine athlete, a born leader') (Rhodes Scholar and Senator). In swimming costume. 38-inch high, coloured plaster. Mill of Kintail, Almonte, Canada.

William P. McKenzie, bronze bust. Copy at Mill of Kintail, Almonte, Canada.

Springfield College Medallion (features "The Joy of Effort")

Frederick George Scott, C.M.G., D.S.O. Bronze portrait plaque.

Dr. Frank Buller, Ophthalmologist. Life size, bronze bust. Royal Victoria Hospital, Montreal, Canada.

1935:   *The Minister and His Wife.* Bronze portrait plaque of McKenzie's parents, set in memorial bench, Almonte, Canada.

The Tumblers. Seated. Hands on ankles. Bronze.

The Tumblers. Head on ground. Bronze.

R.B. Angus (President, Canadian Pacific Railway Company) 3-foot × 2-foot bronze portrait plaque. Royal Victoria Hospital, Montreal, Canada.

1936:   *Robert Henry Michelet,* 38-inch high bronze statue. Part of William Irvine Memorial at Mercersburg Academy, Mercersburg, Pa.

International Congress for Mathematics Medal. 2-1/2-inch diameter medal for outstanding contribution to mathematics. Two medals in 14-carat gold were issued for the 1936 Congress by the Canada Royal Mint.

Strength and Speed, Society of Medalists 13th Issue Medallion. 12-inch diameter, bronze. Also available in 3-inch diameter medal.

Mary Baker Eddy, bronze bust. Gift of William P. McKenzie to First Church, Christ Science, Boston, Mass.

Passing the Baton. 50.5-inch × 15-inch bronze frieze in low relief Commemorating 40th Anniversary of the Penn Relay Carnival, University of Pennsylvania, Philadelphia.

"The Pipes of War" Memorial. 52-inch × 22-1/2-inch, bronze frieze, set in Georgia pink marble monument, City of Darien, Ga.

Jesse Owens (1936 Olympic champion broadjumper). 9-inch, coloured plaster statuette.

Skating Club of New York Medal. 5-inch diameter, bronze. 3-inch reduction.

1937:   *Henry H. Donaldson,* Ph.D., M.D. Bronze portrait plaque.

John Sinnock medal.

Tom Daly ("Laureate of the Lowly") Portrait Medallion.

Wrestling Group, 10-inch high, bronze.

Amherst College Pratt Pool Award. 8-inch diameter plaster medallion. 1-3/4-inch bronze reduction.

1938:   *Column of Youth Herm.* Plaster (later cast in marble for National Education Headquarters in Washington, D.C.)

American Association of Anatomists 50-year Medal. Bronze portrait medallion of Joseph Leidy, first president of the association. 2-1/2-inch reduction.

University of Pennsylvania Bicentennial Medal. 3-inch diameter bronze.

Sir Arthur Doughty. Portrait bust. Unfinished. (Completed by Emannuel Hahn) Public Archives of Canada, Ottawa, Canada.

Duke Kahanamoku. 12-inch high working model of Olympic Hawaiian swimming champion. Unfinished. (Being completed now)

Additional works for which details are not at present known:

George Gibbs (artist). Portrait medallion.

Walter Taylor, portrait medallion.

Mrs. Spellisy, bas-relief portrait.

Dr. Leonard Pearson, bas-relief portrait.

Dr. Paul A. Lewis (Pathologist) Portrait medallion.

The Esquimaux Princess. Mask. For Dr. George Bryson, Curator of the University of Pennsylvania Museum.

Death Masks of John L. Sullivan and Dr. George Bryson, former Curator of the University of Pennsylvania Museum. Both of these were part of the University of Pennsylvania collection of sculpture by Dr. McKenzie.

Bibliography

Primary Sources

(1)   Autobiograhpical unpublished diaries, notes and manuscripts, corre-
      spondence, newspaper clippings, photos, and other memorabilia in the R.
      Tait McKenzie Collection, Archives, University of Pennsylvania, Pa.
      Personal interviews and correspondence with former students, associates,
      relatives, and others who knew Dr. Tait McKenzie and his work.

(2)   Books written by R. Tait McKenzie:

      Exercise in Education and Medicine, 1909, 1915, 1924. W.B. Saunders,
      Philadelphia.
      Reclaiming the Maimed: A Handbook of Physical Therapy, 1918. The
      Macmillan Company, New York.

(3)   Articles written by or about Dr. Tait McKenzie:

1890   "Helps in Teaching the Running High Jump," *Triangle,* November
1891   "The Growth of Gymnastics in Montreal"; *Dominion Illustrated
       Monthly,* 16 May.
1892   "Rugby Football in Canada"; *Dominion Illustrated Monthly,* Feb.
1894   "Therapeutic Uses of Exercise in Education"; *Montreal Medical
       Journal,* February.
       "Report on Physical Education in McGill University."
       "Regulation of Athletic Sports in Colleges"; *This Week,* Jan.
1895   "The Anatomical Characteristics of Speed Skaters", *Popular Science
       Monthly,* December.
       "Hockey in Eastern Canada", *Dominion Illustrated Monthly.*
       "The Typical Speed Skater"; *Popular Science Monthly,* December.
1896   "Notes on the Examination and Measurement of Athletes"; *Montreal
       Medico-Chirurgical Society,* November.
1897   "The Speed Skater and His Art"; McClure's Syndicate, 1897.
       "International Speed Skating"; *Outing Magazine,* December.
       "Natural Selection as Shown in the Typical Speed Skater"; *Journal of
       Anatomy,* Vol. XXXII.
       "The Dissection of Two Club Feet"; *Journal of Anatomy,* Vol. XXXIV.
1898   "Accurate Measurement of Lateral Curvature"; *Montreal Medical
       Journal,* February.
1899   "Influence of School Life on Curvature of the Spine"; National
       Education Proceedings, *Montreal Medical Journal,* March.
1900   "Strain, Breathlessness and Fatigue as shown by the Face"; Interna-
       tional Education Congress, Paris.
       "The Place of Physical Training in the School System"; *Montreal
       Medical Journal,* January.

1901 "The Treatment of Spinal Deformities by Exercise and Posture"; *Montreal Medical Journal*, October.
"A Modern Gymnasium"; *McGill University Magazine*, December.

1902 "The Art of Breathing"; *Outing*, Vol. XL, April.
"Study of Face in Breathlessness"; *Outing*, Vol. XXXIX, January.

1904 "Relation of Thoracic Type to Chest Capacity"; *Montreal Medical Journal*, April.
"Address at the Opening of the Gymnasium of the University of Pennsylvania," Philadelphia, December 14.

1905 "The Facial Expressions of the Emotions with Special reference to Violent Effort and Fatigue;" Lecture. Printed in *Journal of Anatomy and Physiology*, London, England, October.
"Physical Education at Pennsylvania"; *Red and Blue*, October.
"Building the Physical Side of College Men"; *Illustrated Sporting News*, August 12.

1906 The Legacy of the Samourai. Pamphlet. Reprinted from *American Physical Education Review*, December.
"The Relation of Athletics to Longevity"; *Medical Examiner*.

1907 "The Development of Physical Efficiency Among College Men"; Address at Opening Exercises of Queen's University Gymnasium, February, Queen's University, Kingston, Ontario.
"Systematic Physical Exercises for College Students"; Second International Congress on School Hygiene.
"The Anatomical Basis for the Treatment of Scoliosis by Exercise"; Proceedings of the College of Physicians of Philadelphia.
"The Isolation of Muscular Action"; *American Physical Education Review*, November.

1908 "The Regulation of Physical Instruction in Schools and Colleges from the Standpoint of Hygiene" (with Drs. Storey, Lee and Hough); Americal Physiological Convention, December.
"Results of the Examination of Students' Eyes" (with Dr. William Campbell Posey); *Journal of American Medical Association*, March 23.
"Physical Therapeutics"; *American Journal of Medical Sciences*, October.

1909 "Regulation of Physical Instruction in Schools and Colleges from the Standpoint of Hygiene"; *American Physical Education Review*, April.

1910 "Annual Address by the President of the Society of Physical Directors of Physical Education in Colleges"; *American Physical Education Review*, February.
"Report on the Department of Physical Education at the University of Pennsylvania"; *Old Penn*, April 30.
"The City and Fresh Air"; *Fresh Air Magazine*, March.

1911 "The Chronicle of the Amateur Spirit" presented before National Collegiate Athletic Association, December. Reprinted in *The American Physical Education Review*, Vol. XVI, No. 2, February.
"A Visit to the Home of Archibald Maclaren"; read at a meeting of the Directors of Physical Education in Colleges, December.

1912 "Value of Exercises in Treating certain Cases of Acquired Inquinal Hernia"; *International Clinics*, Vol. III, 22nd Series, January.
"Constructive Patriotism"; *American Physical Education Review*, April 1912.

1913 "Influence of Exercise on the Heart"; *American Journal of Medical Sciences*, January.

"The Royal Central Institute at Stockholm"; Pamphlet. Reprinted from the *American Physical Education Review,* March.

"The Mission of the Artist"; Address to Philadelphia School of Design, May.

"The Quest for Eldorado"; *American Physical Education Review,* May.

"The Wisdom of Health"; *Old Penn,* November 8.

1914   "A New View of Benjamin Franklin"; *Century Magazine,* July.

"Non-Military Preparation for National Defence"; *The Standard,* December.

1915   "The Search for Physical Perfection"; Delivered during Free Public Lecture Course at University of Pennsylvania, 1914-15. Reprinted from *Old Penn* in pamphlet.

"Physical Training of the New British Armies"; *American Physical Education Review,* December.

1916   "Hate" (with Sir Arthur Shipley); *The Cornhill Magazine,* September.

"A National Scheme of Physical Education"; *Journal of Royal Sanitary Institute.*

"Treatment of Convalescent Soldiers by Physical Means"; *Proceedings of the Royal Society of Medicine,* Vol. XX, p. 31.

1917   "Making and Remaking of a Fighting Man"; *American Physical Education Review,* March.

"Treatment of Nerve, Muscle and Joint Injuries in Soldiers by Physical Means"; *Canadian Medical Association Journal,* December.

1918   "Treatment of Nerve, Muscle and Joint Injuries in Soldiers by Physical Means"; *American Physical Education Review,* June.

"Mechanical Aids to Reconstruction."

"Reclaiming the Maimed in War"; Meeting of the College of Physicians, Philadelphia, Feb. 7.

"Functional Re-education of the Wounded"; *N.Y. Medical Journal,* October.

"Reconstruction and Rehabilitation of Disabled Soldiers"; *Pennsylvania Medical Journal,* March.

1919   "Functional Re-education of the British Soldier"; reprinted from the *N.Y. Medical Record,* May 17. Booklet. (William Wood & Co., New York)

1921   "The Basis of Our System of Physical Education"; communicated to the Medico-Chirurgical Society of Edinburgh, July 6. Reprinted in *Edinburgh Medical Journal,* December 1921 and *Pennsylvania Gazette,* May 12, 1922.

"The Wisdom of Health"; *Youth's Companion,* May.

"Treatment of Physical Defects"; *How to Live,* March.

1922   "Variations of Athletic Types"; *The Outlook,* June.

1924   Report — *Physical Education in Europe.*

"The University and the Meaning of Education"; *Pennsylvania Gazette,* October 17.

1925   "Le Masque Facial dans l'Effort"; *Aesculape,* February.

1926   "An Address on the Functions and Limits of Sport in Education"; Paper read before National Congress on Education and Citizenship, Montreal, Canada, April 10, 1926. Reprinted from *The Canadian Medical Association Journal,* Vol. XVI, 630-32. Pamphlet.

"Plans for the New Gymnasium at the University of Pennsylvania"; Booklet reprinted from the *Proceedings of the 29th Annual Meeting of the Society of Directors of Physical Education in Colleges.* 1926.

"Address by Professor Tait McKenzie" to the Royal College of Surgeons on occasion of University of Edinburgh Bi-Centenary of Faculty of Medicine (1726-1926); published by University of Edinburgh, 1926. (James Thin, Printers)

"The Modern Discus Thrower"; *International Studio,* May.

1928 "The Place of Physical Education and Athletics in a University"; Address at International Congress of Physical Education and Sports, Amsterdam, August.

"An Address on the Death of the Right Honourable Field Marshal The Earl Haig of Bemersyde" given before the St. Andrew's Society of Philadelphia, Feb. 29, 1928. Pamphlet.

1931 *Physical Education at the University of Pennsylvania from 1904-1931 and the Gates Plan.* Pamphlet. Printed in the *American Education Association Research Quarterly,* June 1932.

1932 "The Athlete in Sculpture"; *Journal of Health and Physical Education,* November.

"Pioneers in Physical Education and the Lessons We May Learn from Them—Edward Hitchcock, Luther H. Gulick, Ernst Herman Arnold, Dudley A. Sargent"; *Journal of Health and Physical Education,* June.

1933 "Reminiscences of James Naismith"; *Journal of Health and Physical Education,* January.

"Posture"; *Hygeia,* November.

1935 "Major General James Wolfe"; Booklet. Reprinted from *Proceedings of the Charaka Club.*

"The Relation of Physical Education and Health Activities to the Academic Program"; Paper read in the discussion of the Joint Session of the National Collegiate Athletic Association and the College Physical Education Society, New York City, December 27, 1935.

1937 "The Column of Youth". Read before American Academy of Physical Education, New York City, April 22, 1937. Printed by *The General Magazine and Historical Chronicle.*

(4) Parochial Registers, New Register House, Edinburgh, Scotland.
Genealogy of MacKenzie Clan, National Library of Scotland, Edinburgh.

(5) *Newspapers*

Almonte Gazette
Boston Globe
Boston Transcript
London Chronicle
Montreal Daily Mail
Montreal Star
Montreal Witness
Morning Telegraph, New York City
New York American
New York Sun
New York Times
Ottawa Citizen
Ottawa Journal
Pennsylvania Gazette
Pennsylvania Evening Bulletin
Philadelphia Evening Ledger
Philadelphia Inquirer
Philadelphia Sunday Bulletin

San Jose Mercury News
Toronto Globe and Mail
Toronto Telegram

(6) *Books, Pamphlets and Periodicals*

Abbott, Brook: "Sculptor from the Medical School"; *Canadian Magazine,* Vol. 75, June 1931.
Adler, Waldo: "A Molder of Clay—and of Men"; *Outing,* July 1915.
Ishbel, Marchioness of Aberdeen and Temair: *The Musings of A Scottish Granny.* (1936) Heath, Cranton Limited, London.
Lady Aberdeen: *Edward Majoribanks: Lord Tweedmouth, K.T. 1849-1909. Notes and Recollections.* (1909) Constable & Co. Ltd. London.
Lord and Lady Aberdeen: *We Twa. Reminiscences of Lord and Lady Aberdeen.* Vols. 1. and 2. (1925) W. Collins, Sons & Co. Ltd. London.
Bourinot, Arthur S.: *Edward William Thomson: A Bibliography and His Letters to Lampman (1849-1924).* (1955) Published by author, Ottawa.
Barr, Robert. "An American Sculptor"; *The Outlook,* March 1905.
Beck, James M.: "The Youthful Franklin". An address at Unveiling of Franklin Memorial, University of Pennsylvania, June 16, 1932. (1932) J.B. Lippincott, Philadelphia, Pamphlet.
Carpenter, E.C.: "Studies From Life: Dr. R. Tait McKenzie"; *Town and Country,* January 27, 1912.
Campbell, Grace: *Highland Heritage* (1962) Collins, London and Glasgow.
Cattell, Henry W.: *Tait McKenzie's Medical Portraits.* (1925) Lippincott, Philadelphia, 16 p. pamphlet.
Collard, Edgar Andrew: "Sir William Van Horne" in *Montreal Yesterdays* (1962) Longmans Canada, Toronto.
Coole, James: *Olympic Report 1968* (1968) Robert Hale, London.
Croskey, John Welsh: Editor: *Historical Catalogue of the St. Andrew's Society of Philadelphia with Biographical Sketches of Deceased Members,* Vol III — 1913-1937, Philadelphia.
Day, James: "Robert Tait McKenzie: Physical Education's Man of the Century", *Journal of the Canadian Association for Health, Physical Education and and Recreation,* Vol. 33, #44, April-May 1967. Reprinted as a booklet.
Donaldson, T.B.: "Robert Tait McKenzie"; Canadian Magazine, June 1905.
Dubuc, F.F.: "A Sculptor of Soldiers and Athletes"; *Arts and Decoration,* June. (1925-1928)
Eberlein, H.D.: "R. Tait McKenzie, Physician and Sculptor", *Century,* December 1918.
Elmore, R.: "Sports in American Sculpture"; *International Studio,* November 1925.
Edwards, Margaret Bunel: "A Man, A Mill, A Memory"; *Onward,* 1963.
Fields, J.C. editor: *Proceedings of the International Mathematical Congress held in Toronto, August 11-16, 1924.* Vol. I and II (1928), University of Toronto Press, Toronto.
Forrer, L.: *R. Tait McKenzie.* Reprinted from *Biographical Notices of Medallists* (1924) Spink & Son Ltd., London.
Fox, Robert Fortescue: *Physical Remedies for Disabled Soldiers* with chapters by Major R. Tait McKenzie. (1917) Bailliere, Tindall and Cox, London.

Gardiner, E. Norman: *Athletics of the Ancient World* (1930) Clarendon Press, Oxford. Reprinted 1955, Oxford University Press, London.

Gardner, Percy: *New Chapters in Greek Art* (1926) Clarendon Press, Oxford.

Gardner, Albert Ten Eyck: American Sculpture: *A Catalogue of the Collection of the Metropolitan Museum of Art* (1965) Booklet.

Gerber, Ellen W.: *Innovators and Institutions in Physical Education* (1971) Lea & Febiger, Philadelphia.

Gregg, Frederick James: "William Henry Drummond", *Putnam's Monthly.*

Harper, J. Russell: *Early Painters and Engravers in Canada* (1970) University of Toronto Press, Toronto.

Harshman, J. Page: "Robert Tait McKenzie: Another Canadian Centennial", *Ontario Medical Review,* July 1967.

Hunter, Adelaide M.: "R. Tait McKenzie: Pioneer in Physical Education." Doctoral Dissertation.

Hunter, Adelaide M.: "R. Tait McKenzie: Portrait of a Pioneer", *The Journal of Health, Physical Education and Recreation,* Vol. 30, November 30, 1959.

Hussey, Christopher: *Tait McKenzie: Sculptor of Youth,* (1929) Country Life Limited, London.

Johnson, D. Wayne: Portfolio on R. Tait McKenzie, Medallic Art Company, Danbury, Conn.

Kelly, Dr. A.D.: "Dr. R. Tait McKenzie and the Mill of Kintail," A Tribute by the Medical Profession from the General Secretary of the Canadian Medical Association. The Journal of the Canadian Association for Health, Physical Education and Recreation, July 1963.

Lerner, Ben: "Scots Industry and the Greek Ideal," *Toronto Telegram,* August 27, 1960.

Leys, James F.: "Theirs Be the Glory" from the Tait McKenzie Memorial Address, CAHPER Convention, McMaster University, Hamilton, Ontario, June 22, 1961.

Leys, James F.: "R. Tait McKenzie", *Journal of Health, Physical Education and Recreation,* April 1960.

Leys, James F.: "Physical Fitness Shrine in Canada," *Canadian Medical Association Journal,* Vol. 82, June 1960.

Le Fanu, William, Librarian of the College: *A Catalogue of the Portraits and Other Paintings, Drawings and Sculpture in the Royal College of Surgeons of England,* (1960) E. & S. Livingstone Ltd., Edinburgh and London.

Leonard, Fred Eugene: *A Guide to the History of Physical Education,* Third Edition revised and enlarged by George B. Affleck, A.M., M.P.E., (1947) Lea & Febiger.

Lyons, Barrow: "Modern Athletes in Sculpture", *The Mentor,* September 1926.

MacBeth, Madge: "Over My Shoulder", column Ottawa *Citizen,* April; 23, 1955.

MacKay, C.C.: "World of Art", *Saturday Night,* November 1, 1930.

Macphail, Sir Andrew: *Official History of the Canadian Forces 1914-19: The Medical Services* (1925) The King's Printer, Ottawa.

Marquis, Albert Nelson, Editor and Director: *Who's Who in Pennsylvania,* Vol. I, (1939) The A.N. Marquis Company, Chicago.

McGarry, W.: "Constructing the Perfect Man", *The Dearborn Indepen-dent, 1927.*

McGill, Jean S.: *A Pioneer History of the County of Lanark,* (1968) Published by the author, Toronto.

Miller, Alec: *Traditions in Sculpture,* (1949) Studio Publications, New York and London.

Mitchell, Elmer D.: " The American Physical Education Association", *The Journal of Health and Physical Education,* January 1932.

Morris, Harrison S.: "Sculpture by R. Tait McKenzie," *The International Studio,* 1920.

Petrie, Alfred E.H.: "In-Depth Study Reveals Important Facet of Medallic Art in Canada." *Coin World,* 1972.

Pentland, Marjorie (Lady): *A Bonnie Fechter: The Life of Ishbel Majoribanks, Marchioness of Aberdeen and Temair, G.B.E., LL.D., J.P. 1857-1939,* (1952) B.T. Batsford Ltd., London.

Price, Hartley d'Oyley: "The Tenth Olympic Games", *The Journal of Health and Physical Education,* November 1932.

Proske, Beatrice Gilman: *Brookgreen Gardens Sculpture,* (1968)|Brook-green Gardens, Murrells Inlet, South Carolina.

Reed, Herbert: "Scraping the Pole Vault Ceiling", *The Sportsman,* May 1927.

Scott, Hew: *Fasti Ecclesiae Scoticanae: The Succession Ministers in The Church of Scotland from the Reformation,* New Edition 1928. Vol. VII, Oliver & Boyd, Edinburgh.

Scott, Rev. David: *Annals & Statistics of the Original Secession Church Till Its Disruption and Union in the Free Church of Scotland in 1852,* (1886) Andrew Elliot, Edinburgh.

Scrymgeour, Norval: "The Story of *The Call:* A Yearly Pilgrimage", *The Scots Magazine,* July 1932.

Small, Robert: *History of the Congregations of the United Presbyterian Church 1733-1900,* Vol. II, (1904) David D. Small, Edinburgh.

Stork, C. Wharton: "R. Tait McKenzie, Sculptor", *The Red and Blue.*

Stork, C. Wharton: "The Joy of Effort", *Century,* 1912.

Thompson, I. Maclaren; "Robert Tait McKenzie" presented before the Medical History Section of the Winnipeg Medical Society, February 23, 1965. Reprinted in *Men and Books.*

Walker, Harry: "The Athlete in Sculpture," *Canadian Homes and Gardens,* December 1934.

Warden, R.V.: "R. Tait McKenzie", *Journal of Health, Physical Education and Recreation,* June 1938.

Wayling, Thomas: "Granny Emeritus Canadian Forever", *Canadian Home Journal,* August 1937.

Wolfe, J.B.: "R. Tait McKenzie, Triune Genius", Canadian Association for Health, Physical Education and Recreation—Proceeding and Research Reports of the 15th Biennial Convention, Saskatoon, 1963.

American Physical Education Review, Vol. 9, December 1904. "Reports of the St. Louis Conference of the American Physical Education Association, St. Louis, Missouri, 1904"

American Physical Education Review, Vol. 17, October 1912. "R. Tait McKenzie, Sculptor."

American Gymnasia, Vol. I, p. 3, September 1904. "Physical Training at St. Louis."

Canadian Medical Journal, November 1938. Obituary of Sir Andrew Macphail.

International Council of Women Bulletin, April 1934. Obituary of Lord Aberdeen.

Franklin Field Illustrated, University of Pennsylvania, 19 June 1938. "Dr. McKenzie's Career."

The Journal of Health and Physical Education: R. Tait McKenzie Memorial Issue, Vol. 15, No. 2, February 1944.

The Journal of Health and Physical Education, Vol. 19, No. 2, February 1948.

The Journal for Health, Physical Education and Recreation: Tait McKenzie Issue, May 1967.

International Studio: "The Revival of Athletic Sculpture: Dr. R. Tait McKenzie's Work". December 1920.

London Times, June 6, 1930. "The Wolfe Statue: A Gift of United Canada."

Mercury Herald, San Jose, California. Nov. 15, 1915. "The Naglee Monument."

MD, "Sculptor of Athletes," April 1975.

New York Magazine, July 1926. "Unveiling of Statue of Former Provost Edgar F. Smith".

Pennsylvania Gazette, July 2, 1926. "Unveiling of Statue of former Provost Edgar F. Smith".

Pennsylvania Gazette, March 25, 1927. "Dr. McKenzie Designs Scotch War Memorial."

The Scotsman, September 1927. "Scots and Americans: Edinburgh Unveiling."

The Scotsman, September 8, 1938. "Sculptor of the Scottish-American War Memorial."

Saturday Night, March 3, 1938. "Medals for Mathematics."

Success Magazine, "Sculpture and the Athlete." 1905.

16th Annual Meeting and Scientific Session of the Academy of Physical Medicine Program, Oct. 24, 25, 26 1938. Willard Hotel, Washington, D.C. Pamphlet.

Minutes of Quadrennial Meeting of the American Olympic Association held at New Willard Hotel, Washington, D.C. Nov 22, 1922.

Catalogue of the International Exhibition of Contemporary Medals of the American Numismatic Society, March 1910. New and Revised Edition 1911. New York.

The Athlete in Sculpture: An Exhibition of Recent Work by Tait McKenzie, Feb. 5 to Feb. 24, 1934 at Grand Central Art Galleries, New York City. Booklet.

Exhibition of Sculpture by R. Tait McKenzie, December 30, 1925 to January 12, 1926, at Doll & Richards, Boston, Mass. Booklet.

Exhibition of Medallions, Medals and Plaques including Portraits of Prominent Philadelphians, by R. Tait McKenzie, March 16-31, 1931, held at Art Alliance, Philadelphia, Program.

Secondary Sources

Schwendener, Norma: *A History of Physical Education in the United States,* (1942) A.S. Barnes and Company, New York.

Van Dalen, Deobold B.; Mitchell, Elmer D.; Bennett, Bruce L.: *A World History of Physical Education,* (1935) Prentice-Hall Inc., New York.

INDEX